Twentieth-Century Ficti

By applying recent trends in literary and language theory to a range of twentieth-century fiction, the contributors to this text make new theoretical insights available to student readers. The analytical and interpretive strategies examined in this book are not intended to be prescriptive, rather they are presented in such a way as to facilitate critical reading and evaluation.

The essays, which are arranged into three groups and focus on a textual, narrative and contextual level, look at a wide range of twentieth-century authors including Fowles, Lessing and Woolf. In addition, this student-friendly text includes a detailed index, a full glossary and helpful suggestions for further reading.

Aimed at beginning students of English Language and Literature and Applied Linguistics, and advanced students of English as a Foreign or Second Language, *Twentieth-Century Fiction* provides an essential introduction to the subject which is both sensitive and enabling.

Peter Verdonk is a Reader in English Language and Literature at the University of Amsterdam. He has contributed widely to periodicals and books on literary stylistics and criticism. His previous publications include *Twentieth-Century Poetry: From Text to Context* (1993).

Jean Jacques Weber is Lecturer in English Language and Literature at University Centre, Luxembourg. He has previously authored *Critical Analysis of Fiction* (1992) and has published a large number of articles on stylistics and discourse.

The INTERFACE Series

A linguist deaf to the poetic function of language and a literary scholar indifferent to linguistic problems and unconversant with linguistic methods, are equally flagrant anachronisms. – Roman Jakobson.

This statement, made over twenty-five years ago, is no less relevant today, and 'flagrant anachronisms' still abound. The aim of the INTERFACE series is to examine topics at the 'interface' of language studies and literary criticism and in so doing to build bridges between these traditionally divided disciplines. Already published in this series:

The Series Editor
Ronald Carter is Professor of Modern English Language at the University of Nottingham and was National Coordinator of the 'Language in the National Curriculum' Project (LINC) from 1989 to 1992.

Twentieth-Century Fiction

From Text to Context

Edited by Peter Verdonk and
Jean Jacques Weber

London and New York

First published 1995
by Routledge
11 New Fetter Lane, London EC4P 4EE

Simultaneously published in the USA and Canada
by Routledge
29 West 35th Street, New York, NY 10001

© 1995 Peter Verdonk and Jean Jacques Weber

Typeset in Baskerville by
Ponting–Green Publishing Services, Chesham, Bucks

Printed and bound in Great Britain by
Biddles Ltd, Guildford and King's Lynn

British Library Cataloguing in Publication Data
A catalogue record for this book is available from the
British Library.

Library of Congress Cataloguing in Publication Data
A catalogue record for this book has been requested

ISBN 0–415–10589–7 (hbk)
ISBN 0–415–10590–0 (pbk)

Contents

Figures

Contributors

Timothy R. Austin is Professor and Assistant Chairperson in the English Department of Loyola University, Chicago. He has published two books on stylistics, *Language Crafted* (Indiana University Press, 1984) and *Poetic Voices* (University of Alabama Press, 1994), and a variety of articles in *Language and Style, Poetics Today* and the *Journal of Literary Semantics*.

David Birch is Professor of Communication and Media Studies at the University of Central Queensland in Rockhampton. He has published widely in stylistics, language and literature, and theatre and drama studies. He is the author of *Language, Literature and Critical Practice* (Routledge, 1989) and of *The Language of Drama* (Macmillan, 1991), as well as the editor, with Michael O'Toole, of *Functions of Style* (Pinter, 1988).

R. A. Buck is Assistant Professor of English Language and Linguistics at Eastern Illinois University. Her research interests lie in the areas of stylistics, socio-linguistics and discourse analysis; she is currently working on a stylistics of literary dialogue in which she examines in particular the novels of E. M. Forster.

Helen Aristar Dry teaches English language and literature at Eastern Michigan University, Ypsilanti. She has published numerous articles on the linguistic analysis of literary narrative. Her most recent work includes 'Ghostly Ambiguity: Presuppositional Constructions in *The Turn of the Screw*' in *Style*, 1991 (with Susan Kucinkas) and 'Foregrounding: An Assessment' in *Studies in Honor of Robert Longacre*, 1992.

Susan Ehrlich is Associate Professor in the Department of Languages, Literatures and Linguistics, York University, Toronto. Her books include *Point of View* (Routledge, 1990) and (with Peter Avery) *Teaching American English Pronunciation* (Oxford University Press,

1992). She has published articles in discourse analysis and language and gender, and is currently working on a book for Blackwell dealing with language, power and gender.

Irene R. Fairley is Professor of English and Linguistics at Northeastern University. Her publications in stylistics have focused on American poets and the reception of texts by the reader. She has also published poems and translations of poems. She is the author of *E. E. Cummings and Ungrammar* (Watermill Press, 1975) and co-author (with Caroline Bloomfield) of the writing textbook *Business Communication: A Process Approach* (Harcourt Brace Jovanovich, 1990).

David A. Lee is Associate Professor of Linguistics in the Department of English, University of Queensland, St Lucia. He has published approximately thirty articles on stylistics and linguistics, and two books: *Language, Children and Society* (Harvester, 1986) and *Competing Discourses: Perspective and Ideology in Language* (Longman, 1991).

Sara Mills is Senior Lecturer in Linguistics and Critical Theory in the Department of English and Drama, University of Loughborough. She has co-written (with L. Pearce, S. Spaull and E. Millard) *Feminist Readings/Feminists Reading* (Harvester, 1989) and written *Discourses of Difference: Women's Travel Writing and Colonialism* (Routledge, 1992). At present she is working on a book entitled *Feminist Stylistics* (Routledge), and is editing two collections: *Language and Gender* (Longman) and *Gendering the Reader* (Harvester).

Martin Montgomery is Senior Lecturer in Literary Linguistics and head of the Department of English at the University of Strathclyde. He is the author of *An Introduction to Language and Society* (Methuen, 1986) and a co-author (with A. Durant, N. Fabb, T. Furniss and S. Mills) of *Ways of Reading* (Routledge, 1992) and *Key Concepts in Communication and Cultural Studies* (Routledge, 1994). He co-edited (with Malcolm Coulthard) *Studies in Discourse Analysis* (Routledge, 1990) and has contributed to a wide range of journals including *Media, Culture and Society*, *Journal of Pragmatics* and *Critical Quarterly*.

Mick Short is Senior Lecturer in the Department of Linguistics and Modern English Language at Lancaster University. He is editor of the journal *Language and Literature*. In addition to numerous articles on stylistic analysis, he wrote *Style in Fiction* (Longman) with Geoffrey Leech in 1981, and edited *Reading, Analysing and Teaching Literature* (Longman) in 1989. He is currently working on an introduction to stylistics, and is planning a book on the stylistics of drama.

Paul Simpson is a Lecturer in the School of English at Queen's University, Belfast, having moved there from Liverpool University in 1992. He teaches undergraduate and postgraduate courses on English language, linguistics and stylistics. He has published on stylistics, critical linguistics and related fields, and his most recent book in this area is *Language, Ideology and Point of View* (Routledge, 1993). He is currently writing a book on stylistics and language teaching.

Michael Toolan is Professor of English at the University of Washington, Seattle. He has published books on narratology and stylistics, recently authoring *Narrative* (Routledge, 1988), *The Stylistics of Fiction* (Routledge, 1990), and editing *Language, Text and Context* (Routledge, 1992). His current research interests include pragmatics and linguistic theory, culminating in the completion of a book-length manuscript provisionally entitled *Taking Language in Context Seriously.*

Peter Verdonk is Reader in the English Department of the University of Amsterdam. He has published widely on literary stylistic criticism in books and journals, and edited *Twentieth-Century Poetry: From Text to Context* (Routledge, 1993). With Roger D. Sell of the Åbo Akademi University (Finland) he has edited *Literature and the New Interdisciplinarity: Poetics, Linguistics, History* (Rodopi, 1994). Recently he has also co-edited and contributed to a course in British and American literature on Dutch radio and television.

Jean Jacques Weber is Lecturer in English Language and Literature at University Centre, Luxembourg. He has published a number of articles on stylistics and discourse analysis in journals and books, and is the author of *Critical Analysis of Fiction* (Rodopi, 1992). He also contributes the Stylistics section to *The Year's Work in English Studies,* and is currently working on a cognitive-stylistic analysis of David Mamet's plays.

Paul Werth is Professor of English Linguistics at the University of Amsterdam, and formerly worked at the Université Libre de Bruxelles and the University of Hull. His research interests centre on the study of discourse, and particularly in its theoretical and stylistic aspects. He is the author of *Focus, Coherence and Emphasis* (Croom Helm, 1984) and has edited a collection called *Conversation and Discourse* (Croom Helm, 1981). His forthcoming book, *Text Worlds: the Conceptual Representation of Discourse,* is to be published by Longman.

Series editor's introduction to the Interface series

There have been many books published this century which have been devoted to the interface of language and literary studies. This is the first series of books devoted to this area commissioned by a major international publisher; it is the first time a group of writers have addressed themselves to issues at the interface of language and literature; and it is the first time an international professional association has worked closely with a publisher to establish such a venture. It is the purpose of this general introduction to the series to outline some of the main guiding principles underlying the books in the series.

The first principle adopted is one of not foreclosing on the many possibilities for the integration of language and literature studies. There are many ways in which the study of language and literature can be combined and many different theoretical, practical and curricular objects to be realized. Obviously, a close relationship with the aims and methods of descriptive linguistics will play a prominent part, so readers will encounter some detailed analysis of language in places. In keeping with a goal of much work in this field, writers will try to make their analysis sufficiently replicable for other analysts to see how they have arrived at the interpretative decisions they have reached and to allow others to reproduce their methods on the same or on other texts. But linguistic science does not have a monopoly in methodology and description any more than linguists can have sole possession of insights into language and its workings. Some contributors to the series adopt quite rigorous linguistic procedures; others proceed less rigorously but no less revealingly. All are, however, united by a belief that detailed scrutiny of the role of language in literary texts can be mutually enriching to language and literary studies.

Series of books are usually written to an overall formula or design. In the case of the Interface series this was considered to be not entirely appropriate. This is for the reasons given above, but also because, as the first series of its kind, it would be wrong to suggest that there are formulaic modes by which integration can be achieved. The fact that all the books address themselves to the integration of language and literature in any case imparts a natural and organic unity to the series. Thus, some of the books in this series will provide descriptive overviews, others will offer detailed case studies of a particular topic, others will involve single author studies, and some will be more pedagogically oriented.

This range of design and procedure means that a wide variety of audiences is envisaged for the series as a whole, though, of course, individual books are necessarily quite specifically targeted. The general level of exposition presumes quite advanced students of language and literature. Approximately, this level covers students of English language and literature (though not exclusively English) at senior high-school/upper sixth-form level to university students in their first or second year of study. Many of the books in the series are designed to be used by students. Some may serve as course books – these will normally contain exercises and suggestions for further work as well as glossaries and graded bibliographies which point the student towards further reading. Some books are also designed to be used by teachers for their own reading and updating, and to supplement courses; in some cases, specific questions of pedagogic theory, teaching procedure and methodology at the interface of language and literature are addressed.

From a pedagogic point of view it is the case in many parts of the world that students focus on literary texts, especially in the mother tongue, before undertaking any formal study of the language. With this fact in mind, contributors to the series have attempted to gloss all new technical terms and to assume on the part of their readers little or no previous knowledge of linguistics or formal language studies. They see no merit in not being detailed and explicit about what they describe in the linguistic properties of texts; but they recognize that formal language study can seem forbidding if it is not properly introduced.

A further characteristic of the series is that the authors engage in a direct relationship with their readers. The overall style of writing is informal and there is above all an attempt to lighten the usual style of academic discourse. In some cases this extends to the way in which notes and guidance for further work are presented. In all cases, the style adopted by authors is judged to be that most appropriate to the mediation of their chosen subject matter.

We now come to two major points of principle which underlie the conceptual scheme for the series. One is that the term 'literature' cannot be defined in isolation from an expression of ideology. In fact, no academic study, and certainly no description of the language of texts, can be neutral and objective, for the socio-cultural positioning of the analyst will mean that the description is unavoidably political. Contributors to the series recognize and, in so far as this accords with the aims of each book, attempt to explore the role of ideology at the interface of language and literature. Second, most writers also prefer the term 'literatures' to a singular notion of literature. Some replace 'literature' altogether with the neutral term 'text'. It is for this reason that readers will not find exclusive discussions of the literary language of canonical literary texts; instead the linguistic heterogeneity of literature and the permeation of many discourses with what is conventionally thought of as poetic or literary language will be a focus. This means that in places as much space can be devoted to examples of word play in jokes, newspaper editorials, advertisements, historical writing, or a popular thriller as to a sonnet by Shakespeare or a passage from Jane Austen. It is also important to stress how the term 'literature' itself is historically variable and how different social and cultural assumptions can condition what is regarded as literature. In this respect the role of linguistic and literary theory is vital. It is an aim of the series to be constantly alert to new developments in the description and theory of texts.

Finally, as series editor, I have to underline the partnership and co-operation of the whole enterprise of the Interface series and acknowledge the advice and assistance received at many stages from the PALA Committee and from Routledge. In turn, we are all fortunate to have the benefit of three associate editors with considerable collective depth of experience in this field in different parts of the world: Professor Roger Fowler, Professor Mary Louise Pratt, Professor Michael Halliday. In spite of their own individual orientations, I am sure that all concerned with the series would want to endorse the statement by Roman Jakobson made over twenty-five years ago but which is no less relevant today:

A linguist deaf to the poetic function of language and a literary scholar indifferent to linguistic problems and unconversant with linguistic methods, are equally flagrant anachronisms.

This volume of the Interface series parallels an earlier book, entitled *Twentieth-Century Poetry*, edited by Peter Verdonk. For this volume Peter Verdonk is joined by Jean Jacques Weber, as co-editors of a book which continues an orientation towards text analysis which takes particular account of the contexts and conditions within which the text and analyses of them are produced. *Twentieth-Century Fiction: From Text to Context* explores a wide and diverse range of texts and contains with each chapter a number of carefully prepared questions, tasks and suggestions for further reading and research which makes the volume highly practical both as a classroom text and as a research resource. The work of the editors and of all the contributors contributes most, however, to ongoing literary-linguistic study of texts which includes systematic and retrievable text-instrinsic treatment but which, crucially, also goes beyond the words on the page to explore the ways in which those words are shaped by different social, cultural and historical contexts of use. During the 1990s work in literary linguistics is rapidly developing the tools to answer charges of narrow formalism. This volume is a significant stage in that development.

Acknowledgements

We have only been able to achieve the aims of this collection with the help of its contributors and we wish to express our sincere thanks for their keen appreciation of our ideas and their inspiring papers. Furthermore we are grateful to Ronald Carter, the series editor, for his encouragement to undertake this project and for the benefit of his wide experience. Jean Jacques Weber would also like to thank Georges Barthel for invaluable help with scanning and computer file conversions. And, last but not least, our thanks go to Julia Hall, Ann Grindrod, Moira Eminton, Alison Foyle and Louise McTaggart for all their kind help in the editorial and production stage at Routledge.

Acknowledgement is due to copyright holders for their kind permission to include the following material in this book: Ablex Publishing Corporation for portions of the chapter 'Repetition and Point of View in Represented Speech and Thought' by Susan Ehrlich from B. Johnstone (ed.) *Repetition in Discourse*; Reed Consumer Books, Sinclair-Stevenson and Richard Scott Simon Limited for an extract from *The Mist in the Mirror*, © 1992 by Susan Hill; Random House UK Ltd, the Estate of the author, the Hogarth Press and Harcourt Brace & Company, copyright 1925, renewed 1953 by Leonard Woolf, for extracts from *Mrs Dalloway* by Virginia Woolf; Random House UK Ltd, the Estate of the author, the Hogarth Press and Harcourt Brace & Company, copyright 1927, renewed 1954 by Leonard Woolf, for an extract from *To the Lighthouse* by Virginia Woolf; Reed Consumer Books, Martin Secker & Warburg Ltd, and Viking Penguin, a division of Penguin Books USA Inc., copyright © 1984 by David Lodge, for an extract from *Small World* by David Lodge; Reed Consumer Books, Martin Secker & Warburg Ltd, and Penguin Books USA Inc. for an extract from *The British Museum is Falling Down* by David Lodge; Laurence Pollinger Ltd, the Estate of Frieda Lawrence Ravagli and Viking Penguin, a division of Penguin Books USA Inc. for extracts from *The Rainbow* by D. H. Lawrence. Copyright 1915 by D. H. Lawrence, renewed 1943 by Frieda Lawrence Ravagli. Laurence Pollinger Ltd, the Estate of Frieda Lawrence Ravagli and Viking Penguin, a division of Penguin Books USA Inc. for extracts from *Sons and Lovers* by D. H. Lawrence. Copyright 1913 by Thomas Seltzer Inc., renewed © 1948 by Frieda Lawrence Ravagli; Paladin/Grafton Books for extracts from 'To Room Nineteen' from *A Man and Two Women* by Doris Lessing; Random House UK Ltd, Jonathan Cape, and Sheil Land Associates Ltd for an extract from *The Ebony Tower* (first published 1974) by John Fowles; The Orion Publishing Group Ltd, Weidenfeld & Nicolson, and Smith/Skolnik USA for an extract from *Lolita* by Vladimir Nabokov; King's College, Cambridge, the Society of Authors as the literary representatives of the E. M. Forster Estate, W. W. Norton & Company Inc., Random House Inc., for extracts from *Howards End*, *Maurice* and *A Passage to India* by E. M. Forster; Charles Scribner's Sons for extracts from 'Hills Like White Elephants' from *The Short Stories of Ernest Hemingway* by Ernest Hemingway; Indiana University Press for an extract from 'You Gotta Do Something' from *Stories, Community and Place* by B. Johnstone; The New York Times Company © 1992 for an extract from 'Rulings Jar France Into Reliving Its Anti-Jewish Role in Nazi-Era' by Alan Riding, 10 May 1992; Scribner, an imprint of Simon & Schuster Inc., and the Hemingway Foreign Rights Trust for an extract from 'A Clean, Well-lighted Place' from *Winner Take Nothing* by Ernest Hemingway. Copyright 1933 by Charles Scribner's Sons; copyright renewed © 1961 by Mary Hemingway; Random House UK Ltd, the Estate of the author, the Hogarth Press and Harcourt Brace & Company, copyright 1944, renewed 1972, for an extract from 'Together and Apart' from *A Haunted House and Other Stories* by Virginia Woolf; Jonathan Clowes Literary Agency for extracts from 'One off the Short List' from *A Man and Two Women* by Doris Lessing; Faber & Faber Ltd, and Harcourt Brace & Company, copyright © 1955 by William Golding, for an extract from *The Inheritors* by William Golding; Random House Inc., Alfred A. Knopf Inc., and International Creative Management Inc., copyright © 1983 by Raymond Carver, renewed in 1993 by Tess Gallagher, for extracts from 'Cathedral' from *Where I'm Calling From: New and Selected Stories* by Raymond Carver, copyright © 1981, 1982, 1983 by Raymond Carver; Random House UK Ltd and Jonathan Cape for extracts from *Cal* by Bernard MacLaverty; Random House UK Ltd, the Estate of the author, the Hogarth Press, and Harcourt Brace & Company for permission to reprint 'Old Mrs Grey' and an excerpt from *The Death of the Moth and Other Essays* by Virginia Woolf, copyright 1942 by Harcourt Brace &

Company, renewed 1970 by Marjorie T. executrix; for excerpts from 'Friday 16 September (1932)' from *The Diary of Virginia Woolf, Volume IV: 1931–1935* by Anne Olivier Bell, copyright © 1982 by Quentin Bell and Angelica Garnett; for excerpts from 'The Modern Essay' from *The Common Reader* by Virginia Woolf, copyright 1925 by Harcourt Brace & Company, renewed 1953 by Leonard Woolf; and for excerpts from *The Letters of Virginia Woolf, Volume V: 1932–1935* by Virginia Woolf, copyright © 1979 by Quentin Bell and Angelica Garnett; Little, Brown and Company (UK) for an extract from *Warsaw Concerto* by D. Jones; Random House UK Ltd., Macmillan, New York, and Scribner, an imprint of Simon & Schuster Inc., copyright 1925 by Charles Scribner's Sons; copyright renewed 1953 by Ernest Hemingway, for an extract from 'The Doctor and the Doctor's Wife' from *In Our Time* by Ernest Hemingway; Reed Consumer Books, William Heinemann and Viking Penguin, a division of Penguin Books USA Inc. for an extract from *The Grapes of Wrath* by John Steinbeck. Copyright 1939, renewed © 1967 by John Steinbeck; Random House UK Ltd, Jonathan Cape, and Scribner, an imprint of Simon & Schuster, Inc., copyright 1940 by Ernest Hemingway; copyright renewed © 1968 by Mary Hemingway, for an extract from *For Whom the Bell Tolls* from the *Essential Hemingway* by Ernest Hemingway; David Higham Associates and William Heinemann for an extract from *The Human Factor* by Graham Greene; HarperCollins Publishers Inc., copyright © 1971 by Harper & Row Inc., for an extract from *The Bell Jar* by Sylvia Plath; Random House UK Limited and Jonathan Cape for an extract from *London Fields* by Martin Amis; Viking Penguin, a division of Penguin Books USA Inc. for extracts from *The Songlines* by Bruce Chatwin, copyright © 1987 by Bruce Chatwin; Victorian AIDS Council/Gay Men's Health Centre © 1990 for the poster When You Say Yes . . . Say Yes To Safe Sex.

While every effort has been made to contact owners of copyright of material which is reproduced in this book, we have not always been successful. In the event of a copyright query, please contact the publishers.

Introduction

Peter Verdonk and Jean Jacques Weber

THE 'FROM TEXT TO CONTEXT' APPROACH: A WAY INTO MODERN LITERARY CRITICISM

This is the second book in the 'From Text to Context' series: just like its predecessor, Peter Verdonk's *Twentieth-Century Poetry* (1993), the present volume on twentieth-century fiction also aims to offer students a way into modern literary criticism. The approach is 'modern', not only because it reflects the current issues in literary and linguistic theory, but also because it provides a teaching methodology which is in keeping with the tendency in recent years to encourage in students greater critical autonomy. To achieve this, students are introduced to a set of analytic and interpretive strategies that open up paths which constrain but do not determine readings and, above all, which *empower* readers. Thus, they put students into a situation of model construction, providing building-blocks and leading them towards the creation of their own personal model, towards the development of a first-hand response to literary texts.

Computer software is evaluated according to its reader-friendliness and its performance; the approach advocated here also tries to be reader-friendly in the sense of being pedagogically oriented and highly replicable (each interpretative step is made explicit so that it can easily be replicated by other readers), and at the same time it is powerful, because it makes possible, at a higher level of awareness, the link with modern literary criticism. It does this by leading students from the textual level, via the narrative level (which deals with the specific characteristics of narrative texts), to the contextual level of worlds and ideologies.

FROM TEXT-ORIENTED TO CONTEXTUALIZED STYLISTICS

This openness to matters of context is characteristic of modern stylistics, which has moved from purely formalist and text-oriented to more functional and contextualized approaches. Similar developments have taken place in literary criticism and linguistic theory. And since stylistics has a long tradition of being an interdisciplinary field, and has always profitably drawn on a mixture of both literary and linguistic theories, it should be no surprise that these sociological trends have given rise to a new movement in stylistics which recognizes the existence of that messy world outside. These stylisticians regard all speech and writing as primarily dialogic, that is, as social discourse in which the words used and the meanings of the words cannot be divorced from their relevant contexts (Macdonell 1986). Accordingly, they also view literary texts as part of a complex social and cultural process (Fowler 1981). There is no doubt that, from a theoretical point of view, this contextualized model has greatly increased the literary critical potential of stylistics and will give more satisfaction in advanced literary studies.[1]

This book presents an introduction to the contextualized approach without, however, simply rejecting the alternative, text-oriented models; on the contrary, it tries to combine the latter's obvious benefits of rigour and systematicity with the deeper insights of the former. Therefore, the contributors were asked to adopt a functional approach to their linguistic descriptions, that is, to take a pragmatic view of language as discourse or social interaction. This implies that the common levels of linguistic analysis (syntax, lexis and semantics) should also include a kind of extension (which, as such, is not a level of formal linguistic organization) accommodating the facets of language in use, which is the business of pragmatics. In other words, pragmatics attempts to explain the facts in the use of language which have a motivation and operation independent of language, but which at the same time function in combination with that language to effect communication (Graham 1992: 185–7).

THE PROCESS OF MEANING CREATION

Implicitly or explicitly, all the contributors to this book see the process of reading as a creative interaction between writer, text, reader and context. Though they may highlight in their analyses one or the other of these factors, they are fully aware that each factor has a contribution to make, that no factor can be discounted, and that therefore each approach is partial and must remain open and sensitive to other approaches.

The result of this construction and negotiation of meaning is the creation of a cognitive text world, but note that the text world will be different for the writer and for each reader (since we all use different assumptions, values, beliefs and expectations in the processing of the text). This by the way is not exclusive to literary discourse, but applies to both literary and non-literary texts, simply because all representation through language is a constructive process. Nor can stylistics nullify the indeterminacy of meaning. What is important, however, is that with a stylistic methodology, this indeterminacy is neither ignored nor allowed to go wild but it is contained, for the stylistic methodology ensures that our reading is both explicit and replicable. It thus allows us to achieve in our reading, not scientific objectivity, but an inter-subjective validity.

ORDERING THE CHAPTERS

We have ordered the chapters into three groups: the first group focuses on the textual level, the second on the narrative level and the third on the contextual level. There is thus, just like in the companion volume on twentieth-century poetry (Verdonk 1993), a gradual widening of the text's contextual orbit.

All the same, also, the first chapters show a thorough awareness of the wider contextual implications of the textual features that they deal with; they simply differ from later chapters in that they concentrate on one particular textual or structural feature in their analysis. Peter Verdonk elaborates on the phenomenon of lexical repetition as an element of meaning production. Because this textual device tends to create an emphatic or emotional style of writing, it is often an easy target for emulation or parody, which then results in what might be called 'intertextual repetition'.[2] Verdonk uses a pragmatic and socio-cognitive theory of language to give a possible explanation for the intriguing disposition of humans to produce these repetitive structures and attach meaning to them. Jean Jacques Weber introduces a method of analysing conceptual metaphors, and demonstrates how the choice of a particular metaphor can have important social and ideological consequences.

Two chapters deal with dialogue, what Mick Short in his chapter calls 'character talk'. Short himself is interested in what we can infer from the verbal interaction about the characters and their relationships. Rosemary Buck and Timothy Austin develop this type of pragmatic analysis of dialogue, focusing upon politeness and power: they study how conversational participants try to gain and maintain power over their interlocutor.

The following five chapters deal with what Short calls 'narrator talk' or, more specifically, with the important question of point of view in narrative. Susan Ehrlich compares oral and literary narratives, and shows how repetition can have the stylistic effect of signalling a shift in point of view in the latter but not in the former. Helen Aristar Dry discusses linguistic point of view, especially free indirect discourse, and how it creates both empathy and also narrative ambiguity or uncertainty. David A. Lee looks at the close connection between visual and cognitive perception, between seeing and interpreting. Michael Toolan focuses even more squarely on the cognitive or ideological dimension of point of view, the aim of his chapter being to define 'the values and attitudinal individuality of [a] text's speaker'. And in the last chapter of this section, Paul Simpson and Martin Montgomery present a model of narrative structure and then study the way in which changes in point of view brought about by translation from one medium to another – here, from narrative to film – significantly affect characterization.

The chapters in the third group also rely on an analysis of textual features or details of narrative technique, but they emphasize the role played by contextual factors in the reader's construction of the fictional world. First, Irene R. Fairley situates the text within the contextual frame of genre, comparing the personal narrative of a diary entry with the more impersonal narrative of a literary essay. Next, Paul Werth proposes to apply the theory of text worlds to the fictional universe projected in novels and short stories. According to this theory, the text of the literary discourse invites the reader to co-operate with the author in constructing a conceptual space in which the fictional state of affairs occurs, i.e. a text world.

The last two chapters share a concern for a greater critical awareness. Sara Mills discusses the role of narrative schemata at the interface between linguistic choices and the wider ideological framework. Her analysis of sexism in discourse also makes explicit the link between stylistic approaches and feminist literary criticism. And David Birch advocates close attention to the political dimension of discourse, insisting that communication is always contingent upon the way in which people assign value to meanings.

TARGET GROUP AND ADVICE ON USING THE BOOK

This book intends to offer an intensive introduction to literary stylistic criticism and is aimed at senior school students of English, under-graduate students of English language and literature, students of applied linguistics, and upper intermediate and advanced students of English as a second or foreign language.

In view of the educational level aimed at, the book contains a detailed index, as well as a glossary providing succinct explanations of the main linguistic and literary terms. Furthermore, there is a list of references at the end of each chapter which enables the student to read up on particular topics.

By way of introduction, we have supplied a preface to each of the chapters. In most cases these prefaces try to give the reader an idea of what the chapter is about, and sometimes they volunteer a piece of information which helps to put the text under discussion in a particular literary or linguistic perspective.

From a pedagogic point of view, the classroom model for teaching literary stylistics is very important. We have found that the seminar format and teaching in groups ensures maximum involvement of the students while the teacher's role is less dominant. As a result the students feel more inclined to share their views and ideas and to co-operate on oral and written assignments.[3]

Finally, we asked the contributors to include a set of assignments in the form of 'suggestions for further work'. We firmly believe that their chapters in combination with these suggestions will foster the students' linguistic awareness as well as their creative interpretation of salient formal and pragmatic features, and that they will be given a very firm foundation for the development of a receptive and sensitive language- and context-based literary criticism.

NOTES

1 In addition to Fowler (1981), some other recent books containing contextualized, i.e. discoursal, stylistic analyses of texts include Carter and Simpson (1989), Sell (1991), Toolan (1992), Weber (1992), Simpson (1993), Verdonk (1993), Sell and Verdonk (1994).
2 Jean Jacques Weber suggested this felicitous term in his reaction to Verdonk's chapter.
3 See Verdonk (1989: 242–5) for a detailed account of a teaching project in literary stylistics carried out with upper intermediate and advanced students of English as a foreign language.

REFERENCES

Carter, R. and Simpson, P. (eds) (1989) *Language, Discourse and Literature: An Introductory Reader in Discourse Stylistics*, London: Unwin Hyman.
Fowler, R. (1981) *Literature as Social Discourse: The Practice of Linguistic Criticism*, London: Batsford.

Graham, J. F. (1992) *Onomatopoetics: Theory of Language and Literature*, Cambridge: Cambridge University Press.

Macdonell, D. (1986) *Theories of Discourse: An Introduction*, Oxford: Blackwell.

Sell, R. D. (1991) *Literary Pragmatics*, London: Routledge.

Sell, R. D. and Verdonk, P. (1994) *Literature and the New Interdisciplinarity: Poetics, Linguistics, History*, Amsterdam: Rodopi.

Simpson, P. (1993) *Language, Ideology and Point of View*, London: Routledge.

Toolan, M. (ed.) (1992) *Language, Text and Context: Essays in Stylistics*, London: Routledge.

Verdonk, P. (1989) 'The Language of Poetry: The Application of Literary Stylistic Theory in University Teaching', in M. Short (ed.) *Reading, Analysing and Teaching Literature*, London: Longman.

—— (ed.) (1993) *Twentieth-Century Poetry: From Text to Context*, London: Routledge.

Weber, J. J. (1992) *Critical Analysis of Fiction: Essays in Discourse Stylistics*, Amsterdam: Rodopi.

1 Words, words, words
A pragmatic and socio-cognitive view of lexical repetition

Peter Verdonk

EDITOR'S PREFACE

There was a crooked man
And he walked a crooked mile;
He found a crooked sixpence
Against a crooked stile;
He bought a crooked cat
Which caught a crooked mouse,
And they all lived together
In a little crooked house.

There is no doubt that from our earliest childhood onward we find great pleasure in playing with the formal structures of language, and as this nursery rhyme illustrates abundantly, the use of lexical repetition appears to be central to this language game. Since this kind of childlore is deeply rooted in ancient superstitions, traditional tales, local customs, folk festivals and the like, and is characteristically still passed on through word of mouth, this simple rhyme furthermore seems to confirm the generally accepted belief that verbal repetition, including such elements as rhythm, metre and rhyme, has its origin in oral cultures. This, of course, raises the question how it is that in cultures in which literacy and the written word are predominant, these rhetorical devices still have a significant aesthetic and social function. For instance, in literary discourse the use of repetition may create thematic or symbolic patterns, while in the case of persuasive discourse like advertising or propaganda, it may lull us into a less critical attitude.

In this chapter I have tried to show that this question cannot be answered with the help of a semantic theory which is focused on meaning as it is produced by the abstract system of language forms, that is, dissociated from the actual situation of a social interaction between language users. Therefore, in my discussion of three different types of lexical repetition in fictional discourse, I have used a pragmatic model of meaning construction, which does not see language as a self-contained conceptual system, but as fundamentally interactive or 'dialogic', and in intimate interaction with a context of use. So we must go beyond the purely formal level of language and take into consideration the wider socio-cultural and ideological contexts of the production and reception of meaning.

Furthermore, extending the field of pragmatics, I have turned to recent work in socio-cognitive science (i.e. the study of the human mind centred upon human acts such as acts of language) to find a possible explanation for the intriguing fact that humans are invariably charmed or, as the case may be, taken in by linguistic quirks involving patterned structures of repetition. Interestingly enough, the cognitive linguists I consulted claim that our innate habit to structure things according to symmetrical patterns, including patterns of repetition, is in fact a projection of our embodied understanding of symmetry in the world around us. So, basically, these cognitivists analyse 'acts of language, including literature, as acts of a human brain in a human body in a human environment which that brain must make intelligible if it is to survive' (Turner 1991: vii–viii).

Yet another topic of interest came out of the very nature of lexical repetition in literary discourse, namely that it may contribute to a very emphatic or emotionally charged style, which in turn may expose writers to the strong temptation of emulation or parody. This then has prompted a discussion of the phenomenon of 'intertextuality', which may be defined as a dialogic interaction not only between books and readers, but also between books and books, each of which, of course, extending even further 'the widening gyre' of the context of signification.

P. V.

INTRODUCTION

Since my subject is lexical repetition as an element of meaning production in literary discourse, Hamlet's tantalizing reply to Polonius' question about what he is reading suitably answers my need of a title for this chapter (*Hamlet*, II.ii.192–3). As a matter of fact, in Shakespeare's age there was a revival of interest in the rhetorical arts of classical antiquity and in contemporary handbooks verbal repetition figured prominently. It was divided up into a lot of sub-categories ranging from the repetition of single words or phrases, located in various places in the sentence, to repetition of words or phrases in concert with recurrent grammatical patterns (see Nash 1989: 116–17 and Wales 1989: 402–3). A quick glance at Shakespeare's plays shows that to put the spectators under the spell of his 'revels', he too made frequent use of the device and to profound effect. This is shown most strikingly in Macbeth's anguished lamentation 'To-morrow, and to-morrow, and to-morrow,/Creeps in this petty pace from day to day', in which a single word repeated three times takes up an entire line (*Macbeth*, V.v.19–20). In the eponymous play, for that matter, the word 'blood' occurs over a hundred times!

Now, before this heyday of rhetoric, verbal repetition had gone through a long history, probably going back to the days when poems and narratives were composed and transmitted orally. In fact, as we can all see for ourselves, it has been in the literary tool box ever since. By its very nature, lexical repetition has always been a fundamental unifying device in poetry, jointly with other elements like rhythm, stress, metre and sound patterns. And, when occurring over longer stretches of text, it may have a similar controlling function in prose, in that it may intensify the overall thematic or symbolic structure of the work. For instance, Virginia Woolf's *Mrs Dalloway* (1925/1976) contains rewarding examples of repeated thematically interesting keywords.

In addition to this unifying function, readers appear to attach meanings to verbal recurrences, and going by what literary critics and my students say, they are chiefly felt to convey emphasis and/or to heighten emotion. That this seems to be the predominant response from readers, is perhaps confirmed by the fact that emotionally-charged poetry or prose is an easy and welcome target for parody, especially when it features the regular beat of one single word or phrase creating a kind of incremental emotional effect. In his book *The Language of Humour* (1985: 74–102), Nash has devoted an insight-ful chapter to this for many writers' irresistible temptation.

As a matter of fact, I was thinking about all this when I came across a recent piece of writing by a British author, who had evidently emulated the highly patterned style, teeming with lexical repetition, of one of the great Victorian novelists. This recognition raised a lot of questions including the following: what exactly is the nature of such an interaction between two novels from different centuries? What is the significance of this reading adventure or intertextuality, as it is now generally called, for my interpretation? What is its relation to the context of the writer, reader and book? Is it really a case of parody in the usual sense of the word? And, most importantly: what kind of theory do we need to account for the meanings arising from inter-textuality and from reiterated verbal patterns? And, last but not least, what is the source of this strong inclination of writers to produce these verbal recurrences and of the equally strong disposition of readers to tolerate them and even enjoy them, if they are artistically sound?

In the following sections, I have tried to find an answer to these questions, though I had better first begin with a brief introduction to some basic concepts such as that of 'word', the distinction between 'content words' or 'lexical items' and 'function words', and between 'open' and 'closed' word classes.

WHAT'S (IN) A WORD?

Everyone knows, in a general sort of way, what a word is and how it is used. However, the matter turns out to be rather problematic when we attempt a consistent definition (see, e.g., Carter 1987: 3–32). Some of the problems relate to decisions over where a word begins and where it ends. For instance, it is questionable whether fixed ex-pressions like 'letter-box' and 'one-parent families' count as one word or as more than one. And in connected speech, for that matter, words may not even have perceptible boundaries at all, that is, if there are no pauses around them. Furthermore, the familiar definition of a word as 'the minimal meaningful unit of language', which goes back to Bloomfield's 'minimum free form' (1933: 178), may well appeal to our intuitive knowledge about words, but it does not cover single units of meaning which are expressed by fixed phrases of two or more words, like the ones above, or idiomatic phrases like 'raise somebody's hackles'. And, what about words like 'the', 'if', 'but', 'because'? Do they have the same status as words like 'apple' or 'cat'?

In view of the overall aim of this chapter, however, this is not the place to go more deeply into what a word exactly is, and in spite of its limitations, I will continue to use the notion 'word' as a common-sense term. On the other hand, we also need a theoretical term, not only to refer to units of meaning that consist of more than one word, but also in case we have to make the kind of differentiation which follows from the questions in the preceding paragraph about the status of words. As to the latter, there is at least some psycho-linguistic evidence justifying the assumption that our socio-cognitive abilities enable us to divide the words we know into two rough categories: content words and function words (Aitchison 1987: 104–6).

CONTENT WORDS ARE EQUAL TO LEXICAL ITEMS

Content words, as the name implies, carry a particular information content, in that they name the persons, things, concepts, qualities, actions, events, processes, etc., which speakers experience in their culture. They include the major word classes of English: nouns ('girl', 'dog', 'politics'), adjectives ('good', 'small'), verbs ('see', 'think') and adverbs ('plainly', 'quickly'). Since these sets easily admit new members by coinage or borrowing, they are commonly called open classes. Not surprisingly, many speakers regard content words as constituting the lexicon proper of their language (cf. Greek *lexikon*, 'dictionary' and *lexis*, 'word'). Therefore, content words are also known as 'lexical items', and it is in fact this theoretical term which is commonly used when the term 'word' is not precise enough. For instance, as units of meaning, lexical items may not only consist of one word but also of multi-word compounds like 'tight-rope walker', idiomatic or other fixed phrases like 'the odd man out' and 'at any rate', as well as phrasal verbs like 'sound out' and 'tidy up'. From this it follows that it is lexical items which are usually listed as headwords in a dictionary.

ALICE'S INTUITION OF FUNCTION WORDS
AND CONTENT WORDS

Function words, on the other hand, constitute a relatively small and closed class to which new words are not usually added. Their primary function is grammatical, in that they structure the relationships between words, phrases, clauses and sentences. They include pronouns ('you', 'they', 'these'), articles ('a', 'the'), auxiliaries ('may', 'must'), conjunctions ('and', 'because') and prepositions ('in', 'over', 'after'). In the following text, the function words are italicized:

> '*T was* brillig, *and the* slithy toves
> *Did* gyre *and* gimble *in the* wabe:
> *All* mimsy *were the* borogroves,
> *And the* mome raths outgrabe.

'*It* seems very pretty,' *she* said *when she had* finished *it*, '*but it's rather* [italics of last word as original] hard *to* understand!' (*You* see *she* didn't like *to* confess, even *to herself, that she couldn't* make *it* out at all.) 'Somehow *it* seems *to* fill *my* head *with* ideas – only *I don't* exactly know *what they* are!'

(Carroll 1871/1970: 197)

I am sure many readers will recognize this passage from Lewis

Carroll's *Through the Looking-Glass*, when Alice has just finished reading (with the help of a mirror, of course!) the poem 'Jabberwocky', which she found in a Looking-Glass book lying near her on the table in Looking-Glass House. No doubt, Alice is a highly imaginative little girl, but it is probably her intuitive awareness of the fact that the grammatical function words and the lexical items in the poem are exactly in the right places in terms of normal English word order, which makes her say that it somehow seems to fill her head (and ours, for that matter) with ideas. Traugott and Pratt (1980: 88–9) rightly observe that much of the poem's pseudo-meaningfulness also derives from the fact that the sound and word structure of the nonsense words are strongly reminiscent of real English nouns, adjectives and verbs, calling up semantic associations.

THE INSTABILITY OF THE LEXICON AS A SOURCE OF LEXICAL CREATIVITY

The grammatical and lexical structure of 'Jabberwocky' also provides a brilliant illustration of another interesting linguistic feature. Because of the closed character of the system to which they belong, the meaning of function words, which is essentially grammatical, is relatively stable. However, through their very openness as a class, the meaning of lexical items is comparatively unstable, with individual items changing or even losing their original meanings and with a constant influx of new items. This fickleness of the lexical system is, of course, grist to the mill of the literary artist because it leaves plenty of scope to create ambiguity, to use words in non-standard senses, and even to coin entirely new words. Examples of such verbal invention in fiction include Newspeak in George Orwell's *Nineteen Eighty-Four* (1949/1954) and 'nadsat' – the teenage argot used in Anthony Burgess's *A Clockwork Orange* (1962). Interestingly enough, this brief sketch of lexical creativity fits in well with the view in cognitive linguistics that originality is not something autonomous, but is firmly grounded in the unoriginal everyday structures of language that inform it (Turner 1991: 19–20).

A PRAGMATIC MODEL OF MEANING: SENTENCE VERSUS UTTERANCE

In the previous paragraphs, the complex issue of meaning has been left more or less implicit, but I have now come to the point where it has to be dealt with explicitly. However, since the concept of meaning covers a vast area of knowledge, the limits of this chapter force me to be very selective, and for reasons which will be revealed presently, I will only make a brief excursion into one model of meaning, namely the pragmatic model.

The study of meaning has traditionally been the field of philosophy and semantics. It goes back to classical times and has many ramifications, but I have to cut down its long intellectual history quite disrespectfully to the summary statement that the primary focus of modern linguistic semantics is on meaning as it comes out of the systematic relations holding between words, phrases, clauses and sentences. In other words, it is concentrated on meaning produced by the abstract system of language forms, divorced from the concrete situation of verbal communication. Of course, depending on the task linguists set themselves, this formal approach to meaning is perfectly legitimate, but it does not suit my purpose because I need a model which can also account for the meaning that arises out of the very act of communication. In his seminal book *Pragmatics* (1983), Stephen Levinson describes the gap left by semantics as follows:

> if the term *meaning* [italics as original] . . . is restricted to the output of a semantic component, those interested in a theory of linguistic communication are likely to be greatly disappointed. For it is becoming increasingly clear that a semantic theory alone can give us only a proportion, and perhaps only a small if essential proportion, of a general account of language understanding.
>
> (Levinson 1983: 38)

Now, it is the discipline of pragmatics which seeks to bridge this gap and to complement semantics by investigating the meaning of language in relation to a context of use and users. If we draw a sharp line between the two complementary disciplines, we could say that where semantics concentrates on the meaning of the *sentence* as an abstract syntactic unit dissociated from a situational context, pragmatics centres on the meaning of the *utterance*, which is the concrete realization of a sentence in a context of use. To put it differently, sentences are types which have utterances as their tokens. For instance, if a piece of language like 'It's cold in here' is produced in, say, ten different situational contexts, then there are ten different utterances or tokens, each with its own utterance or pragmatic meaning, such as: 'Could you turn the heater up?', 'Someone left the door open', or 'Would you mind closing the window?', and many other possible messages which could be inferred. It is important to note here that these pragmatic meanings should not be put exclusively to the account of the speaker, because they are in fact the product of a complex social interaction, a kind of give-and-take exchange between addresser and addressee. In contrast, there is only one sentence or type with its own individual sentence or semantic meaning, which comes out directly from the linguistic structures used and carries a straightforward piece of information to the effect that the temperature in a particular place is very low.[1]

Just to avoid any misunderstanding, it should not be concluded from the foregoing discussion about the sentence/utterance dichotomy that pragmatic or utterance analysis is restricted to sentence-like structures only. If necessary, we may isolate as an utterance any chunk of language which is either too short or too long to be classified as a sentence (Leech 1983: 14). Furthermore, it should be noted that, although the term utterance is likely to be associated with a face-to-face speech situation, it may also refer to written texts. In the latter case, it may apply to interactions between speakers and interlocutors within the text as well as to the relation between text and reader (Pearce 1994: 81). So the fundamentally interactive or 'dialogic' nature of the utterance, which I have already referred to, remains operative in all types of communicative situation.

PRAGMATICS AND THE BAKHTINIAN DIALOGIC UTTERANCE

The term dialogic, for that matter, is a key concept in the theoretical writings of 'The Bakhtin circle' and in my view it ties in with the pragmatic model of meaning I have summarized above, while it also provides support for the type of discourse analysis underlying this book.[2] Consider, for instance, what one of Bakhtin's associates, Voloshinov, has to say on the matter:

> Dialogue, in the narrow sense of the word, is, of course, only one of the forms – a very important form, to be sure – of verbal interaction. But dialogue can also be understood in a broader sense, meaning not only direct, face-to-face, vocalized verbal communication between persons, but also verbal communication of any type whatsoever. A book, i.e., *a verbal performance in print* [italics as original], is also an element of verbal communication. It is something discussable in actual, real-life dialogue, but aside from that, it is calculated for actual perception, involving attentive reading and inner responsiveness, and for organized *printed* [italics as original] reaction in the various forms devised by the particular sphere of verbal communication in question (book reviews, critical surveys,

defining influence on subsequent works, and so on). Moreover, a verbal performance of this kind also inevitably orients itself with respect to previous performances in the same sphere, both those by the same author and those by other authors.

(Voloshinov 1930/1973: 95)

So the dialogic interaction as defined by Voloshinov is twofold, i.e. not only between books and readers, but also between books and books, each of which, of course, causes just so many ripples in the contextual pond. Interestingly, the latter type of interaction anticipates the present-day literary critical notion of 'intertextuality', which holds that texts are produced and interpreted through our conscious or unconscious experience of other texts. The texts in such an intertextual network can relate to each other for various reasons. For instance, a strong bond between texts (and, of course, between other modes of communication such as film, television and video) can be that they hail from the same genre. In this case, they are either genre specific (e.g. sonnet, epic, sermon, soap, western) or one genre infringes upon another (e.g. mock-epic, parody, advertising). As McCarthy and Carter (1994: 115) rightly say, the ability to refer across discourse or text worlds may be looked upon as a particular aspect of lexical competence.

INTERTEXTUALITY AND THE RELATIVENESS OF MEANING

The phenomenon of intertextuality is also a good illustration of the relativeness of all meaning in the sense that it is never absolute, but is always determined by or arising from something else, and this something else, as we have seen, is an inexhaustible variety of contexts. This fundamental notion rose to my consciousness again the other day, when I was reading Susan Hill's latest novel *The Mist in the Mirror* (1993) and felt quite pleased when I recognized the following extract as an imitation of the magnificent style of the opening chapter of Dickens's *Bleak House* (1853/1971). I realized that if I had failed to notice the echo, I would have missed not only the fun of it but also an extra source of contextual meaning:[3]

Rain, rain all day, all evening, all night, pouring autumn rain. Out in the country, over field and fen and moorland, sweet-smelling rain, borne on the wind. Rain in London, rolling along gutters, gurgling down drains. Street lamps blurred by rain. A policeman walking by in a cape, rain gleaming silver on its shoulders. Rain bouncing on roofs and pavements, soft rain falling secretly in woodland and on dark heath. Rain on London's river, and slanting among the sheds, wharves and quays. Rain on suburban gardens, dense with laurel and rhododendron. Rain from north to south and from east to west, as though it had never rained until now, and now might never stop.

Rain on all the silent streets and squares, alleys and courts, gardens and churchyards and stone steps and nooks and crannies of the city.

Rain. London. The back end of the year.

(Hill 1993: 9)

PARODY OR STYLIZATION?

In Bakhtin's theory of dialogism, Susan Hill's imitation.of Dickens's style is referred to as 'doubly-voiced' discourse, because she enters into a dialogic relationship by mingling her voice with that of another writer, and 'in keeping with its task, [the other voice] must be perceived as belonging to someone else' (Bakhtin 1963/1984: 189).[4] This category of doubly-oriented discourse is subdivided into several subcategories, which include, among others, stylization and parody. I have hesitated between these two, but I now think Hill's verbal imitation is a matter of stylization rather than parody. As a rule, the latter implies borrowing somebody else's discourse but turning it 'to a purpose opposite to or incongruous with the intention of the original' (Lodge 1990: 59), whereas stylization occurs when the writer borrows another's discourse but 'uses it for his [or her] own purposes – with the same general intention as the original' (ibid.).

Dickens is a master at beginning novels, and setting the scene. In the frightening opening pages of *Bleak House*, he leads the reader into a sinister and polluted world; the perfect image for this is the November fog in London, penetrating everywhere and soiling every-thing it touches, as the forces of evil and corruption pervade and infect the public institutions of Victorian society and its members. Susan Hill's novel is a classic ghost story also set in Victorian London. Quite appropriately, the hero enters the scene on a dark and rainy night at 'the back end of the year', and from then on his life is shrouded in a mist of mystery. So what could serve her purpose better than modelling the beginning of her novel on the splendid opening of *Bleak House*?

LEXICAL REPETITION EMBEDDED IN SCHEMES

Though the extract from Susan Hill's novel gave rise to some interesting thoughts on intertextuality and the related issues of parody and stylization, the primary reason why I have cited it is that it invites comment on the unrestrained overuse of one and the same word: rain. In everyday discourse, lexical recurrence is common enough to express emphasis, but here one wonders why Hill's readers would tolerate this almost obsessive repetition. The answer is that the writer gets away with it by incorporating the reiterated lexical item into 'schemes'. According to the traditional handbooks, schemes (from the Greek word for 'form') are rhetorical figures which show fore-grounded repetitions of formal expression. So they usually involve parallelistic or symmetrical structures on the level of phonology and/ or syntax.[5]

Thus, we can set out the dominant syntactic schemes that Hill uses in the following way:

rain	in London	rolling	along gutters
		gurgling	down drains
rain		gleaming silver	on its shoulders
rain		bouncing	on roofs and
			pavements
soft rain		falling secretly	in woodland and
			on dark heath
rain	on London's river	slanting	among the sheds,
			wharves and
			quays
rain	on suburban gardens	(dense)	with laurel and
			rhododendron
rain	from north to south and		
	from east to west		
rain	on all the silent streets and squares,		
	alleys and courts,		
	gardens and churchyards and stone steps		
	and nooks and crannies of the city		

Though the first two sentences of the Hill text are also richly equipped with replicated words and phrases, involving syntactic parallelism underpinned by phonological patterns, in a way they appear to serve only as a prelude to the ostentatious outburst of parallelistic structures laid out above. Our minds are literally soaked with the downpour of elaborate details about the relentless and all-pervading rain. It is not just a spate of detail, it is a spate of lexical items invoking a dazzling variety of contexts taking us from the outlying countryside to every nook and cranny of the Victorian metropolis.

As the above layout also shows, Hill has exploited two dominant syntactic schemes. One construction consists of the undefined noun 'rain' (i.e. without a preceding article or other determiner) modified attributively by one or more locative prepositional phrases, e.g. 'Rain on London's river'. The other is composed of the same undefined noun, but now modified by one or more non-finite clauses (i.e. not marked for tense); these consist of a present participle followed by another locative prepositional phrase, which is here adverbial in function, e.g. 'Rain bouncing on roofs and pavements'. It will be perceived, of course, that in some phrases this syntactic symmetry is further reinforced by sound patterns, e.g. 'Rain in London, rolling along gutters, gurgling down drains'.

This last sentence also shows that Hill sometimes blends the two major schemes, probably, so as to alleviate the drone of monotony. For the same reason, it seems, she uses the present participle construction all right, but replaces the reiterated noun 'rain' by a different word: 'A policeman walking by in a cape'. And so there are a few other variations on the two basic schemes, which may hold up the 'theme tune' for a while, but we know all the time that it will soon be resumed at full blast.

It is remarkable that the complexity of the above replicative, parallelistic structures can still be added to by yet another kind of syntactic extension, for which Nash (1971: 180) proposes the term 'elaboration'. It is most conspicuous in the phrase, 'Rain on all the silent streets and squares, alleys and courts, gardens and churchyards and stone steps and nooks and crannies of the city', in which the first modifying prepositional phrase 'on all the silent streets and squares' is amplified by an almost interminable list of elaborative noun phrases, which may comprise in themselves further instances of replication. For instance, the explicit and repeated use of the co-ordinating conjunction 'and', which is traditionally termed 'syndeton', may be felt to intensify the 'listing' of all the places where the rain falls, and thereby its omnipresence. Yet another instance of replication that will be noticed in this structure of elaborations is the pattern of alliterating hissing sounds. Anyway, the cathartic power of this piling detail on detail is suddenly reduced to the bare bones of the narration in the stark one-word sentences 'Rain', 'London', and in the portentous phrasal sentence 'The back end of the year', which echoes the final phrase of the first sentence: 'pouring autumn rain'.

Still this is not the end, I'm afraid, of my comment on the construction of this text, for it is built on an overarching structuring element which, perhaps, I should have started with, but left till now in order not to disturb a particular line in my argument. What I am hinting at is the striking feature that from virtually all sentences a crucial element is missing, namely forms of verbs which grammatically correlate with either present or past time, like for instance in 'the rain pours down' or 'the rain poured down'. In this connection, it will be noted that, in spite of their 'past tense' appearance, the verb forms 'had' and 'might', which are tucked away in the two neatly balanced subordinate clauses 'as though it had never rained until now, and [as though] [it] now might never stop', are no grammatical indication of the fact that the speaker talks about some actual past time occurrence. On the contrary, she makes a kind of hypothetical comparison to express her amazement at the incessant downpour.

Grammatically, present participles are not fixed in time and, as we have seen earlier, in this text they act as adjectival modifiers, that is, they are descriptive. (This also applies, for that matter, to the past participle 'borne' in the phrase 'sweet-smelling rain, borne on the wind'.) Interestingly, though, the experience of time can be inferred from lexical items other than verbs, namely from phrases like 'all day, all evening, all night', 'pouring autumn rain', 'street lamps blurred by rain', 'on dark heath', the repeated adverb 'never', and, last but not least, the phrase 'the back end of the year'. All these features taken together pragmatically suggest that the rain is felt to be self-contained, something existing in its own right.

Now, one thing we can learn from our reading of the Hill text is that there is often an intimate interaction between the semantic and pragmatic effects produced by lexical items and those produced by grammatical and phonological patterns. Since they usually have a high concentration of semantic and pragmatic meaning, this reciprocal influencing is particularly apparent in literary texts.

OUR EMBODIED UNDERSTANDING OF SYMMETRY: A SOCIO-COGNITIVE VIEW

Of course, if we resume our line of thought that communicative or pragmatic meaning is the product of a dialogic interaction between an addresser and addressee, Susan Hill's formal *tour de force* cannot be intended merely as a show of rhetorical skill. On the contrary, it must be taken as a linguistic signal alerting us to the social activity in which the writer and we as readers are engaged. Now, in this interactional communicative process, linguistic signals as a rule are only picked up if the addresser and addressee share more or less the same socio-cultural and cognitive context, which includes, among many other factors, the general background knowledge required for an understanding of the discourse, the abilities and beliefs of the participants, and knowledge of the socialized linguistic conventions of the genre of the discourse, which is here the novel.

So the question arises what is the source of this mutual ability of writers and readers to recognize these patterned structures?[6] For an answer to this question we can turn to the recent theories and findings of a number of cognitive linguists. Mark Turner (1991: 68–98), among them, holds that our intuitive ease in recognizing symmetries of all kinds, as well as our inclination to structure things according to symmetries whenever we can, are anchored in our bodily knowledge of symmetry and therewith in the basic perceptive habits of our daily lives. We project this embodied understanding of symmetry meta-phorically on to all our perceptions, actions and imaginings, so as to make sense of the world. Not surprisingly, this ingrained disposition is stimulated maximally by symmetric structures in art of various forms such as literature, music, painting, sculpture, architecture, etc.[7] And, for that matter, if we think that advertisements fulfil a need for language play, the discourse of advertising is also a rich quarry for parallelism on the levels of sound, grammar and meaning (see in particular Cook 1992: 120–45).

Our ability to recognize symmetry is inseparably linked with our ability to recognize the breaking of it, though we can never tell when or where this happens. Again, due to our daily physical experience and interactional relation with the external world, we are disposed to project symmetrical structures metaphorically on to all sorts of things around us. However, the more successful we are in doing so, the more strongly alerted we are to just those places where the symmetry breaks down. It is obvious that creative artists, and Susan Hill, as we have seen, is no exception, exploit this habitual disposition by lulling us into a false sense of continued and complete symmetry. When they then break the symmetry, we are challenged to account for it.

REPETITION THROUGH WORDS WITH SIMILAR MEANINGS

In addition to the type of lexical repetition involving reiteration of the same words or phrases, there are at least two other types which are of interest from a literary linguistic point of view. The first type occurs when there is a pattern of lexical items which are more or less synonymous. For instance, 'poison', 'venom', 'virus', 'toxin' and 'bane' are listed under the same entry in *Webster's New Dictionary of Synonyms*, which provides as the common denotation of all these words 'matter or a substance that when present in an organism or introduced into it produces an injurious or deadly effect'. I used the restrictive 'more or less synonymous', because total synonymy would involve lexical items which are identical both semantically, i.e. in terms of their denotations, and pragmatically, i.e. in terms of their connotations and therefore interchangeable in all contexts of use. Since this is an unlikely possibility, the pragmatic, contextually inspired choice which a speaker makes from lexical items coinciding or nearly coinciding in their semantic meaning is a significant factor of style. So because lexical items are associated with certain contexts, it is worthwhile to scrutinize the interplay between the actual and potential lexical choices in a specific context. It will be understood, though, that it is virtually impossible to give anything like an exhaustive list of all the contextual considerations which may determine a speaker's choice of words. Therefore, the following instances are only a random selection.

Thus, there may be a semantic proximity between 'poison', 'venom', 'toxin' and 'bane', but pragmatically they should be differentiated according to their contexts of use: 'keep poisons out of the reach of children' (common usage); 'man spurns the worm, but pauses ere he wake the slumbering *venom* of the folded snake' (literary and emotive – Byron); 'bacterial *toxins*, such as those of botulism and tetanus' (technical usage: medical); 'that journalist is regarded by some as the *bane* of Whitehall' (literary and attitudinal).

These few examples suffice to show that a particular choice of words reflects how we experience and comprehend the world, how we respond to it and behave as a social being. Particularly 'attitudinal' words may carry revealing pragmatic meanings. For instance, in a recent article in the *Daily Telegraph* about the outbreak of anti-foreigner sentiment in Europe I found the following pattern of words with the same or roughly the same semantic identity but articulating pragmatically widely divergent social and political attitudes: 'illegal aliens', 'foreigners', 'refugees', 'asylum-shoppers', 'illegal immigrants', 'illegals' and 'political asylum seekers' (cf. Verdonk 1993: 122–5).

The predominant French origin of the two series of examples of near synonyms cited in this section reminds me of another rich source of synonymous repetition, namely the well-known fact that the English language possesses almost a double lexicon in which items from Germanic origin coexist with items derived from the Romance languages. It is again the inexhaustible source of Shakespeare's genius which provides a splendid illustration of the two hemispheres of the English language. In *As You Like It* (V.i.52–60) the jester Touchstone

speaks to the rustic William as follows: 'Therefore, you clown, abandon, – which is in the vulgar, leave, – the society, – which in the boorish
is, company, – of this female, – which in the common is, woman; which
together is, abandon the society of this female, or, clown, thou
perishest; or, to thy better understanding, diest.'

It is, of course, a sweeping and unallowable generalization, but the
words of native Anglo-Saxon origin tend to have a stronger hold on
everything that is fundamental, familiar, concrete or emotional in our
lives, whereas the French or Latinate derivatives are generally associated with greater formality and abstraction. For instance, we say 'Help
me!' rather than 'Aid me!', and 'hearty', as in 'He had a big hearty
laugh', appears to sound warmer than 'cordial', as in 'They seemed
to be on cordial terms'.[8]

REPETITION THROUGH WORDS WITH
RELATED MEANINGS

The somewhat loose synonymy between some of the naming words for
'foreign-born people', listed in the previous section, makes an appropriate transition to the second type of semantic and pragmatic
repetition. It occurs when there is a grouping of lexical items which
are not semantically synonymous but associatively related because they
tend to recur in similar contexts. In fact, they build up or, to put it
more theoretically, they categorize, the areas of social and cognitive
experience that exist in our culture. In this case, the lexical items
involved are said to form a lexical set. They are called a 'set' because
together they give linguistic structure to a conceptual or semantic field
(e.g. 'appeal', 'prosecution', 'defence', 'plaintiff', 'defendant', 'accused' and 'witness' are lexical categories relating to the concept of
a court of law).

Interestingly enough, this theory seems to be confirmed by the
results of psycho-linguistic experiments which suggest that our socio-
cognitive abilities allow us to organize lexical items in such topic areas
of word storage (Aitchison 1987: 82–5).

Let us now consider the following extract from Virginia Woolf's *Mrs
Dalloway* (1925/1976):

> The hall of the house was cool as a vault. Mrs Dalloway raised her
> hand to her eyes, and, as the maid shut the door to, she heard the
> swish of Lucy's skirts, she felt like a nun who has left the world and
> feels fold round her the familiar veils and the response to old
> devotions. The cook was whistling in the kitchen. She heard the

click of the typewriter. It was her life, and, bending her head over the hall table, she bowed beneath the influence, felt blessed and purified.

(Woolf 1925/1976: 27)

Thus, through the close bonds which either already exist or, if necessary, are temporarily brought about in our mental lexicon between words which are felt to structure a particular semantic field, we are able to perceive in the above text a chain of inferential associations between the lexical items 'nun', 'left the world', 'veils', 'devotions', 'blessed' and 'purified'. Because both this lexical set as a whole and its reinforcing member items call up certain pragmatic or connotational references, they evoke a particular image or, perhaps, a series of images: e.g. nuns live in a convent, an austere and cold place lacking comfort; they renounce the world to devote their lives to religious duties, prayer, and often social or medical work; they have made vows of poverty, chastity, and obedience to a set of rules; they are uniformly dressed in a plain habit; and so there are, no doubt, many other associations.

ONLY CONNECT: ASSOCIATIVE LINKS
BETWEEN DIFFERENT SEMANTIC FIELDS

For our literary linguistic purposes, it is furthermore important to know that, according to the outcome of the psycho-linguistic experiments I referred to before, we are also able to make connections on the spot between different semantic fields by means of an active process of inferential association (Aitchison 1987: 85). This ability, then, would allow us to explore possible associative links between the lexical set building up the topic area of the 'nun' and other lexical items in the text. So we may wonder if it is 'the hall of the house . . . cool as a vault' which sets Mrs Dalloway's train of thought in motion. Does 'the swish of Lucy's skirts' evoke the rustling sound of a nun's veil or habit? And did we not expect 'bending her head in prayer; in obedience; in devotion, or over some object of worship', instead of 'over the hall table'? Similar associations, for that matter, may be produced by the clause 'she bowed beneath the influence', especially because one of the earlier meanings of 'influence' is 'the inflow of a divine force', as in the biblical line 'A pure influence flowing from the glory of the Almighty' (*Authorized Version, Wisdom*, 7:25). Again, this is just an example of a limited number of associations that may be triggered off by this kind of lexical analysis.

We have seen in the Susan Hill text that we may expect syntactic patterns and phonological links to reinforce the meanings generated by lexical strings. Considering Virginia Woolf's poetic style, it is therefore not surprising that this text, too, contains quite a few of such rhetorical schemes. For instance, the syntactic pattern 'Mrs Dalloway raised' is followed by the reiterated structures 'she heard', 'she felt', 'she heard', 'she bowed', and '[she] felt', while there are also quite a number of alliterating sounds intensifying the semantic and pragmatic meaning production of the text.

Obviously, the foregoing lexical analysis only reveals a single drop of the fountain of meaning of the novel as a whole. Therefore, I restrict myself to the observation that throughout the book regularly recurrent lexical items such as 'cold', 'coldness', 'petrified', 'contracted', 'rigid', 'impenetrability', 'woodenness' and, three times repeated, 'the death of her soul' (Woolf 1925/1976: 53–5) seem to hint at Clarissa Dalloway's supposed frigidity. Furthermore, it is repeatedly suggested that she is out of touch with the real world. It would seem, then, that the brief glimpse we have just caught of Clarissa's state of mind is a fragment that fits into the rich tapestry of recurrent narrative motifs in the novel.

SUGGESTIONS FOR FURTHER WORK

1 In an appendix to his novel *Nineteen Eighty-Four* (1949/1954: 241–51), George Orwell discusses the principles of Newspeak, a language that had been devised to meet the ideological needs of a totalitarian system called Ingsoc, or English Socialism. Read this appendix carefully and answer the following questions:

(a) The idea was that once Newspeak had been adopted, a dissenting thought should be literally unthinkable. In fact, it was devised not to extend but to diminish the range of thought. Considering the nature of language, do you think this is possible? Argue your answer from the point of view of the socio-cognitive approach to language which underlies this chapter.

(b) In what way was Newspeak utilized to make it impossible to use figures of speech such as irony or metaphor?

(c) What was the idea behind the interchangeability between different parts of speech, including content words and grammatical function words such as 'if' and 'when'? Are there examples in English in which function words are used as content words? Is it possible for particular content words to become function words? Give some examples of present-day function words which went through such a development. Relate your answer to question (a).

2 In terms of intertextuality, a strong bond between texts can be that they are associated with the same genre. In this case, such texts are either genre specific or they exploit another genre to create a particular effect. Read the opening of John Fowles's story 'The Enigma' (1974/1986: 185–239). Does it belong to a particular genre? If it does, read the whole story to find out whether it is genre specific or just utilizes another genre to achieve some specific literary effect. Work out this effect in case it is a matter of genre infringement.

3 The comic novel *The British Museum is Falling Down* (1965/1983) by David Lodge contains a strong element of literary parody and pastiche. In 'An Afterword' to a later edition, the author makes the following interesting comment on this aspect of the book:

> No doubt the use of parody in this book was also, for me, a way of coping with what the American critic Harold Bloom has called 'Anxiety of Influence' – the sense every young writer must have of the daunting weight of the literary tradition he has inherited, the necessity and yet seeming impossibility of doing something in writing that has not been done before.
>
> (Lodge 1965/1983: 168)

The novel contains several passages of parody or pastiche, mimicking, among other writers, Joseph Conrad, Graham Greene, Ernest Hemingway, Henry James, James Joyce, D. H. Lawrence and Virginia Woolf. Write an essay on the function of these parodied sections in the novel as a whole. As a theoretical framework, you can use Bakhtin's essay 'From the prehistory of novelistic discourse' (Bakhtin 1940/1981), which sees parody as one of the key types of intertextuality or double-voiced discourse in the modern novel. You could also make profitable use of Bakhtin's *Problems of Dostoevsky's Poetics* (1963/1984), which I referred to earlier in this chapter.

4 The passage below is an example of one of the parodied writers in David Lodge's *The British Museum is Falling Down* (see assignment 3):

> He was getting tired with trekking backwards and forwards to the telephone. After the coolness of the foyer, the atmosphere of the Reading Room, when he re-entered it, struck him as oppressively hot. The dome seemed screwed down tightly on the stale air, sealing

it in. It hung over the scene like a tropical sky before a storm; and the faint, sour smell of mouldering books and bindings was like the reek of rotting vegetation in some foetid oriental backwater. Appleby cast a gloomy eye on the Indians and Africans working busily in their striped suits and starched collars.

There comes a moment in the life of even the most unimaginative man – and Appleby was not that – when Destiny confronts him with the unexpected and the inexplicable, when the basis of his universe, like a chair which has so habitually offered its comforting support to his limbs that he no longer troubles to assure himself of its presence before entrusting his weight to it, is silently and swiftly withdrawn, and the victim feels himself falling with dismaying velocity into an infinite space of doubt. This was the sensation of Appleby as, mopping away with a soiled handkerchief the perspiration which beaded his forehead like the drops of moisture on the interior of a ship's hull that warn the knowledgeable mariner that he is approaching the equatorial line, he came in sight of the desk where he had left his books and papers. He staggered to a halt.

(Lodge 1965/1983: 52)

Make a lexical analysis and set out any phonological or syntactic schemes reinforcing the semantic and pragmatic meanings of the passage. Try to track down which of the authors mentioned in assignment 3 is being mimicked here, and if you have found her or him, try to find a piece of her or his writing that comes closest to the style of Lodge's imitation. Finally, explain why this is an instance of parody rather than stylization.

5 Considering the profusion of lexical repetition and rhetorical schemes of sounds and syntax, the following deeply moving passage from the final paragraph of James Joyce's story 'The Dead' in *Dubliners* (1914/1956) offers interesting material for comparison and intertextual association with the abstract from Susan Hill's novel *The Mist in the Mirror*, which I have analysed in this chapter. Analyse and interpret the Joyce passage along similar lines and show how its mood fits into the theme of the story as a whole. Note that Wales (1992: 37–55) contains a very interesting section on repetition in Joyce's *Dubliners*. The passage reads as follows:

Yes, the newspapers were right: snow was general all over Ireland. It was falling on every part of the dark central plain, on the treeless hills, falling softly upon the Bog of Allen and, farther westward, softly falling into the dark mutinous Shannon waves. It was falling, too, upon every part of the lonely churchyard on the hill where Michael Furey lay buried. It lay thickly drifted on the crooked crosses and headstones, on the spears of the little gate, on the barren thorns. His soul swooned slowly as he heard the snow falling faintly through the universe and faintly falling, like the descent of their last end, upon all the living and the dead.

(Joyce 1914/1956: 220)

6 In his novel *The Rainbow* (1915/1981), D. H. Lawrence uses a kind of style which he himself called 'violent'. Its most obvious feature is relentless repetition. The following passage from the opening of the book offers a good illustration:

So the Brangwens came and went without fear of necessity, working hard because of the life that was in them, not for want of the money. Neither were they thriftless. They were aware of the last halfpenny, and instinct made them not waste the peeling of their apple, for it would help to feed the cattle. But heaven and earth was teeming around them, and how should this cease? They felt the rush of the sap in spring, they knew the wave which cannot halt, but every year throws forward the seed to begetting, and, falling back, leaves the young-born on the earth. They knew the intercourse between heaven and earth, sunshine drawn into the breast and bowels, the rain sucked up in the daytime, nakedness that comes under the wind in autumn, showing the birds' nests no longer worth hiding. Their life and interrelations were such; feeling the pulse and body of the soil, that opened to their furrow for the grain, and became smooth and supple after their ploughing, and clung to their feet with a weight that pulled like desire, lying hard and unresponsive when the crops were to be shorn away. The young corn waved and was silken, and the lustre slid along the limbs of the men who saw it. They took the udder of the cows, the cows yielded milk and pulse against the hands of the men, the pulse of the blood of the teats of the cows beat into the pulse of the hands of the men. They mounted their horses, and held life between the grip of their knees, they harnessed their horses at the wagon, and, with hand on the bridle-rings, drew the heaving of the horses after their will.

(Lawrence 1915/1981: 41–2)

Identify the different types of lexical repetition and the parallelistic structures on the levels of phonology and syntax in which they are embedded. Relate these to the semantic and pragmatic meanings of the text, and establish the main images that are evoked to convey the intimate relationship of the Brangwens with nature. You can use the analytic method I have applied to the pieces by Susan Hill and Virginia Woolf.

7 Virginia Woolf's *Mrs Dalloway* (1925/1976) presents one day in the life of Clarissa Dalloway, a middle-aged wife of an MP, who prepares and gives an important party in the City of London just after the Great War. In spite of the novel's extremely brief time-scheme, its sense of the passage of time is particularly strong. This is brought about by mingling subjective time, filled in by the past and present-time experiences in the minds of the characters, with clock time, which is indicated by the recurring chimes of Big Ben. In several places in the book, the striking of the clock is accompanied by a kind of refrain: 'First a warning, musical; then the hour, irrevocable'. Another refrain repeated several times is 'Fear no more. Fear no more the heat o' the sun', sometimes abbreviated to 'Fear no more', which is an echo from Shakespeare's *Cymbeline*. Furthermore, the book contains many repetitions of single lexical items as well as lexical sets giving shape to recurrent images. Read the novel carefully and write an essay on the function and meaning of these various forms of repetition in the context of the novel as a whole.

NOTES

1 It will be noted that, strictly speaking, even a simple statement like 'It's cold in here' cannot be fully interpreted on the basis of its linguistic or semantic meaning, because we can only determine the pragmatic meaning of the present tense 'is' and the locative phrase 'in here' if we take into account the real context of use from which we can then infer the time and place of the utterance.

2 'The Bakhtin circle' refers to a body of writings by Mikhail Bakhtin (1895–1975) and his friends and associates V. N. Voloshinov (1884/5–1936) and P. N. Medvedev (1891–1938). They published their major works under the extremely difficult conditions in the Soviet Union of the 1920s and 1930s, and only became widely known in the West after they had been translated into English during the 1970s and 1980s. Because of the hazardous political situation at the time, there is uncertainty about the authorship of the writings of the group. Some scholars claim that Bakhtin published most of his earlier works under the names of his associates. For further details on this question, see Holquist (1990). In an interesting article, Hall (1989) proposes to use the Bakhtinian approach as a theoretical foundation for literature teaching. Wales (1988) describes lucidly where the works of the Bakhtin circle tie in with some recent developments in stylistics and discourse analysis, while also providing a

useful working bibliography for further reading. For an accessible introduction to Bakhtinian dialogic theory, supported by readings of some literary texts, see Pearce (1994). Morris (1994) provides a convenient selection of writings of Bakhtin and his associates.

3 To be honest, it was easy enough for me to spot the resemblance because the 'Fog everywhere' piece from *Bleak House* has long been a stock-in-trade of countless stylisticians. The passage, which has been thoroughly exhausted but will never lose its fascination, runs as follows:

Fog everywhere. Fog up the river, where it flows among green aits and meadows; fog down the river, where it rolls defiled among the tiers of shipping, and the waterside pollutions of a great (and dirty) city. Fog on the Essex Marshes, fog on the Kentish heights. Fog creeping into the cabooses of collier-brigs; fog lying out on the yards, and hovering in the rigging of great ships; fog drooping on the gunwales of barges and small boats. Fog in the eyes and throats of ancient Greenwich pensioners, wheezing by the firesides of their wards; fog in the stem and bowl of the afternoon pipe of the wrathful skipper, down in his close cabin; fog cruelly pinching the toes and fingers of his shivering little 'prentice boy on deck. Chance people on the bridges peeping over the parapets into a nether sky of fog, with fog all round them, as if they were up in a balloon, and hanging in the misty clouds.

(Dickens 1853/1971: 49)

Though it is, of course, a matter of personal preference, the most enlightening analysis of this passage I have seen so far is the one produced by Walter Nash (1971: 178–80). Interestingly enough, Nash has later used the same passage to illustrate the phenomenon of 'pseudoparodies', i.e. 'texts that are not centrally parodic, in terms of a clearly definable model, but which wear a parodic *aura* [italics as original], and are full of echoes of half-remembered writings' (Nash 1985: 99–102).

4 The translation Emerson published in 1984 is based on the 1963 edition, entitled *Problems of Dostoevsky's Poetics*, which in turn is a revision Bakhtin made of his *Problems of Dostoevsky's Art*. He had published this study as early as 1929; the same year he was arrested and sent into exile.

5 The semantic counterpart of the scheme is the 'trope' (from the Greek word for 'turn' or 'conversion'), i.e. a foregrounded irregularity of content, in which lexical items are used in such a way that their standard meaning is changed conspicuously. Examples include metaphor and metonymy.

6 Van Peer (1986) presents a rewarding empirical investigation (involving psychological testing) into formally and semantically foregrounded structures.

7 As Jean Jacques Weber clearly shows in his chapter, the recurrent patterns which are anchored in our bodily experience and our everyday perceptual interactions with the external world, can also be metaphorically extended to the more abstract and less-well-understood domains of human experience.

8 An extremely useful study of the double lexicon of English is Sylvia Adamson's article 'With double tongue: diglossia, stylistics and the teaching of English' in Short (1989).

REFERENCES

Adamson, S. (1989) 'With double tongue: diglossia, stylistics and the teaching of English', in M. Short (ed.) *Reading, Analysing and Teaching Literature*, London: Longman.

Aitchison, J. (1987) *Words in the Mind: An Introduction to the Mental Lexicon*, Oxford: Blackwell.

Bakhtin, M. (1929) *Problems of Dostoevsky's Art*, Leningrad: Priboi.

—— (1940/1981) 'From the prehistory of novelistic discourse', in Michael Holquist (ed.), trans. Caryl Emerson and Michael Holquist *The Dialogic Imagination: Four Essays by M. M. Bakhtin*, Austin: University of Texas Press.

—— (1963/1984) *Problems of Dostoevsky's Poetics* (ed. and trans. C. Emerson), Minneapolis: University of Minnesota Press.

Bloomfield, L. (1933) *Language*, London: Allen and Unwin.

Burgess, A. (1962) *A Clockwork Orange*, Harmondsworth: Penguin.

Carroll, L. (1871) *Through the Looking-Glass, and What Alice Found There*, in M. Gardner (1970) *The Annotated Alice*, Harmondsworth: Penguin.

Carter, R. (1987) *Vocabulary: Applied Linguistic Perspectives*, London: Allen and Unwin.

Cook, G. (1992) *The Discourse of Advertising*, London: Routledge.

Dickens, C. (1853/1971) *Bleak House*, Harmondsworth: Penguin.

Fowles, J. (1974/1986) 'The Enigma', in J. Fowles, *The Ebony Tower*, London: Pan Books.

Hall, G. (1989) 'Mikhail Bakhtin's language based approach to literature: A theoretical intervention', in R. Carter, R. Walker and C. Brumfit (eds) *Literature and the Learner: Methodological Approaches*, London: Modern English Publications and the British Council.

Hill, S. (1993) *The Mist in the Mirror*, London: Reed Consumer Books.

Holquist, M. (1990) *Dialogism: Bakhtin and his World*, London: Routledge.

Joyce, J. (1914/1956) 'The Dead', in J. Joyce, *Dubliners*, Harmondsworth: Penguin.

Lawrence, D. H. (1915/1981) *The Rainbow*, Harmondsworth: Penguin.

Leech, G. N. (1983) *Principles of Pragmatics*, London: Longman.

Levinson, S. C. (1983) *Pragmatics*, Cambridge: Cambridge University Press.

Lodge, D. (1965/1983) *The British Museum is Falling Down*, Harmondsworth: Penguin.

—— (1990) *After Bakhtin: Essays on Fiction and Criticism*, London: Routledge.

McCarthy, M. and Carter, R. (1994) *Language as Discourse: Perspectives for Language Teaching*, London: Longman.

Morris, P. (1994) *The Bakhtin Reader: Selected Writings of Bakhtin, Medvedev and Voloshinov*, London: Edward Arnold.

Nash, W. (1971) *Our Experience of Language*, London: Batsford.

—— (1985) *The Language of Humour*, London: Longman.

—— (1989) *Rhetoric: The Wit of Persuasion*, Oxford: Basil Blackwell.

Orwell, G. (1949/1954) *Nineteen Eighty-Four*, Harmondsworth: Penguin.

Pearce, L. (1994) *Reading Dialogics*, London: Edward Arnold.

Peer, W. van (1986) *Stylistics and Psychology: Investigations of Foregrounding*, London: Croom Helm.

Traugott, E. Closs and Pratt, M. L. (1980) *Linguistics for Students of Literature*, New York: Harcourt Brace Jovanovich.

Turner, M. (1991) *Reading Minds: The Study of English in the Age of Cognitive Science*, Princeton: Princeton University Press.

Verdonk, P. (1993) 'Poetry and public life: a contextualized reading of Seamus Heaney's "Punishment"', in P. Verdonk (ed.) *Twentieth-Century Poetry: From Text to Context*, London: Routledge.

Voloshinov, V. N. (1930/1973) *Marxism and the Philosophy of Language*, trans. L. Matejka and I. R. Titunik, New York and London: Seminar Press.

Wales, K. (1988) 'Back to the future: Bakhtin, stylistics and discourse', in W. van Peer (ed.) *The Taming of the Text: Explorations in Language, Literature and Culture*, London: Routledge.

—— (1989) *A Dictionary of Stylistics*, London: Longman.

—— (1992) *The Language of James Joyce*, London: Macmillan.

Woolf, V. (1925/1976) *Mrs Dalloway*, London: Granada Publishing Limited.

2 How metaphor leads Susan Rawlings into suicide

A cognitive-linguistic analysis of Doris Lessing's 'To Room Nineteen'

Jean Jacques Weber

EDITOR'S PREFACE

In the 'Afterword, or end-paper' to her novel *Briefing for a Descent into Hell* (1971/1972: 251–2), which explores a man's mental breakdown and society's conditioned and unimaginative reaction to it, Doris Lessing observes wryly that it needs a particular training to instil in people the belief that putting a label on some feeling or thing and defining it, is equivalent to 'understanding and experiencing it'. It is precisely the kind of training, she continues, children receive in our schools where they are taught 'how to use labels, to choose words, to define'. This appears to be an informal way of saying that such rigid categorization imposes severe constraints on the human potential to conceive of the world in other ways.

Lessing's intuition that there must be something wrong with this way of defining and understanding our experiences in the world, happens to fall in with the results of recent empirical studies conducted by a group of cognitive linguists of which George Lakoff, Mark Johnson and Mark Turner are the leading exponents.

The following very brief summary of their views must be introduced by the important observation that since language is the vehicle for expressing the conceptual system which we use in thinking and acting, it is the main source of information about the structure of that system.

Lakoff and his colleagues share the common assumption, which goes back to classical times, that humans categorize their experience into general concepts so as to make sense of the astounding variety of the world. But they contest the traditional idea that our categorized concepts are an objective representation of reality and therefore primary, which means that all imaginative conceptualizations are derivative, and to be labelled figurative, poetic or metaphorical. In the cognitivist view it is just the other way round: metaphor is not some rhetorical by-product of objective thinking, but in fact the foundation of the human conceptual system. In other words, metaphors can be expressed in language precisely because human thought processes are essentially metaphorical.

Though we may no longer see them as metaphorical, there are numerous common expressions which show how metaphors structure our everyday concepts. Of course, this metaphorical structuring of our thinking is culturally and ideologically determined. For instance, how we experience one thing in terms of another, 'a heart of stone'; how we give a concept a spatial orientation (up–down, on–off, near–far, right–left, in–out, forward–back, centre–periphery, etc.) based on our everyday physical experience, e.g. 'This is hard, uphill work'; how we project our experiences with physical objects in the world on to non-physical experiences such as activities, emotions, ideas, etc., so as to be able to refer to them, to quantify them, to identify them, in short, to reason them out, e.g. 'Her mind broke down' (we have this experience with machines!).

These are all examples of metaphors which have become linguistically ossified because they structure the conceptualization of our everyday realities. Other metaphors, of course, have not been assimilated into routine conceptualizations because they are too evocative and creative. Though they provide new insights into our social, ideological and cultural realities, it must be noticed that such fresh metaphors are embedded in the same conceptual system as their conventionalized counterparts, that is, they, too, originate from the same experiential basis of the knowledge of our body, our sense perceptions, mental images as well as other experiences of a physical or social nature.

Within the limits of this preface, the foregoing could only be a thumbnail sketch of the general theories underlying the cognitive-linguistic model of analysis or, what Turner (1991: 148) called, 'cognitive rhetoric' on which Jean Jacques Weber has based his stimulating reading of Doris Lessing's short story 'To Room Nineteen' (1958/1992). This story, too, reveals the author's preoccupation with the way in which her characters define and understand their experiences.

P. V.

A number of linguists, in particular George Lakoff, Mark Johnson and Mark Turner, have developed a new approach in linguistics which they call cognitive linguistics. They contrast their own, cognitivist view of meaning with the traditional, 'objectivist' view. According to the latter, meaning resides in the relationship between words and the world, independently of human cognition and conceptual systems. In other words, meaning is characterized via reference to an objective, 'mind-free' reality. However, such a view, as Lakoff and his co-workers have repeatedly pointed out, ignores all experiential aspects of the human psyche, such as human perception, mental imagery, bodily experiences, motor movements, desires and intentions, personal or social experiences, etc. Their own, cognitivist view stipulates that meaning is experientially-based, grounded in patterns of human experience.

Mark Johnson has provided detailed studies of what he calls the image-schematic bases of meaning, by which he means the extent to which our mental concepts depend on, among other things, our bodily experience. Image-schemata are the recurrent patternings of our everyday perceptual interactions and bodily experiences, such as the centre–periphery (or figure–ground) relation or the notion of containment. For example, we experience the centre–periphery distinction whenever we look at something: at any one time, we can only focus on one object, and the remainder is backgrounded, made peripheral. We also experience the in–out distinction many times daily, when we go into or out of a particular containing space such as a house or a room, and when we move an object from the outside to the inside of something or vice versa (e.g. putting money into a wallet or taking it out of the wallet). We use these image-schemata as a way of imposing order upon the chaos of reality, but note that they are not fixed and static but dynamic patterns, which are constantly updated and modified in our encounters with new types of situations. Such image-schemata can also be metaphorically extended to more abstract or less-well-understood domains of experience. So the centre–periphery distinction is extended from the concrete domain of seeing an object to the epistemic domain of understanding an idea, with the visually central object finding its counterpart in the epistemically 'central' (or significant) idea. And the domain of physical contain-ment metaphorically structures the domain of psychological contain-ment, so that we may feel psychologically 'imprisoned' or feel a need to 'break out' of our lives.

In the short story that will be analysed below, Doris Lessing's 'To Room Nineteen' (1958/1992), we find a related example that draws upon both image-schemata of centre–periphery and containment: namely, our psychological experience of the self. Susan Rawlings, the heroine of the story, sees her self as a container with certain elements, especially the rational ones, central to it, whereas other, unconscious, irrational elements are kept outside, in the periphery and hence under control. I guess many people would share her view to some extent, though other people might prefer different metaphors, such as a metaphor of balance, to represent the different components of the self.

For Susan and her husband Matthew, a healthy self is definitely a matter of control rather than balance. The narrator tells us that with Susan and Matthew all 'inner storms and quicksands were understood and charted' (255).[1] 'Charted' is reminiscent of the phonologically and etymologically related 'chartered', which occurs at the beginning of William Blake's 'London' (1794/1971):

I wander thro' each charter'd street,
Near where the charter'd Thames does flow.

In Blake, both the world of man ('street') and even the world of nature ('Thames') are controlled by the forces of the law. And in Lessing's image, it is human nature that is controlled by the forces of the Freudian super-ego. The image emphasizes the idea of control being re-established after brief periods of psychological turbulence.

Such an image-schema of the self can lead to the development of one or more conventional, conceptual metaphors. For instance, we can now look upon neurosis as a military invasion of the self. The source domain is that of an invasion: there is a particular territory, which is considered to be the 'interior' space and which is threatened and aggressed by an external enemy. The idea of an invasion thus pre-supposes an externalization of the enemy. It also implies a destructive warring of opposed forces. These are some of the assumptions which are mapped on to the less-well-understood target domain of neurosis. The latter can then be seen, too, as an invasion of the inner territory of the self by alien, external forces. The result is a destructive confrontation between the rational elements of the self, which defend the inner territory, and the irrational, unconscious instincts and impulses, which attack it.

In this way, the image-schematic structure of the source domain is transferred on to the target domain. Note that the image-schematic structure of the target (neurosis) is not pre-existent, but is actively constructed, created by the reader in his/her interpretation of the metaphor. Only the self has some pre-existent image-schematic structure as a container with an inside and an outside. Therefore the *neurosis as military invasion* metaphor only works because the (constructed) structure of the self as a territory is compatible with the (pre-existent) structure of the self as a container. In general, we can say that only as much knowledge about the source domain as is consistent with the target domain is transferred in the metaphorical mapping. This is a constraint on metaphorical mappings that Lakoff (1990) has called the 'invariance hypothesis'.

Metaphor is thus defined as an ontological and epistemic mapping across conceptual domains, from a source domain (military invasion) on to a target domain (neurosis). The conceptualization of neurosis as military invasion is realized in a number of different linguistic expressions. In Lessing's 'To Room Nineteen', these include the notions of facing, defeating, being taken over, being besieged, being attacked as well as the basic being invaded:

> When I go into the garden, that is, if the children are not there, I feel as if there is an enemy there waiting to *invade* me.
>
> (1958/1992: 260)
>
> she returned to the house determined to *face* the enemy wherever he was, in the house, or the garden or – where?
>
> (262)
>
> She sat *defeating* the enemy, restlessness.
>
> (262)
>
> He is lurking in the garden and sometimes even in the house, and he wants to get into me and to *take me over.*
>
> (267)
>
> I'm *besieged* by seven devils.
>
> (269)
>
> she came face to face with her own craziness which might *attack* her in the broadest valleys.
>
> (271)

Because of this wide range of possible linguistic realizations of one and the same conceptual metaphor, Lakoff and his co-workers emphasize that metaphor is not just a matter of language but a matter of thought and reason. It is a way of understanding or thinking about a particular domain of experience in terms of another.

A conceptual metaphor also sets up what Lakoff and his co-workers call an 'idealized cognitive model' (ICM) of the target domain: the ICM combines the pre-existent image-schematic structure of the domain with the structure imported by the metaphorical mapping. We have seen that in the case of the self, this is a bounded space with an interior – containing the rational elements of the self – and an exterior, where the unconscious, irrational elements are located. And neurosis involves the external forces staging an attack in order to conquer the inner territory of the self. Such a concept of neurosis is thus irretrievably metaphorical. However, this does not imply some form of determinism, as if we could not conceive of neurosis in any other way; on the contrary, a domain of experience may have, and usually has, different and competing metaphorical ICMs. For instance, even within Lessing's short story, neurosis is not only conceptualized as a military invasion but also as an economic take-over bid. Indeed, the 'take over' expression quoted above is ambiguous and could equally well fit into an economic as into a military ICM. And the presence of such an economic ICM is confirmed by the following quotation:

> The demons were not here. They had gone forever, because she was *buying* her freedom from them.
>
> (285)

There is an underlying compatibility here: both neurosis and business can be seen as war, hence neurosis can also be seen as a business deal. Yet another ICM – of neurosis as rape – is suggested by 'he wants to get into me', the expression that precedes 'to take me over'. And again, the presence of such an ICM is confirmed by the following passage:

> She had to go right away to the bottom of the garden until the devils of exasperation had finished their *dance* in her blood.
>
> (266)

Here the underlying ICM of neurosis as orgy, revelry is still basically an image of certain elements no longer under control, but the emphasis has shifted: now the uncontrolled elements are no longer attacking, invading, conquering the inner core but staging a wild dance, perhaps as a celebration of a first victory.

It is important to realize that all these ICMs are not natural but highly ideological structures, integral parts of a particular world-view. In Lessing's 'To Room Nineteen', the narrator establishes a liberal–bourgeois, upper-middle-class ideology as the dominant one and, at the same time, expresses an ironic attitude towards it. It is epitomized by the words 'intelligent' and 'sensible'. Both Susan and Matthew do 'everything right, appropriate' (253), even down to the number and gender of their children! Both are highly conscious of the basic assumptions of this ideology, as evidenced by the frequent repetition of 'know' constructions:

[Children] can be a thousand things that are delightful, interesting, satisfying, but they can't be a well-spring to live from. Or they shouldn't be. Susan and Matthew *knew* that well enough.

(254)

both *knew* of the hidden resentments and deprivations of the woman who has lived her own life and, above all, has earned her own living, and is now dependent on a husband for outside interests and money.

(255)

Children needed their mother to a certain age, that both parents *knew* and agreed on.

(255)

Susan would work again, because she *knew*, and so did he, what happened to women of fifty at the height of their energy and ability, with grown-up children who no longer needed their full devotion.

(255)

The 'know' constructions set up what seems to be a liberal twentieth-century revision of the Victorian 'angel-in-the-house' ideology, built around the image of the dutiful, self-denying mother-figure. Both versions of the ideology imply repressed feelings of fear and anger ('hidden resentments and deprivations') for the woman during her home-bound phase as angelic wife and mother. As many feminist critics (e.g. Gilbert and Gubar 1979) have pointed out, these feelings, caused by the woman's social confinements, often lead to a schizophrenic split and tend to be embodied in a dark double, who represents the depths of her nature. This is exactly what happens to Susan: she, too, is faced by her dark double, a 'gingery green-eyed demon with his dry meagre smile' (272).

In the story, the angel-in-the-house ideology is characterized by a complete domination of the rational and is symbolized by the house, which is set in opposition to the garden with its 'wild sullied river' (258). The geographical locations not only symbolize psychic configurations but are also congruent with the container schema discussed above: the house is the inner core, the central self; as such, it represents the husband's (and middle-class society's) sensible, intelligent, rational, civilized values, which have been interiorized by Susan. The inner demon, on the other hand, has been exteriorized, and is now associated with the garden, so that all irrational elements and demonic values are located in the outer periphery.

At the beginning of the story, as the inner core of Susan's self is being besieged by the alien, demonic forces of otherness, Susan tries to avoid the garden, where the demon is freed, while in the house he (or it) is contained. But gradually she actively seeks out the garden:

> When she heard Harry and Matthew explaining it to the twins with Mrs Parkes coming in: 'Yes, well a family sometimes gets on top of a woman . . .' she had to go right away to the bottom of the garden until the devils of exasperation had finished their dance in her blood.
>
> (266)

She becomes more and more aware of the house as a form of social confinement: 'it was like living out a prison sentence' (264). She realizes that what she considered to be her innermost self is only a set of superficial social roles, and that 'essential Susan' is 'in cold storage' (259) or being sacrificed ('nailed . . . to her cross' 271). Eventually she rejects social responsibility and the pressure to be what she is not.

So the invasion of the centre results in an inversion of inner and outer. The demons gradually take over the inner territory, whereas the civilized values are pushed outside, to the periphery. This is the moment in the story when Susan feels that she has become other, 'a stranger' (273):

> She felt as if Susan had been spirited away. She disliked very much this woman who lay here, cold and indifferent beside a suffering man, but she could not change her.
>
> (273)

Note the lack of co-reference between 'she' and 'her' in the final sentence, which foreshadows the fact that ultimately Susan will be unable to accept her demon as her truest self, to live her own otherness. In a gesture of sterile escapism, she flees from her invading alter ego and takes refuge in no man's land, the neutral ground of Fred's seedy hotel, where she can survive like a war refugee. The hotel room is a sanctuary where she finds a sterile and false psychic unity, although the narrator also hints in one passage that she at least glimpses the possibility of an alternative, non-split self here: '[She] let go into the dark creative trance (or whatever it was) that she had found there' (280).

Matthew's inquiries into Susan's whereabouts put an end to all this. Metaphorically they involve an extension of the realm of the civilized forces, so that the hotel room is as it were 'colonized'. As a result, Susan feels imprisoned here too, just like in her own house:

> she was impelling herself from point to point like a moth dashing

itself against a window-pane, sliding to the bottom, fluttering off on broken wings, then crashing into the invisible barrier again. And again and again.

(280)

And inevitably, the demonic forces take over here, too:

Several times she returned to the room, to look for herself there, but instead she found the unnamed spirit of restlessness.

(280)

Susan does not realize that the 'unnamed spirit' is a key element of her own self and that it needs to be balanced with its rational elements. On the contrary, she is still on the run, still unable to face her true otherness. Now she tries to find self-fulfilment through an illusory and destructive search for dissolution; and so the story ends with her 'drift[ing] off into the dark river' (286) of unconsciousness and death.

Our analysis of the image-schematic structure underlying the conceptual metaphor of neurosis as military invasion – as it is actualized in Lessing's story – has provided us with an insight into the heroine's assumptions, values and attitudes. It is not a natural but a highly ideological model, which has important consequences for the way Susan Rawlings acts and lives. Indeed, the liberal–bourgeois conceptualization of the self as a contained territory and of neurosis as a military invasion of this territory at least predisposes Susan to act in certain ways rather than others. After all, her Manichean division of the self into good and evil can only be resolved by either total victory or total defeat, but not for instance by integration. And so, because total victory seems impossible to sustain, Susan is faced with a limited, false and misguided choice between ignominious destruction of the self in defeat and the martyrdom of death as the only way of securing victory over the conquering forces of irrationality.

Lessing thus shows how a particular idealized cognitive model leads Susan into self-destruction. At the same time, she promotes social and personal awareness in the reader by hinting at the possibility and desirability of different world-views, different ways of conceiving of the self and neurosis. *Neurosis as military invasion* is only the most visible surface metaphor, whose source domain has an explicit linguistic realization (the verb 'invade' is actually used in the story to refer metaphorically to the onset of neurosis). And hence its underlying idealized cognitive model is part of the dominant ideology in Susan's life. But there is also a latent undercurrent in 'To Room Nineteen': a deeper, more invisible metaphor, whose source domain has to be retrieved by inference.[2] It is associated with the imagery of the snake, which is used at three different places in the story, charting the development of Susan's self.

At the beginning, Susan and Matthew's life is said to be 'like a snake biting its tail' (253), an image of ineffectiveness, stagnation and sterility. Later in the story, Susan has a vision of her demon prodding an unhealthy-looking snake with a stick (267). The snake might still symbolize Susan's self – unhealthy because of too much repression – and so the demon could be seen as shaking her unhealthy self out of its stagnation. In other words, what might be suggested here is a kind of awakening. And indeed, the next time we come across the snake image, Susan's dormant self has been awakened:

> she was running the brush over her hair again and again, lifting fine black clouds in a small hiss of electricity. She was peering in and smiling as if she were amused at the clinging hissing hair that followed the brush.
>
> (272–3)
>
> She thought this out, as she brushed her hair, watching the fine black stuff fly up to make its little clouds of electricity, hiss, hiss, hiss.
>
> (278–9)

Here Susan's snake-like black hair hissing with electricity can be seen as a metaphorical expression of her new, fierce, powerful self.

Our brief analysis of the snake imagery suggests a re-interpretation of the *neurosis as military invasion* metaphor; neurosis – or rather what from a conventional viewpoint is considered to be neurosis – is now seen in a much more positive light as an awakening. However, the source domain of awakening is not linguistically realized in the text; it has to be inferred from the context by the reader. It is part of an alternative, but non-dominant ideology in Susan's mind, and therefore not strong enough to influence her actions. On the contrary, the dominant ideology leads her to reject her newly awakened self and to choose instead the sleep of unconsciousness and death. Like Edna Pontellier's (Chopin 1899/1986), Susan's awakening ultimately ends in suicide.

Even more positive, more constructive alternative conceptualizations of the self and neurosis are markedly absent from the text. For instance, a conceptualization in terms of the process of artistic creation, equating the creation of the self with the creation of a work of art, would have been possible: here inner conflicts and demon-possession would be seen as necessary steps in a process leading to the creation of a balanced, integrated work of art (or self, respectively).

Susan Rawlings, however, because of her conventional understanding of the self and neurosis, is unable to come to terms with the unconscious elements of her self, to move through (necessary) dissolution towards integration and a creative balance between rational and irrational elements. She is, quite literally, propelled into suicide by the wrong metaphors.[3]

SUGGESTIONS FOR FURTHER WORK

1 What 'idealized cognitive models' (ICMs) underlie such expressions as 'to go mad' (consider the difference between 'go' and 'come') and 'the terrible madness that overtook the king' (*Source: Collins Cobuild English Language Dictionary,* 1987)? Look for more expressions connected with madness, neurosis, etc. What ICMs underlie them? To what extent are they compatible with the ICMs underlying Doris Lessing's story 'To Room Nineteen'?

2 Find out something about Freud's theory of the mind. What does he call the ego, the super-ego, the id? What metaphor is his view of the mind based on (a metaphor of control, balance, etc.)? Is his view of the mind compatible with Susan Rawlings's in Lessing's story?

3 A major contention of this chapter has been that conceptual metaphors provide an insight into the speaker's assumptions, values and world-view.

  (a) Study any other metaphors in 'To Room Nineteen' not discussed above and see whether they throw further light upon the structure of Susan Rawlings's (or the narrator's) cognitive universe.

  (b) Read other short stories and find out what conceptual metaphors (if any) underlie them. Examples include the simile of 'Hills Like White Elephants' (1925/1966) in Ernest Hemingway's short story of that name or the simile of the sky and the ocean 'like a flat screen' in Margaret Atwood's 'A Travel Piece' (1975/ 1985). Consider, first, whose world-views the similes characterize (the author's, the narrator's or a particular character's) and secondly, what they reveal about this person's world-view.

4 Margaret Atwood is a prime example of a writer who uses metaphors to express her narrators' and characters' world-views. Read any short story or novel by Atwood and carry out the following tasks:

  (a) Collect all the metaphors in the text and group them according to who uses them (the narrator, a particular character).

  (b) Metaphor being a mapping from an old or well-understood

source domain on to a new or less-well-understood target domain, identify the source and target domains for each metaphor that you have found. In particular, consider what source domains each 'metaphor user' relies on in his/her metaphorical mappings, and what target domains they are used to explain. (For readers who are confused about the distinction between source and target domains: in the *neurosis as military invasion* metaphor, *military invasion* is the source domain and *neurosis* is the target domain.)

(c) What insights does your analysis of source and target domains give you into the narrator's or the particular character's way of conceiving of the world? (If you feel safer comparing your results with somebody else's analysis, study Atwood's novel *Surfacing* (1972/1990) and then read 'The Metaphorical Selfscape of Atwood's Narrator' in Weber 1992: 68–74.)

5 Conceptual metaphors are also common in non-literary discourse types such as political discourse and newspaper language. For instance, Fairclough (1989: 120) discusses a newspaper article which describes riots in terms of the spread of cancer. He points out that this discursive practice has social and ideological consequences: 'one does not arrive at a negotiated settlement with cancer . . . Cancer has to be eliminated, cut out.'

Look through some newspapers and find articles that represent social or political problems metaphorically. What ideological implications does the choice of metaphor have?

NOTES

1 Quotations are from the Paladin (1992) edition of 'To Room Nineteen'. All italics and words within square brackets are mine.
2 The distinction between surface and deep, visible and invisible metaphors is taken from Stockwell (1992: 53).
3 I should like to thank Clara Calvo, Marion Colas-Blaise, Donald Hardy and Neal Norrick for their most useful comments on an earlier version of this chapter.

REFERENCES

Atwood, M. (1972/1990) *Surfacing*, London: Virago.
—— (1975/1985) 'A Travel Piece', in *Dancing Girls and Other Stories*, New York: Bantam.
Blake, W. (1794/1971) 'London', in J. Bronowski (ed.) *William Blake: A Selection of Poems and Letters*, Harmondsworth: Penguin.
Chopin, K. (1899/1986) *The Awakening and Selected Stories*, London: Penguin.

Fairclough, N. (1989) *Language and Power*, London: Longman.

Gilbert, S. and Gubar, S. (1979) *The Madwoman in the Attic*, New Haven: Yale University Press.

Hemingway, E. (1925/1966) 'Hills Like White Elephants', in *The Short Stories of Ernest Hemingway*, New York: Charles Scribner's Sons.

Hunter, E. (1987) 'Madness in Doris Lessing's '"To Room Nineteen"', *English Studies in Africa* 30: 91–104.

Johnson, M. (1987) *The Body in the Mind: The Bodily Basis of Meaning, Imagination and Reason*, Chicago: University of Chicago Press.

—— (1989) 'Image-Schematic Bases of Meaning', *Recherches Sémiotiques-Semiotic Inquiry* 9: 109–18.

—— (1992) 'Philosophical Implications of Cognitive Semantics', *Cognitive Linguistics* 3: 345–66.

—— (1993) *Moral Imagination: Implications of Cognitive Science for Moral Understanding*, Chicago: University of Chicago Press.

Lakoff, G. (1987) *Women, Fire and Dangerous Things: What Categories Reveal About the Mind*, Chicago: University of Chicago Press.

—— (1990) 'The Invariance Hypothesis: Is Abstract Reason Based on Image-Schemas?', *Cognitive Linguistics* 1: 39–74.

Lakoff, G. and Johnson, M. (1980) *Metaphors We Live By*, Chicago: University of Chicago Press.

Lakoff, G. and Turner, M. (1989) *More Than Cool Reason: A Field Guide to Poetic Metaphor*, Chicago: University of Chicago Press.

Lessing, D. (1958/1992) 'To Room Nineteen', in *A Man and Two Women*, London: Paladin: 252–86.

—— (1971/1972) *Briefing for a Descent into Hell*, London: Grafton Books.

Stockwell, P. (1992) 'The Metaphorics of Literary Reading', *Liverpool Papers in Language and Discourse* 4: 52–80.

Tiger, V. (1990) "Taking hands and dancing in (dis)unity": Story to Storied in Doris Lessing's "To Room Nineteen" and "A Room"', *Modern Fiction Studies* 36: 421–33.

Turner, M. (1987) *Death is the Mother of Beauty: Mind, Metaphor, Criticism*, Chicago: University of Chicago Press.

—— (1991) *Reading Minds: The Study of English in the Age of Cognitive Science*, Princeton: Princeton University Press.

Weber, J. J. (1992) *Critical Analysis of Fiction: Essays in Discourse Stylistics*, Amsterdam: Rodopi.

3 Understanding conversational undercurrents in 'The Ebony Tower' by John Fowles

Mick Short

EDITOR'S PREFACE

Traditionally, linguists have always studied the structure and meaning of single sentences regardless of their use in actual communication. In the last few decades, however, there has been a growing interest in the properties of whole texts and their communicative functions and uses in particular contexts. This shift in emphasis has given rise to the relatively new discipline of discourse analysis, which regards all types of spoken and written texts, for example, conversations, interviews, leaflets, poems, novels, etc., as discourses, that is, as interpersonal communicative activities performed for a specific social purpose and situated in a particular context.

Discourse analysts identify particular linguistic patterns in spoken and written texts, and then relate these to a context of use so as to infer the meanings worked out or rather negotiated by the speaker/writer and hearer/reader in a social interaction, i.e. a discourse. Instances of such recurrent patterns include the switch in roles from hearer to speaker (turn-taking); pairs of utterances which are commonly connected (adjacency pairs); formal linking devices marking clausal and sentential relationships (cohesion); the arrangement of information in sentences (given/new information); and formal structures typifying particular types of discourse (genre).

Because the full meaning of these linguistic building blocks of discourses cannot be dealt with on the level of text-internal semantics, discourse analysts must turn to the findings of the study of language used in context (pragmatics). This enables them to make sense of the extra-linguistic motivations and cognitive assumptions of language users. These include the sense that uttering language involves certain deeds, not merely words, and the ability to identify the functional intention of such deeds (speech acts); in association herewith, the inclination to co-operate in the use of language so as to communicate successfully (the co-operative principle); the dependence on polite behaviour in social interaction (the politeness principle), and, in connection herewith, the selection of forms of address (vocatives/ address); the need to 'save face' in conversational interaction (face); the ability to make sense of discourse which lacks cohesion (coherence); the stereotypical assumptions about frequently encountered situations (schema), and, last but not least, the ability to refer to or understand any one text through a conscious or unconscious awareness of other texts (intertextuality).

This is a reasonably adequate overview (the bracketed concepts are meant as cross-references to the corresponding entries in the glossary) of the theoretical framework which Mick Short has used for his perceptive analysis of a piece of dialogue, or 'character talk' as he calls it himself, from John Fowles's short story 'The Ebony Tower' (1974).

In the continuation of the argument between the characters quoted by Short, the old painter Henry Breasley presses his attack on abstraction by calling it the greatest betrayal in the history of art. Summarizing his attack, he brands this betrayal as the 'ebony tower', which has replaced the ivory tower of art pursued for art's sake. Probably, he associates its blackness with anything obscure in modern art which the abstract artist is scared to be clear about (Fowles 1974/ 1986: 50–3). This debate about art turns out to be so closely interwoven with the action of the story, with the relations between its characters and the actual characterization, that Short's 'critical game', i.e. his special interest in the story's dialogic aspects, proves highly relevant to the story as a whole.

P. V.

INTRODUCTION

In this chapter I will discuss a short interaction involving four characters from a short story. To show satisfactorily what is going on 'underneath' this interaction, I will need to make use of a number of different approaches thrown up by discourse analysis and pragmatics in recent years. I do not have the space to describe those approaches in detail here, but if you are not already familiar with them you will need some introduction to them. Hence, I will describe the approaches very briefly in the next section, giving enough information for you to follow my discussion of the extract, and also referring to work which you can read later, if you wish, to fill in the analytical and methodological gaps which I am bound to leave trailing in my descriptive wake.

Before we move on to discuss the extract itself, let us note a major distinction in novels and stories between the talk of the characters and the 'talk' of the narrator, in which that character communication is embedded. The majority of critical work on fictional prose, including stylistic analysis, concentrates rather more on narrator 'talk' than character talk. For example, Leech and Short (1981) devote one chapter out of ten to describing 'Conversation in the novel', and Toolan (1990) has only one chapter out of thirteen ('Monologue and dialogue') on related matters. The reasons for this are not difficult to see. First, most twentieth-century criticism of the novel has concentrated on matters related to 'point of view', which is most interestingly realized in the narrative portions of novels. In this context, it is almost too obvious to bother to say, for example, that when Mrs Norris talks in Jane Austen's *Mansfield Park* (1814/1966), she does so from her point of view. Second, discussion of authorial style, which has also been commonplace in the twentieth century, works best with relatively large stretches of text, all emanating from the same producer. This again has led critics towards narration and away from character talk. Finally, the analytical linguistic tools needed to cope sensibly with character talk were developed by linguists after the kinds of analysis which have helped stylisticians to characterize critical concepts like style and viewpoint in reasonably exact ways.

THE APPROACHES

Discourse analysis concentrates on describing the 'structure' of spoken and written discourse above the level of the sentence, including, for example, the unwritten 'rules' by which people take turns in conversation. Pragmatics explores how utterances are interpreted in context, giving meanings for utterances which are different from the meanings of the individual sentences which comprise them. Hence pragmatics helps to explain how, on leaving a theatre, 'The costumes were very nice', in answer to the question 'What did you think of the performance?', indirectly means 'I didn't think much of it'. Although their basic aims are different, discourse analysis and pragmatics overlap to some extent in that discourse structure is meaningful. For example, turn-taking patterns in a particular conversation will be interpreted as significant. Hence if A always speaks first and always interrupts B, who in turn never interrupts A, this behaviour tells us something about the relationship between A and B. Wardhaugh (1985) is an accessible general introduction to these areas, and Brown and Yule (1983) and Levinson (1983) are fuller, and more advanced introductions. Leech and Short (1981: chapter 9) and Fowler (1986: chapter 8) are accessible accounts of how these sorts of approaches can be used in the study of conversation in literature.

Turn-taking mechanisms

All conversational encounters are based upon the notion of speakers taking turns, and there is a tendency for the most powerful speaker to have the longest turns and to initiate sub-parts of conversations. In teacher–student interactions, for example, teachers initiate and students respond, and teachers often say more than all of the students put together (see Sinclair and Coulthard 1975, and Burton 1980 for a modification of their analysis of teacher–pupil talk for use on dramatic dialogue). The initiation–response structure is a general one in that many conversations can be analysed as sequences of connected pairs of contributions (often called 'adjacency pairs': e.g. question–answer, greeting–greeting). The sub-parts of this two-part structure are called 'first pair-part' and 'second pair-part', and the second pair-part will often have a conversationally preferred outcome, based on the assumptions of social harmony and polite behaviour. Hence a request will normally be followed by an agreement to the request, rather than a refusal, and an offer by its acceptance. Adjacency pair structures can also have other structures embedded inside them. Pretend, for example, that you ask me the best way to get to my house. This first pair-part assumes a relevant answer, but before I am able sensibly to give you the most appropriate set of directions I may need more information from you, for example whether you are walking or coming by car, in which case I will need to ask you a question (another first pair-part) to which you will need to reply (another second pair-part) before I can supply the second pair-part demanded by your original question. For more reading and references see Levinson (1983: chapter 6). Bennison (1993), Herman (1991) and Toolan (1989) use turn-taking theory in stylistic analysis.

Speech acts

Talk is a kind of action. If I utter the sentence 'Can I have a lick of your lolly?' in appropriate circumstances (i.e. when you and I are together, and when you have a lolly in your hand), I have at the same time performed the speech act of requesting permission from you. And you, in agreeing or refusing, will also perform a speech act. Note also that these speech acts can sometimes be performed non-verbally:

you could agree to my request by nodding your head. Meaningful behaviour realized by body movements like this is usually called kinesic behaviour. Speech acts are often realized by sentences, but can also be realized by parts of, or groups of, sentences. A political speech, for example, may count as a whole as an act of persuasion, but have within it a number of constituent speech acts like accusing the opposing political party of incompetence, and telling a joke at their expense. The turns in the adjacency-pair analysis set out above are usually speech acts, and the distinction between grammatical structure and speech act force helps us to understand why, traditionally, we have overlapping terms to describe sentence types. Thus 'command' is a speech act label and 'imperative' is a grammatical label describing a grammatical structure often used to make commands with. Because imperatives are so often used to make commands, the two terms are often used interchangeably. But, given appropriate contextual circumstances, an imperative structure can be used to make a request ('Give me a dime, buddy') and a declarative structure can be used to deliver a command (consider 'You can go now, Jones' uttered by a teacher to a pupil who has been detained after school for misbehaviour).

Because of the partial fit between grammatical structure and speech act force, utterances can often be ambiguous. 'Give me a dime, buddy' could be a command or a request. We often use this ambiguity to see how much we can get away with while not disturbing the social fabric. Hence if someone says to you 'Give me a dime' and you say 'You can't tell me what to do', it is possible for the person talking to you to defuse the situation by saying he was asking, not telling you. It will be clear from this discussion that analysing the acts of speech used can tell us a lot about the inter-relations between characters, for example if one character uses lots of requests, and a second character always agrees to those requests. For more work on speech acts see Searle (1975), Levinson (1983: chapter 5), and for stylistic work using speech act analysis see Hurst (1987), Leech and Short (1981: 290–4) and Short (1989).

Politeness

Social interaction depends crucially on polite behaviour. To get anything done technically involves being impolite to others in that you prevent them from doing what they might otherwise want to do while they accede to your wishes. We usually 'mitigate' our impolite behaviour by linguistic (and other) means, for example by apologizing for an intrusion, or by being indirect or saying 'please' when telling someone what to do. My local railway station has a notice which says 'Please do not leave luggage unattended or it will be removed. Thank you.' Unattended luggage might hide a terrorist bomb, so British Rail have good reasons for such notices, but they still feel the need to surround the imposition on their customers by politeness markers. The most influential discussions of politeness phenomena are Brown and Levinson (1987) and Leech (1983). Bennison (1993), Brown and Gilman (1989), Leech (1992) and Simpson (1989) use politeness theory to discuss drama.

Other markers of social relations

It will be clear from the above that social relations are influenced by a large variety of linguistic forms. Being more formal, or more informal, than normal in some context, for example, will indicate disturbed social relations. A common way in which people mark their social relations is by the terms which they use to address one another or to refer to others. There is a system of terms of address in English, so that, for example, title and last name (e.g. 'Dr Short') suggests formality, social distance and respect, whereas last name only ('Short') usually suggests social distance and less respect, and first name only ('Mick') suggests informality and social closeness between addresser and addressee.

Inferring meaning

Texts do not have meaning in themselves. They are patterned assemblages of linguistic information and structure which need to be interpreted by the reader, who brings along background knowledge of the world and an understanding of the meaning of words and structures and the procedures which we habitually use to encode and decode meaning. Authors write in the knowledge that readers have this knowledge and abilities, and readers make similar assumptions about authors when they read their works. The ways in which we infer meaning are many and complex, but one influential account of how we infer meaning is Grice (1967/1975). He suggests that when we talk we obey at least four maxims of conversational behaviour, which can be crudely summarized as:

(a) Say what you believe to be true (maxim of quality);
(b) Give the appropriate amount of information (not too much and not too little) for your hearer (maxim of quantity);

(c) Be relevant (maxim of relation);
(d) Speak clearly and concisely (maxim of manner).

We can break these maxims secretly (breaking (a) secretly would be to lie, and breaking (b) by giving insufficient information would be to be 'economical with the truth'). But, more importantly for conversational meaning, these maxims can be broken *flagrantly*, in a way which is clear to both speaker and hearer, or reader and writer. This *flouting* of the conversational maxims allows speakers/writers to imply and hearers/readers to infer unstated information. The conversation about the play above produces the inferred meaning described by applying the maxim of relation to the reply. The most relevant way to answer the question 'What did you think of the performance?' would be to give an assessment straightforwardly. To praise the costumes is thus not maximally relevant. However, costumes are a relatively minor aspect of staging a play, and if the speaker praises this aspect and not others, it is easy to infer that he or she cannot openly assess these more important aspects without appearing impolite, and must therefore be criticizing the performance indirectly. For fuller discussion of this kind of approach, see Levinson (1983: chapter 3), Brown and Yule (1983: chapter 2), and for applications to literature see Cooper (1981) and Short (1989, 1990).

THE TEXT TO BE ANALYSED

'The Ebony Tower' (1974/1986) is about an art critic, David Williams, who goes to France to interview a British painter called Henry Breasley in connection with a book he is writing about Breasley's painting. When David arrives at Breasley's house, he discovers that the painter, who is also a notorious womanizer, has two attractive young women living with him, who are sunbathing in the nude in the garden when he arrives. Breasley, a rather unpleasant and domineering man, calls his two companions, both ex-art students, the Mouse and the Freak (their real names are Diana and Anne). The third-person narrator, who, by and large, shares David's viewpoint, also uses Breasley's designations for the girls in the first part of the story, when David does not know the girls well. It is only when David has become more involved with them that the narrator refers to them by their first names. At the first evening meal of David's short stay in the house, Breasley takes a dislike to David because the critic admits to painting abstracts. The short extract quoted below comes at the end of the meal

(I have numbered the sentences for ease of reference). It begins to reveal the inter-relations and tensions among the characters, and hence how they are portrayed in terms of characterization. Breasley, fairly drunk by this time, is staring at David, and the Freak asks the painter if she can leave the table:

(1) 'Henry, can I get down?'
(2) He remained staring at David. (3) 'Why?'
(4) 'I want to read my book.'
(5) 'You're a fucking little ninny.'
(6) 'Please.'
(7) 'Bugger off then.'
(8) He had not looked at her. (9) The Mouse came back with the third bottle, and the Freak looked nervously up at her, as if her permission was needed as well. (10) There was a little nod, then David felt his thigh being briefly squeezed. (11) The Freak's hand had reached along beneath the table, apparently to give him courage. (12) She stood up and went down the room and up the stairs. (13) Breasley pushed the bottle towards David. (14) It was not a politeness, but a challenge.

(15) 'Not for me, thanks. (16) I've had enough.'
(17) 'Cognac? (18) Calvados?'
(19) 'No thanks.'
(20) The old man poured himself another full glass of wine.
(21) 'This pot stuff?' (22) He nodded sideways down the room. (23) 'That's the book she wants to read.'
(24) The Mouse said quietly, 'She's given it up. (25) You know that perfectly well.'
(26) He took a mouthful of wine.
(27) 'Thought all you young whiz-kids indulged.'
(28) David said lightly, 'Not personally.'
(29) 'Interferes with the slide-rule stuff, does it?'
(30) 'I imagine. (31) But I'm not a mathematician.'
(32) 'What do you call it then?'
(33) The Mouse waited, eyes down. (34) Evidently she could not help him now, except as a silent witness. (35) It was not worth pretending one did not know what that 'it' meant. (36) David met the old man's stare.
(37) 'Mr Breasley, most of us feel abstraction has become a meaningless term. (38) Since our conception of reality has changed so much this last fifty years.'

(Fowles 1974/1986: 44–5)

THE ANALYSIS

Before discussing the passage, let us make sure we know which critical 'game' we are playing. Stylistic analysis, unlike more traditional forms of practical criticism, is not interested primarily in coming up with new and startling interpretations of the texts it examines. Rather, its main aim is to explicate how our understanding of a text is achieved, by examining in detail the linguistic organization of the text and how a reader needs to interact with that linguistic organization to make sense of it. Often, such a detailed examination of a text does reveal new aspects of interpretation or help us to see more clearly how a text achieves what it does. But the main purpose of stylistics is to show how interpretation is achieved, and hence provide support for a particular view of the work under discussion. As you read what I have to say about the extract, you may at times say to yourself 'I knew that already'. I often say the same thing to myself as my analysis reveals what is going on in a text. But the 'news' comes from knowing explicitly something that you had only understood intuitively, and from understanding in detail how the author has constructed the text so that it works on us in the way that it does.

I have chosen this passage because the contributions made by the characters are all in direct speech, and there is also relatively little narrative description. I will not ignore the narrative in what follows, but analyse it using the same methodology that is used to describe the conversation. The speech and the narrative in fact form a conversational whole in this extract. Some of the turns in the conversation are realized not by speech, but by actions described in the narrative. In what follows I will go through the extract a chunk at a time, quoting each chunk for ease of reference.

(1) 'Henry, can I get down?'
(2) He remained staring at David. (3) 'Why?'
(4) 'I want to read my book.'
(5) 'You're a fucking little ninny.'
(6) 'Please.'
(7) 'Bugger off then.'

The Freak's first utterance uses a first-name vocative, which assumes a relatively close relationship between two adults, but the speech act to which the vocative is attached is a request to leave the table, a speech act normally addressed by children to their parents. This suggests a rather different relationship: the reader is thus likely to hypothesize that Breasley dominates the Freak in fairly extreme ways and that she goes along with this relationship. Normally we look at one another when we communicate, but the narrative tells us that Breasley continues to stare at David as he replies. This suggests either that he is preoccupied by David, or that he is being rude to the Freak, or both. Moreover, his response is not the preferred second pair-part to the Freak's question. He should either say 'yes' or 'no', and in terms of polite social relations, preferably 'yes'. Instead he asks a question about her reason for wanting to get down, which she then answers immediately. Given that she has given a perfectly reasonable reason for wanting to leave the table, we would now expect him to answer the original question, but instead of doing so he abuses her. The utterance he uses refers to her as a 'ninny', someone who is silly, and he elaborates that rude designation with an extreme swear word and a diminutive adjective. He is thus being maximally rude, allowing us to infer that he is contemptuous of her. This behaviour of Breasley's is consistent with what we have already seen, and the fact that the Freak does not react verbally against his utterance again suggests that she must be completely dominated by him. With sentence (6), 'Please', we infer that she reiterates her original plea, and in sentence (7) Breasley at last gives the preferred answer to the original request, saying that she can go. But even here, he produces that speech act in a form which involves a term of abuse. We can thus infer that Breasley dominates the Freak in a very overbearing fashion, that he thinks very little of her, and that she apparently acquiesces in her treatment of him. From this small conversational extract we are thus able to infer character and character-relations, and are set up by the interaction to want to know how this non-normal set of social relations came into being and why the Freak does not merely leave.

> (8) He had not looked at her. (9) The Mouse came back with the third bottle, and the Freak looked nervously up at her, as if her permission was needed as well. (10) There was a little nod, then David felt his thigh being briefly squeezed. (11) The Freak's hand had reached along beneath the table, apparently to give him courage. (12) She stood up and went down the room and up the stairs.

The next narrative sentence reiterates what we have already been told about Breasley's kinesic behaviour. The quasi-repetition of that information increases the force of our assumption that Breasley is contemptuous of the Freak and much more interested in David. The 'as if' clause at the end of the next sentence indicates that the Freak does not need the Mouse's permission to leave the table, but that she is acting, from David's viewpoint, as if she does. Although it is just conceivable at this point in the passage that the Freak also needs the permission of the Mouse to leave the table, this interpretation becomes less likely a few lines later in the passage, allowing us to infer that the Freak and the Mouse are colluding in some undeclared way. Perhaps they have an agreement about how they interact with Breasley? This 'conversational turn' is done entirely silently. The Freak's look towards the Mouse counts as a first pair-part, a request or question, and the Mouse's nod counts as the response, the preferred second pair-part, adding weight to the assumption that the two young women are, unbeknown to Breasley, colluding in some way. This allows us to infer that the Freak cannot just be allowing herself to be dominated by Breasley because she is weak-willed. There must be some higher-order reason for her apparently pusillanimous behaviour.

The second half of sentence (10) represents a completely different exchange in the interaction. The Freak now 'addresses' David by squeezing his thigh. Her action is technically impolite: English people do not normally touch one another, particularly in areas of the body near the sexual organs, unless they are on fairly intimate terms. This cannot be the case, as David and the Freak have only recently met for the first time. The fact that the Freak acts as if she is on intimate terms with David thus suggests that she probably wants to be. Moreover, given that this information is juxtaposed, within the same sentence, with the Mouse's response to the Freak's request/question, we also have to conclude that the Freak's squeezing of David's thigh is a way of including him in the young women's conspiracy in some way. Sentence (11), with the non-factive adverb marking David's personal understanding of the event, spells out what must logically have happened if she had stroked his thigh, namely that she had stretched out under the table to do so, and gives a much more innocent interpretation of the event. This in turn helps us to infer (a) that David is probably something of an innocent and (b) that he has been affected significantly by the Freak's action. Otherwise there would have been no need to break Grice's maxim of quantity by spelling out what we can easily infer. The quantity maxim is broken again in sentence (12). Fowles could merely have said that the Freak went up the stairs. But by spelling out the sub-parts of her action he suggests that David is very aware of her actions, and also that the room is probably quite large.

(13) Breasley pushed the bottle towards David. (14) It was not a politeness, but a challenge.

(15) 'Not for me, thanks. (16) I've had enough.'
(17) 'Cognac? (18) Calvados?'
(19) 'No thanks.'
(20) The old man poured himself another full glass of wine.
(21) 'This pot stuff?' (22) He nodded sideways down the room.
(23) 'That's the book she wants to read.'

This chunk starts with another non-verbal turn, as sentence (14) makes clear, specifying the speech act force we should assign to the potentially ambiguous action. However, although the value rejected by the narrator would be the socially polite default value, the one supplied is consistent with everything else we have seen so far, and so the narrator appears to be supplying too much information, in order to underline Breasley's discourteous attitude. Breasley has used the potential ambiguity to be rude in a way which would be difficult to challenge. The contrast in the narrator's attitude towards the two characters is also made clear by the differential ways of referring to them, first name (close, sympathetic) for David and last name only, for Breasley, signifying more distance, and, in context, considerably less sympathy.

David replies negatively to the offer/challenge, thus confirming that the action described in (13) was the first pair-part of a conversational exchange. It is impolite to turn down an offer, and David, conforming to politeness rules, mitigates the negative response to that interpretation of Breasley's action by using a politeness marker and supplying an explanation for his refusal. However, if, as we are told, Breasley's action was a challenge, David in effect responds to that challenge, despite the politeness markers, with another challenge. A subtle social game is being played here, a game which is continued in the next two sentences, which constitute a re-offer/challenge on Breasley's part and a re-refusal/challenge on David's. A battle of wills between the men is clearly developing, and the double adjacency-pair sequence echoes to some extent, and, in terms of outcome, contrasts with, the earlier interaction between Breasley and the Freak. This contrast becomes even clearer when Breasley produces a third offer/challenge in (21), which David does not even answer. Breasley's nodding towards the part of the room the Freak has just walked through on her way out indicates a change in the sub-topic of Breasley's talk, and explains the otherwise unanchored 'she' in (23), a sentence which contains an obvious untruth, and hence a flout of Grice's maxim of quality. The clear inference to be made is that although the Freak said she was going to read her book, the real reason for her departure was that she wanted to smoke marijuana.

(24) The Mouse said quietly, 'She's given it up. (25) You know that perfectly well.'
(26) He took a mouthful of wine.
(27) 'Thought all you young whiz-kids indulged.'
(28) David said lightly, 'Not personally.'
(29) 'Interferes with the slide-rule stuff, does it?'
(30) 'I imagine. (31) But I'm not a mathematician.'

Sentence (24) is the Mouse's first verbal contribution of the extract, and the first time she addresses Breasley (she has, of course, communicated non-verbally with the Freak). She corrects Breasley's interpretation, and then in the next sentence makes it clear that he must have known that his ostensible interpretation of the Freak's action was wrong. Hence she accuses Breasley of lying and in challenging him in this way, sides with David against him. Breasley drinks his wine, but does not respond to the challenge she has made. It is difficult to be sure what inference we are intended to draw from this. It could be that he has no reply, and so the Mouse has beaten him in the exchange, or that by ignoring her contribution he implies that her views are unimportant, even if they are correct.

Breasley instead addresses David. The vocative 'you young whiz-kids' is clearly rude, and if all young whiz-kids indulge in drugs, then David, being a whiz-kid, must also indulge. The sentence is thus another challenge to David, being an indirect insult. David denies that he takes drugs, and Breasley then suggests a reason for his non-indulgence. But again Breasley's contribution contains an implied insult with the phrase 'the slide-rule stuff'. David is an art critic and an abstract artist, not a mathematician, and Breasley's suggestion that he uses a slide-rule in his work suggests that he uses an over-mechanistic approach.

(32) 'What do you call it then?'
(33) The Mouse waited, eyes down. (34) Evidently she could not help him now, except as a silent witness. (35) It was not worth pretending one did not know what that 'it' meant. (36) David met the old man's stare.
(37) 'Mr Breasley, most of us feel abstraction has become a meaningless term. (38) Since our conception of reality has changed so much this last fifty years.'

David denies straightforwardly what Breasley has implied, and this leads to another challenge on Breasley's part. By inference, the 'it' in

(32) must be David's work as an art critic, the fact that he paints abstracts, or both, and the sentence is thus a re-stating of the previous insult.

The narrative focus now switches to the Mouse, a clear flouting by the narrator of the maxim of relation. After all, the battle of wills is between the two men. The fact that the Mouse's reaction is described, from David's point of view (cf. 'Evidently'), helps us to infer her interest in David and David's awareness of, and thus interest in, the Mouse, even in the middle of David's tense interchange with Breasley. Sentence (34) also presupposes that the Mouse's challenge to Breasley in (24) and (25) was perceived by David as a move to support him.

We now move briefly inside David's head, with the indication that he is not going to continue with the strategy of polite avoidance of antipathy while holding his own position. The next narrative sentence tells us that he meets Breasley's stare, kinesic information which suggests confrontation. Then, in the last sentence of the extract, we get the response to Breasley's challenge in (32), a response which itself is a challenge, as it suggests that Breasley's attitude is out of date. This is the first time that David has verbally indicated his disapproval of Breasley. Until now he has merely fended off personal challenges made by Breasley towards him. But even now, he obeys the normal politeness 'rules' by phrasing the challenge in a way which plays it down. The vocative used (title and last name) is formal, distant and polite, and David follows Breasley's strategy of (27) by making a general statement rather than a personal accusation. Breasley, and the reader, can only 'realize' the insult by inferring that Breasley is not included in 'most of us' and that his understanding of reality has not kept pace with others in the art world.

CONCLUSION

A close look at the discoursal and pragmatic aspects of this short piece of dialogue has revealed quite a lot about the individual traits of the characters and their relationships. Breasley is domineering towards both the women who live with him and his guest. He has taken a dislike to David, and probably disapproves of art critics in general. He is prejudiced and is prepared to lie in order to win the conversational games he plays. The Freak, who has some kind of history of drug-taking, is the most submissive of the characters, but she appears, in collusion with the Mouse, to be humouring Breasley for some reason, and she is forward in her secret 'approach' to David. The Mouse seems more reserved and more in control of herself and her environment than the Freak. In some ways, these three characters are like a family. If Breasley's behaviour reminds us of a stereotypical domineering father-figure, the Freak is the most like a child in the scene, and the Mouse's characterization resembles that of a traditional mother-figure, calm, supportive and trying to control family relations in more indirect ways. David, the guest, is challenged continually by Breasley, but rebuffs those challenges while labouring to observe normal polite social relations. We are thus likely to sympathize with him, not just because the narrator's description of what happens often shares David's viewpoint, but also because he behaves in a reasonable way both in social terms and in not giving in to bullying tactics.

That we can infer so much about characterization and character-relations from such a short piece of dialogue is salutary in itself. There are considerable undercurrents in the dialogue, which our analysis has helped to bring out. But the interaction also provides us with narrative puzzles which we will want to resolve as the story unfolds. What exactly is the relationship in Breasley's *ménage à trois*? Is Breasley having sexual relationships with both of the young women? Why do they stay when he behaves so unreasonably? What is the importance of the different roles of the two women? Will David be able to get the information he needs from Breasley for his book? Will David and the Freak become sexually involved? How might this affect the relationship between Breasley and David, and between Breasley and the girls? We may not find the answer to all these puzzles as we read on. Some of the questions may even become irrelevant. But analysing this conversation from a discoursal and pragmatic viewpoint does not just help us to understand what is going on under the surface of the conversation. It also shows us how dialogue, as well as narrative action, can be of crucial importance in creating narrative tension, a tension for which we will seek resolution. Now read on.

SUGGESTIONS FOR FURTHER WORK

1 Re-write the passage from 'The Ebony Tower' so that David reacts more forcibly to Breasley's challenges. Now compare your version with the original and, using the approaches outlined in the above chapter, analyse (preferably in discussion with another student) the detailed changes you have made and how they affect the text as a whole.

2 Analyse the conversation below from Vladimir Nabokov's *Lolita* (1955/1973), using the approaches used in the passage from 'The

Ebony Tower'. *Lolita* is a comic novel narrated in the first person by a man called Humbert Humbert. He is in love with a teenage girl called Lolita who is still legally a minor. He has murdered Lolita's mother in order to gain legal control over her as her guardian. They have now set out on a journey across the USA, and have stopped for the first night at a motel. Humbert Humbert is contemplating drugging Lolita after she has gone to sleep, so that he can make love to her unawares. He has let her go to the motel room to go to sleep, and while waiting for her sees another young girl, almost, but not quite, as attractive as Lolita amid a large and noisy party in the motel lobby. Feeling somewhat guilty, he goes outside, where a man he cannot see properly in the darkness addresses him:

'Where the devil did you get her?'
'I beg your pardon?'
'I said: the weather is getting better.'
'Seems so.'
'Who's the lassie?'
'My daughter.'
'You lie – she's not.'
'I beg your pardon?'
'I said: July was hot. Where's her mother?'
'Dead.'
'I see. Sorry. By the way, why don't you two lunch with me tomorrow. That dreadful crowd will be gone by then.'
'We'll be gone too. Good night.'
'Sorry. I'm pretty drunk. Goodnight. That child of yours needs a lot of sleep. Sleep is a rose, as the Persians say. Smoke?'
'Not now.'

(Nabokov 1955/1973: chapter 28)

3 Examine in detail the following passage from *Alice's Adventures in Wonderland* (1865). What rules of polite behaviour can you deduce from the impolite way in which the characters behave towards one another? Then use what you have discovered as the basis for a brief handbook called *How to be Rude in Conversation*.

The March Hare, the Mad Hatter and the Dormouse are sitting having tea at a table under a tree:

The table was a large one, but the three were all crowded together at one corner of it. 'No room! No room!' they cried out when they saw Alice coming. 'There's *plenty* of room!' said Alice indignantly, and she sat down in a large arm-chair at one end of the table.

'Have some wine,' the March Hare said in an encouraging tone. Alice looked all round the table, but there was nothing on it but tea. 'I don't see any wine,' she remarked.

'There isn't any,' said the March Hare.

'Then it wasn't very civil of you to offer it,' said Alice angrily.

'It wasn't very civil of you to sit down without being invited,' said the March Hare.

'I didn't know it was *your* table,' said Alice: 'it's laid for a great many more than three.'

'Your hair wants cutting,' said the Hatter. He had been looking at Alice for some time with great curiosity, and this was his first speech.

'You shouldn't make personal remarks,' Alice said with some severity; 'it's very rude.'

The Hatter opened his eyes very wide on hearing this; but all he *said* was, 'Why is a raven like a writing desk?'

'Come, we shall have some fun now!' thought Alice. 'I'm glad they've begun asking riddles. – I believe I can guess that,' she added aloud.

'Do you mean that you think you can find out the answer to it?' said the March Hare.

'Exactly so,' said Alice.

'Then you should say what you mean,' the March Hare went on.

'I do,' Alice hastily replied; 'at least – at least I mean what I say – that's the same thing, you know.'

'Not the same thing a bit!' said the Hatter. 'You might just as well say that "I see what I eat" is the same thing as "I eat what I see"!'

(Carroll 1865: chapter 7)

REFERENCES

Austen, J. (1814/1966) *Mansfield Park*, Harmondsworth: Penguin.

Bennison, N. (1993) 'Discourse Analysis, Pragmatics and the Dramatic Character: Tom Stoppard's *Professional Foul*', *Language and Literature* 2, 2: 79–99.

Brown, G. and Yule, G. (1983) *Discourse Analysis*, Cambridge: Cambridge University Press.

Brown, P. and Levinson, S. C. (1987) *Politeness: Some Universals in Language Usage*, Cambridge: Cambridge University Press.

Brown, R. and Gilman, A. (1989) 'Politeness Theory and Shakespeare's Four Major Tragedies', *Language in Society* 18: 159–212.

Burton, D. (1980) *Dialogue and Discourse*, London: Routledge and Kegan Paul.

Carroll, L. (1865) *Alice's Adventures in Wonderland*, London: Dent.

Carter, R. and Simpson, P. (eds) (1989) *Language, Discourse and Literature*, London: Unwin Hyman.

Cooper, M. (1981) 'Implicature, Convention and *The Taming of the Shrew*', *Poetics* 10: 1–14.

Fowler, R. (1986) *Linguistic Criticism*, Oxford: Oxford University Press.

Fowles, J. (1974/1986) *The Ebony Tower*, London: Pan Books.

Grice, H. P. (1967/1975) 'Logic and Conversation', in P. Cole and J. Morgan (eds) *Syntax and Semantics 3: Speech Acts*, New York: Academic Press: 41–58.

Herman, V. (1991) 'Dramatic Dialogue and the Systematics of Turn-taking', *Semiotica* 83: 97–121.

Hurst, M. (1987) 'Speech Acts in Ivy Compton-Burnett's *A Family and a Fortune*', *Language and Style* 20: 342–58.

Leech, G. N. (1983) *Principles of Pragmatics*, London: Longman.

—— (1992) 'Pragmatic Principles in Shaw's *You Never Can Tell*', in M. Toolan (ed.) *Language, Text and Context*, London and New York: Routledge: 259–80.

Leech, G. and Short, M. (1981) *Style in Fiction*, London: Longman.

Levinson, S. C. (1983) *Pragmatics*, Cambridge: Cambridge University Press.

Nabokov, V. (1955/1973) *Lolita*, London: Corgi.

Searle, J. (1975) 'What is a Speech Act?', in P. Giglioli (ed.) *Language and Social Context*, Harmondsworth: Penguin: 136–54.

Short, M. (1989) 'Discourse Analysis and the Analysis of Drama', in Carter and Simpson: 139–68.

—— (1990) 'Literature and Language', in M. Coyle, P. Garside, M. Kelsall and J. Peck (eds) *Encyclopedia of Literature and Criticism*, London: Routledge: 1082–97.

Simpson, P. (1989) 'Politeness Phenomena in Ionesco's *The Lesson*', in Carter and Simpson: 171–93.

Sinclair, J. and Coulthard, R. (1975) *Towards an Analysis of Discourse*, Oxford: Oxford University Press.

Toolan, M. (1989) 'Analysing Conversation in Fiction: An Example from Joyce's *Portrait*', in Carter and Simpson: 195–211.

—— (1990) *The Stylistics of Fiction*, London and New York: Routledge.

Wardhaugh, R. (1985) *How Conversation Works*, Oxford: Basil Blackwell.

4 Dialogue and power in E. M. Forster's *Howards End*

R. A. Buck and Timothy R. Austin

EDITOR'S PREFACE

E. M. Forster's novel *Howards End* (1910/1973) is about the relationship between two families, the Schlegels and the Wilcoxes, and their relationships with a number of houses, of which Howards End is the most important one. It is also about the resilience of the artistically-minded Schlegels: paradoxically, it is they who inherit Howards End, whereas the property-conscious, commercially-minded Wilcoxes are dispossessed. At the beginning, though, Henry Wilcox had acted against his wife's last wish, when she wanted to bequeath Howards End to Margaret Schlegel, and had kept the house in the Wilcox family. But after Henry marries Margaret, the latter becomes the mistress of Howards End after all, and on her death the property will pass on to the son of Helen Schlegel, Margaret's sister.

In this way, the values of the Schlegels turn out to be stronger than the values of the Wilcoxes. The fundamental clash of values, between the feminine world of culture and the masculine world of business, as well as Margaret's resilience, is already evident in the scene studied in this chapter by Rosemary Buck and Timothy Austin. They analyse the lunchtime conversation between Henry Wilcox and Margaret Schlegel at Simpson's restaurant in chapter 17 of *Howards End* and show how social power is not something given, but constantly has to be re-negotiated by the conversational participants. Margaret Schlegel turns out to be surprisingly resilient, not afraid of retaliating against the verbal onslaughts of her conversational partner.

In their description of the underlying mechanisms of this verbal battle, Buck and Austin rely on Brown and Levinson's politeness model. In particular, they focus upon the speech acts by which the speaker threatens the hearer's *face* (the self-image that the latter hopes to maintain in social interaction). They consider whether the speaker attempts to minimize the threat, and what redressive strategies s/he uses to achieve this. They distinguish between three types of strategies:

- negative face strategies: choosing more polite forms;
- positive face strategies: emphasizing one's high regard for the hearer;
- off-record strategies: performing the face-threatening act in an indirect way.

The result is a systematic model for the analysis of politeness, power and distance in any (literary or non-literary) dialogue.

J. J. W.

In the 1960s and 1970s, most theoretical linguists paid little attention to language units longer than the single sentence. They compiled highly detailed studies of how speakers deploy individual sounds, syllables, words and clauses. But they deferred the challenge of analysing either the longer formal units typical of written discourse (such as the paragraph) or the sustained exchanges of spoken language that we call dialogue or conversation.

More recently, however, linguists have focused on the fact that human beings do not generally speak simply in order 'to record or impart straightforward information'; instead, they contrive 'to do things with words' (J. L. Austin 1962: 2). They conduct ceremonies, instruct classes, or swear 'to tell the whole truth'; and, most commonly of all, they participate in conversations. Performing any of these activities minimally requires the sequencing of several sentences and is by no means always the sole responsibility of a single speaker.

One branch of research in the broad area of discourse analysis derives from the observation that among the 'things' that participants in an everyday conversation 'do' is build, maintain and modify sophisticated interpersonal relationships. Since both dialogue and evolving relationships between individuals lie at the heart of much nineteenth- and twentieth-century prose fiction, it seems reasonable to expect that linguists' theories in this area should throw light on the workings of those novels and short stories. In this chapter, we demonstrate how one particular socio-linguistic model of discourse provides a valuable tool for exploring the function of dialogue in one of E. M. Forster's novels.

Linguists Penelope Brown and Stephen Levinson (1987), elaborating on the work of anthropologist Erving Goffman, propose that an abstract social principle guides and constrains each speaker's unconscious language choices in casual conversation. This principle effectively articulates the collective will of society to regulate the behaviour of individual members. It presumes that all individuals have a right to be treated by others with respect, and it provides for this right to be upheld by participants in conversation. The principle, in other words, safeguards an individual's *face*, the public social value or self-image that a person attempts to maintain in interactions with others (Goffman 1967: 15).

Speakers thus come to conversations with two categories of social expectations, called *face wants* in Brown and Levinson's system. The first reflects their desire to be able to act freely and to avoid having their privacy and possessions violated; these are called *negative face wants*. The second category, called *positive face wants*, reflects speakers' aspirations to be respected and liked by those around them.

To succeed in satisfying their own face wants in these two areas, participants in a conversation must, in theory, win the collaboration of their fellow conversationalists. In practice, however, this balancing act is no easy task, for the legitimate pursuit of one's own face needs often leads one to perform acts that by their very nature threaten the face needs of others. Any command or request, for example, threatens one's hearer's wish to be free to act unhindered, while any act of criticism, disapproval or disagreement on a speaker's part threatens the hearer's desire to be liked and respected. All such acts – acts that are inherently threatening to the hearer – are called by Brown and Levinson *face-threatening acts* or *FTAs*.

Speakers can also perform acts that are *self-threatening*. Expressing thanks and accepting offers are acts that impose on speakers' own negative face wants, for they imply or even impel future obligation; apologies and confessions, among other self-humiliating acts, compromise the self-image of those who utter them, thus encroaching on those individuals' positive face wants.

As speakers, we adopt *strategies* that enable us to manage this complex aspect of our discourse effectively. If we foresee that some act we are about to perform may appear threatening to our hearer's face, for instance, we may *redress* it in various ways. We can soften FTAs by making them sound less imposing or by preceding them with polite conventional forms (*negative face strategies*). 'Please could you come in and close the door?' is far less likely to cause offence than 'Harry! Close that door!' Alternatively, we can use *positive face strategies*, appealing to our hearers' desire for solidarity and emphasizing our high opinion of them: 'Why don't we close the door and keep this little chat between the two of us?' A third kind of strategy involves performing FTAs only indirectly (*off-record strategies*). Still with the intent of having our hearer shut the door, for example, we might say, 'That door is open again'; under the right circumstances, the self-evident truth of that assertion will be heard as a hint that an FTA is at stake, though it would remain for our hearer to decide if this is really what we intended.

Even when no specific FTAs are employed, speakers still rely on utterances to convey solidarity or to express distance or reserve, constantly responding to and refining their immediate social context (Buck 1993: 50). Inevitably, factors extrinsic to language affect the conversational strategies that speakers select for doing this. The *social distance* between participants (whether they are strangers, acquaintances, friends or intimates) influences the choices they make, as does their relative *social power* (the freedom to impose on another's face wants that derives from such factors as gender, age, culture, wealth or class). Thus even discourse between the most casual acquaintances ('small talk') displays complex organizational structure, each conversational *move* or *turn* being related to preceding utterances on the basis of an evolving interpersonal framework.

Many scholars have pointed out that literary dialogue is almost never merely a bald transcript of everyday conversation. But as Michael Toolan (1990: 275) remarks, 'it is hard to see how we could recognize and respond to the former as a version of the latter' if the two did not share significant structural properties (see also Hurst 1987: 356; Halliday 1989: 41, 79; Bialostosky 1994; T. R. Austin 1994: chapter 2). In the pages that follow, we rely on this observation of Toolan's as the a priori justification for applying a version of Brown and Levinson's model of discourse to a passage of literary dialogue with the goal of tracing subtle shifts in the dynamic social context in which it occurs.

In chapter 17 of E. M. Forster's *Howards End* (1910/1973), Margaret Schlegel accepts an invitation to lunch at 'Simpson's restaurant in the Strand' (147) from Evie Wilcox.[1] Evie's avowed purpose in extending the invitation is to introduce Margaret to her fiancé, Percy Cahill, but when Margaret arrives, she learns that they are to be joined by Evie's father, Henry Wilcox. Since she felt very close to Henry's late wife Ruth before her death some two years earlier and has met Henry briefly on several occasions since, she greets his appearance with 'a smile of pleasure' (148) – a detail which enables the reader to gauge the degree of intimacy (the social distance) between them even before their conversation begins.

Evie and Percy soon '[fall] into a conversation of the . . . type . . . which . . . neither desires nor deserves the attention of others' (148), leaving Margaret and Henry to establish a separate discourse at their end of the table. Henry's early turns at talk confirm what we have learned from earlier episodes – that he regards himself as entitled to counsel and protect unmarried women, Margaret in particular. In the Edwardian society that Forster portrays in this novel, men in general exercise rights and privileges that depend solely on their gender and 'women are by definition inferior' (Finkelstein 1975: 89). In addition, though, Henry lays explicit, if overstated, claim to an unusual breadth of experience 'in the East' (148). At the lunch table, he immediately exploits the considerable social power conferred by these factors, even to the extent of overruling what he views as Margaret's unwise selections from the lunch menu.

As we shall see, however, this initial, socially pre-determined basis for their relationship is neither entirely stable nor Henry's alone to control. For, even as Margaret and Henry eat their lunch and indulge in talk on a variety of unrelated topics (many of them seemingly trivial), each also attempts to re-negotiate the balance of social power in her or his favour, deploying a series of FTAs accompanied (though not in all cases) by an array of positive, negative and off-record redressive strategies.

Initially, Margaret acquiesces in Henry's boorish behaviour even where she clearly disagrees with his pronouncements, but when he is distracted by the need to make 'inquiries about cheese' (149), we sense her preparing to assert herself.

> 'Next time,' she said to Mr Wilcox, 'you shall come to lunch with me at Mr Eustace Miles's.'
> 'With pleasure.'
> 'No, you'd hate it,' she said, pushing her glass towards him for some more cider. 'It's all proteids and body-buildings, and people come up to you and beg your pardon, but you have such a beautiful aura.'
>
> (150)

In this brief exchange, Margaret displays a formidable arsenal of conversational weaponry. Some of her techniques are apparent even without detailed linguistic analysis. For example, she knows from previous encounters with the Wilcox family that adopting the spiritual avant-garde as a subject for discussion will put Henry at a disadvantage. But she also opts to initiate this new topic by extending an invitation. As we have seen, this gesture represents a mild imposition on Henry's negative face since for him to accept will entail his surrendering a small measure of his independence. Significantly,

Margaret compounds her imposition by ignoring the opportunity to redress her FTA. She rejects a wide range of relatively gracious conventional forms for invitations ('would you come to lunch?'; 'you could come to lunch') in favour of the directive 'you shall come to lunch'. Indeed, her use of the modal auxiliary 'shall' strongly emphasizes the obligation that her proposal will impose and thus significantly increases the risk that her remark will cause some offence.

Henry temporarily defuses this situation, politely accepting both her invitation and the imposition that it entails. But when he does so, Margaret promptly reverses direction on him. After all, however accurate her perception that 'you'd hate it' may be, uttering those words in this context has the practical effect of withdrawing the invitation just when Henry has accepted it, blatantly threatening Henry's positive face by making him look foolish. Not content with this, Margaret presses her advantage by moving from the mention of Mr Miles's restaurant into a detailed discussion of auras and astral planes, concepts that she knows Henry will probably not recognize. Finally, having ridiculed his ignorance, she unleashes an off-record (but unmistakable) attack on his positive face. To Henry's suggestion that he may perhaps have no aura, she responds:

> 'You're bound to have one, but it may be such a terrible colour that no one dares mention it.'
>
> (150)

Henry ignores this remark altogether and begins a counterattack in the next passage of dialogue (dialogue punctuated, significantly, by a brief discussion of what cheese Margaret should order in which he once again magisterially overrides her initial selection). He seizes on one of Margaret's few redressive gestures, her self-threatening ridicule of her own behaviour at Mr Miles's ('I just sat with my handkerchief in my mouth' 150) and seeks to turn her own humour against her, defying her three times to disavow 'the supernatural and all that' (150).

The first of these challenges takes the overall form of a question, a form that in itself would threaten Margaret's negative face: 'Tell me, though, Miss Schlegel, do you really believe in the supernatural and all that?' (150). He prefaces the question, furthermore, by demanding an answer ('Tell me . . .'), and implies by his use of 'really' and 'and all that' his own sceptical views, thus establishing a significant distance between his position and hers. Henry's second gambit involves a still more abrupt affront to both Margaret's negative and her positive face. When she begins to answer his first question:

'though I don't believe in auras, and think Theosophy's only a halfway-house'

(150)

he blatantly interrupts her, completing what he takes to be her line of thought:

'Yet there may be something in it all the same,' he concluded.

(150)

Margaret calmly endures Henry's incursion into her discourse space and his implicit presumption of a right to voice her opinions, framing a sophisticated but non-committal reply. Henry, however, perceiving her graciousness as a sign of weakness, presses a third time for a definitive response:

'So you couldn't give me your word that you *don't* hold with astral bodies and all the rest of it?'

(151, italics are Forster's)

This time, Margaret's response to Henry's persistence betrays rising impatience:

'I could,' said Margaret . . . 'Indeed, I will.'

(151)

She initially accepts the modal auxiliary 'could(n't)' that Henry himself introduced in his probing question. But she quickly substitutes for it the more assertive 'will', a choice that enables her to repair some of the recent damage to her own positive face. For by employing 'will', she makes clear that she is not merely indicating to Henry which of his variants accurately reflects her beliefs; rather, she is exercising voluntary control over what she will commit herself to (at least in matters of greater significance than choosing from the menu).

In terms of face-relations, Margaret and Henry's discourse to this point may be compared to two tactical manoeuvres on a battlefield where Henry initially held the socially ceded 'high ground'. Through aggressive management of the discussion of 'the supernatural and all that', as we saw, Margaret succeeded in driving him from that position. But Henry then resorted to a stubborn frontal assault and made some headway, though his attack finally bogs down in an inconclusive exchange of accusations in which Margaret gets the last word:

'But why do you want all this settled?' [asked Margaret].
'I don't know.'
'Now, Mr Wilcox, you do know.'

(151)

The next section of dialogue illustrates an interesting subtlety of face negotiation: the potential for rich irony when an FTA is perceived by a hearer even though none was intended by the speaker.

After a brief interruption, Margaret chooses a new topic of conversation by asking, 'How's your house?' (151). Henry's response ('Much the same as when you honoured it last week' (151)) reveals that he has interpreted her question as referring to his London house on Ducie Street and thus as face-threatening only in the minimal sense that it requires him to supply an answer. However, Margaret quickly corrects an underlying misunderstanding: 'I don't mean Ducie Street. Howards End, of course' (151). From Margaret's viewpoint, this clarification does absolutely nothing to increase the degree of threat implied in the question. But Henry sees things quite differently. At the time of his wife's death, Henry persuaded the rest of the family to disregard her clear intention of bequeathing Howards End to Margaret. To him, therefore, Margaret's question appears suspiciously pointed.

His instinctive reaction in his next, lengthy turn at talk is to weave furiously from side to side – and in any case away from a topic which he views as inherently face-threatening. He reminds Margaret of her preference for living in London; he offers advice about house-hunting in general; and he introduces the names of two properties that he owns in addition to Howards End – Ducie Street (again) and Oniton (twice).

But Margaret has no idea what could have motivated this burst of talk. She therefore picks up on Henry's counsel that house-hunters should decide what they want to pay and where they want to live and then not 'budge' (151), and complains that houses overcome her best intentions by 'mesmerizing' (151) her: 'Houses are alive. No?' (151). As luck would have it, this unorthodox notion so closely resembles ideas voiced by Ruth Wilcox before her death, that Henry sees it too as potentially threatening. This time, however, he elects to abort the subject altogether, using the lame excuse, 'I'm out of my depth' (151).

Having 'lost' this minor skirmish (which Margaret 'won' without ever knowing she had come under hostile fire), Henry takes the offensive, accusing Margaret of having talked in the same poetic vein to 'your office boy' (151), Leonard Bast, a clerk to whose life the Schlegel sisters had indeed tried to bring a little culture. Margaret concedes his point, but launches into a lengthy self-justification which she bases on the notion that one should 'talk the same way to everyone – or try to' (151). In passing, she censures the concept of a mode of discourse specifically tailored to 'the lower classes' (152), but she is already far beyond that point when Henry interrupts her in mid-sentence for the second time during this luncheon:

> 'Lower classes,' interrupted Mr Wilcox, as it were thrusting his hand into her speech. 'Well, you do admit that there are rich and poor. That's something.'
>
> (152)

Margaret is dumbfounded ('Margaret could not reply' 152) both by the obviousness of Henry's point ('everyone admits that' (152), she points out) and by the brutality of his conversational affront to her negative and her positive face – brutality captured in Forster's brilliant simile for that speech-act ('as it were thrusting his hand into her speech' 152). But Henry presses forward. 'Your socialists don't [admit it]' (152), he alleges, openly challenging her assertion and stressing again the lack of common ground between them, which draws from Margaret the taut – and equally face-threatening – rejoinder:

> 'My socialists do. Yours mayn't; but I strongly suspect yours of being not socialists, but ninepins . . . I can't imagine any living creature who would bowl over quite so easily.'
>
> (152)

At this point, both participants have resorted to outright assaults on the other's positive face and the social order within which the conversation began lies in tatters. In a final, futile attempt to patch things up, Henry falls back on the supremely ironic rationalization that 'women may say anything – it was one of his holiest beliefs' (152). The irony lies, of course, in the fact that such a broad principle of discourse management would assign to women a priori the power to threaten others' faces with impunity, while all the evidence in the novel – not least Henry's own behaviour in the conversation we have examined – demonstrates precisely the opposite.

In many important respects, readers of this passage from *Howards End* treat the dialogue it contains as if it were spontaneous conversation. As we have seen, Brown and Levinson's model helps us to appreciate some of the subtleties that this may involve. In particular, their attention to face concerns clarifies the fact that much more is at stake here than where the Schlegel sisters are to live or what Socialists may or may not 'admit'. For Forster's characters are seeking continuously to empower themselves through the language they use and to modify the status that society has assigned them to better suit their aspirations. In Forster's dialogue, in short, as in all socially contextualized speech, power is not given; it is something that must be continually negotiated for, something that is lost and regained with each shift and turn of conversation.

SUGGESTIONS FOR FURTHER WORK

1 The social encounter in *Howards End* that we analysed in this chapter occurs when Margaret Schlegel accepts Evie Wilcox's invitation to lunch. In turn, the passage also includes the issuance of another invitation – Margaret's invitation to Henry which she promptly withdraws as a conversational ploy. Briefly review our discussion of that exchange and consider, in the context of your own experience of invitations, the implications of uttering an invitation for both (potential) host and (intended) guest. In terms of our understanding of positive and negative face wants, how is the act of inviting a face-threatening act (FTA)? Who is most threatened, the host or the guest? And what will be the face implications if the invitation is accepted, or if it is refused? (Hancher 1979 offers an analysis with which you might want to compare your own intuitions.)

Forster's later novel, *A Passage to India* (1924/1974), is set in Chandrapore, India, towards the end of the period of British colonial rule. At the end of chapter 6, Aziz, a Muslim doctor at the Government Hospital, returns home to find a note from Fielding, the English Principal at the Government College, inviting him to tea. 'Fielding had asked him to tea a month ago', Aziz recalls, 'and he had forgotten about it – never answered, never gone, just forgotten' (59–60).

Consider the several factors that complicate the dynamics of the incipient relationship between Aziz and Fielding as compared to that between most participants in invitation rituals. What implications for the face concerns of each are entailed by their relative social power in light of the colonial setting? What impact will Aziz's previous negligence have on their interaction if he now accepts this second invitation (for that is precisely what he does)?

When Aziz arrives (at the beginning of chapter 7), Fielding is still dressing and his first words are shouted from the bedroom:

'Please make yourself at home.' The remark was unpremeditated, like most of his actions; it was what he felt inclined to say.

To Aziz it had a very definite meaning. 'May I really, Mr Fielding? It's very good of you,' he called back; 'I like unconventional behaviour so extremely . . . . The fact is I have long wanted to meet you,' he continued. 'I have heard so much about your warm heart from the Nawab Bahadur. But where is one to meet in a wretched hole like Chandrapore?' He came close up to the door. 'When I was greener here, I'll tell you what. I used to wish you to fall ill so that we could meet that way.' They laughed.

(Forster 1924/1974: 63)

Given the unusual circumstances surrounding this exchange, analyse the face-tending and face-threatening acts that it contains. How do Fielding and Aziz separately perceive the function of Fielding's greeting? Whose face (if anyone's) do they view it as threatening? In what ways could Aziz's remarks be seen as attempts to redress face imbalances that existed prior to this meeting? And what might be the connection between the face implications of Aziz's last sentence in this extract and the laughter that follows it?

More broadly, invitations of various kinds abound in *A Passage to India*. The chief British administrator in Chandrapore invites selected Indians to a Bridge Party at 'the Club'; the party is a disaster (chapter 5). Visiting Englishwomen Adela Quested and Mrs Moore are invited to the household of an Indian couple, the Bhattacharyas, but their putative hosts fail to provide the necessary transportation at the agreed-upon time (chapters 5 and 7). And the novel's crisis occurs during an ill-fated expedition to see the Marabar Caves, an expedition that results from Aziz's ambitious invitation to the English visitors. Compare several of the passages in which these invitations are extended and accepted in terms of the ways in which the characters involved handle the face considerations that inevitably accompany their actions.

2 It can be argued that simply indulging in conversation *at all* imposes on the privacy (and thus the negative face) of the person one is speaking with, and also that this is particularly true when one attempts to revive a conversation that has apparently died. The awkwardness of 'breaking the ice' at the beginning of a party results in part from our awareness of just this dynamic in that discourse situation.

In chapter 6 of Forster's novel *Maurice* (1971/1988), the protagonist first meets Clive Durham. Both are undergraduates at Cambridge University and they meet by accident in the room of a third student named Risley. Durham is looking for a pianola record that Risley owns, but is doing so in Risley's absence and apparently without his permission; Maurice has arrived on an unannounced visit. Both feel somewhat awkward, therefore, and, as virtual strangers, must negotiate some common ground if they are to establish a discourse.

Study the following brief excerpt and then outline the ways in which each character balances FTAs with redressive strategies in an effort to achieve a basis for continued conversation:

'Have you found that music yet?' [asked Maurice].
'No.'
'Because I must be going'; he was in no hurry, but his heart, which had never stopped beating quickly, impelled him to say this.
'Oh. All right.'
This was not what Maurice had intended. 'What is it you want?' he asked, advancing.
'The March out of the Pathétique –'
'That means nothing to me. So you like this style of music.'
'I do.'
'A good waltz is more my style.'
'Mine too,' said Durham, meeting his eye.
(Forster 1971/1988: 38)

Among the questions you may want to consider are the following: in what sense does the word 'yet' in Maurice's first question accentuate the implied threat to Durham's face? After Durham replies to that question with a curt 'No', Maurice responds 'Because I must be going'; what face-tending function does this utterance serve, and how is the word 'because' crucial to its correct interpretation?

Forster informs his readers that, despite having said that he 'must be going', Maurice was in fact 'in no hurry'; what do we infer from this about Maurice's purpose in speaking as he does? How is that impression confirmed when we learn just two lines later that his utterance does not have the effect that he 'had intended'?

In discussing the passage from *Howards End* in this chapter, we noted the implications for face-relations when one speaker interrupts another. If we understand the dash after the word 'Pathétique' in this excerpt to signal an interruption, how would we expect this act of Maurice's to affect the developing conversation? What other features of his interruption might also be seen as face-threatening? (Recall Henry Wilcox's dismissive reference to 'astral bodies *and all the rest of it*'.)

And how does the glance described in the last three words of the excerpt mirror what seems to have happened at the level of face negotiation during the preceding four turns at talk?

3 As in so many other areas, Herman Melville's short story 'Bartleby the Scrivener' (1853/1981) furnishes superb material for discourse

analysis on the basis of face needs. Read the whole story and consider the following questions:

(a) The narrator in 'Bartleby' devotes considerable time initially to describing his own character, claiming that 'such description is indispensable to an adequate understanding of the chief character about to be presented' (that is, Bartleby; 75). He introduces himself as a man 'filled with a profound conviction that the easiest way of life is the best' (75). What expectations does he thus establish regarding the way in which he will handle whatever face concerns may arise between himself and others?

(b) The narrator is Bartleby's employer and a 'Master in Chancery' (a lawyer) while Bartleby is merely a scrivener or copyist. When we first meet Bartleby, furthermore, he is responding to a job advertisement. What initial social distance and social power relationships are suggested by these circumstances?

(c) In our own everyday conversations, 'I'd rather not go to the party' represents a relatively unthreatening way to reject an unwanted invitation. Why is that? What strategies are invoked to redress the underlying FTA by someone who utters those words?

(d) When Bartleby repeatedly responds to the narrator's requests for assistance by saying 'I would prefer not to', do we interpret *his utterances* as face-threatening? To what extent is any implicit threat redressed? And what clues does Melville offer in the text to help us assess the face implications of Bartleby's replies? (Consider, for example, the reactions of the various overhearers present on each occasion.)

(e) In what ways is Bartleby's discourse an extension of his other inappropriate behaviour in the narrator's chambers? What does this imply about the function of discourse as a facet of human conduct in general?

(f) Finally, why does the narrator delay in reacting to Bartleby's actions (both verbal and non-verbal)? Which of the narrator's face wants is finally violated in a way that makes reaction unavoidable? And what is the long-term consequence for Bartleby of the narrator's insistence on respecting his own face needs? (Michael Toolan 1985 conducts a detailed analysis of part of 'Bartleby' which may help you in formulating your own conclusions.)

4 In discussing negative face wants in this chapter, we listed *privacy* as one of the rights that individuals seek to protect in discourse (as well as by other means, of course). They typically regard their life

stories and their emotional states, for example, as their own concern and resist attempts by others to manipulate or analyse them. As a result, the discussion of sensitive or intimate topics, though sometimes unavoidable, puts an inordinate strain on strategies for face negotiation.

In Ernest Hemingway's 'Hills Like White Elephants' (1925/1954), an unnamed man and girl sit and talk at a table in the restaurant outside a small railway station. Their conversation is of two kinds: sometimes they chat about such trivial subjects as the flavour of the aperitif they are drinking or the appearance of the hills on the far side of the valley; at other times they far more warily discuss the possibility that the girl might elect to undergo an abortion (referred to only as 'an operation' or as 'it' throughout the story).

Early in the dialogue, the girl '[looks] off at the line of hills' (273) in the distance:

> 'They look like white elephants,' she said.
> 'I've never seen one,' the man drank his beer.
> 'No, you wouldn't have.'
> 'I might have,' the man said. 'Just because you say I wouldn't have doesn't prove anything.'
> The girl looked at the bead curtain. 'They've painted something on it,' she said. 'What does it say?'
>
> (Hemingway 1925/1954: 273)

Later on, after they have begun to discuss the abortion itself and emotions on both sides have intensified, the man tries to calm the girl down:

> 'Come on back in the shade,' he said. 'You mustn't feel that way.'
> 'I don't feel any way,' the girl said. 'I just know things.'
> 'I don't want you to do anything that you don't want to do –'
> 'Nor that isn't good for me,' she said. 'I know. Could we have another beer?'
> 'All right. But you've got to realize –'
> 'I realize,' the girl said. 'Can't we stop talking?'
>
> (Hemingway 1925/1954: 276)

Consider how each of these characters seeks to protect her or his negative face. Which utterances does each perceive as face-threatening? Were they apparently intended in that way? Which character employs the more explicit strategies, which the more off-record methods? And what is the girl's ultimate conversational weapon when she feels most threatened?

NOTE

1 The passage to which reference is made throughout this chapter appears on pages 147–53 in the Abinger edition of *Howards End*, edited by Oliver Stallybrass (London: Edward Arnold, 1973). Readers are advised to acquaint themselves with the scene as a whole since it is too lengthy to be quoted here in full.

REFERENCES

Austin, J. L. (1962) *How to Do Things with Words*, Cambridge, Mass.: Harvard.
Austin, T. R. (1994) *Poetic Voices: Discourse Linguistics and the Poetic Text*, Tuscaloosa: University of Alabama Press.
Bialostosky, D. H. (1994) 'Dialogics of the Lyric: A Symposium on Wordsworth's "Westminster Bridge" and "Beauteous Evening"', in M. Macovski (ed.) *Textual Voices, Vocative Texts: Dialogue, Linguistics, and Literature*, Oxford: Oxford University Press.
Brown, P. and Levinson, S. C. (1987) *Politeness: Some Universals in Language Usage*, Cambridge: Cambridge University Press.
Buck, R. A. (1993) 'Politeness, Invitations, and Discourse Structure: A Sociolinguistic Approach to the Novels of E. M. Forster', unpublished Ph.D. dissertation, Northwestern University.
Finkelstein, B. B. (1975) *Forster's Women: Eternal Differences*, New York: Columbia University Press.
Forster, E. M. (1910/1973) *Howards End*, London: Edward Arnold.
—— (1924/1974) *A Passage to India*, Harmondsworth: Penguin.
—— (1971/1988) *Maurice*, Harmondsworth: Penguin.
Goffman, E. (1967) *Interaction Ritual: Essays on Face-to-Face Ritual*, New York: Doubleday.
Halliday, M. A. K. (1989) *Spoken and Written Language*, Oxford: Oxford University Press.
Hancher, M. (1979) 'The Classification of Cooperative Illocutionary Acts', *Language and Society* 8, 1: 1–14.
Hemingway, E. (1925/1954) 'Hills Like White Elephants', in *The Short Stories of Ernest Hemingway*, New York: Charles Scribner's Sons: 273–8.
Hurst, M. J. (1987) 'Speech Acts in Ivy Compton-Burnett's *A Family and a Fortune*', *Language and Style* 20, 4: 342–58.
Melville, H. (1853/1981) 'Bartleby the Scrivener', in J. Cochrane (ed.) *The Penguin Book of American Short Stories*, Harmondsworth: Penguin: 75–112.
Toolan, M. J. (1985) 'Analysing Fictional Dialogue', *Language and Communication* 5, 3: 193–206.
—— (1990) *The Stylistics of Fiction: A Literary–Linguistic Approach*, London and New York: Routledge.

5 Narrative iconicity and repetition in oral and literary narratives

Susan Ehrlich

EDITOR'S PREFACE

In many modernist and postmodernist novels, it is a daunting task for the reader to decide which character's subjective impressions are articulated in a particular passage. Sometimes it may even be imposs- ible to decide whether to attribute a particular passage to the narrator or a particular character. Such ambiguous passages are not un- common in the novels of Virginia Woolf, for example. But often the presence of one or more linguistic feature (e.g. a change in diction) helps us to solve the problem of attribution. In this chapter, Susan Ehrlich presents a detailed discussion of one of these linguistic features: namely, the repetition of narrative events.

Normally, narrative events are narrated only once in the text, and the order in which narrative events are presented in the text corres- ponds to their order of occurrence in the real or a fictional world. Thus, if event A is narrated before event B, the reader will assume – unless there is evidence to the contrary – that event A occurred before event B in the fictional world depicted by the text. However, this basic narrative convention of iconicity (or imitation) can be violated by novelists: for instance, event A can be narrated twice in the text, although it only occurred once in the fictional world of the novel. Ehrlich considers examples of this in the novels of Virginia Woolf, where it is quite clear that the second mention of the event is not simply a flashback.

Ehrlich suggests that in these cases the reader is initially dis- concerted by a sense of superficial incoherence. But since readers approach literary texts such as Virginia Woolf's novels with an assumption of coherence, an expectation that every linguistic choice is highly significant, their search for meaning and coherence leads them towards the following interpretation: in its second mention, the event in question is seen again as new but this time from a different perspective. In other words, the repetition of the narrative event signals a shift in (visual) point of view. In this way, the reader has succeeded in restoring coherence to the text.

This is the stylistic or rhetorical effect that a particular linguistic feature (the repetition of narrative events) has in literary narratives. In the second part of her chapter, Ehrlich considers whether the repetition of narrative events produces the same effect in oral narratives. Her analysis leads her to the interesting conclusion that the same linguistic feature can have different functions in literary and oral narratives.

J. J. W.

INTRODUCTION: TEMPORAL STRUCTURE
OF NARRATIVES

Of increasing interest in text linguistics and discourse analysis is the identification of linguistic properties of narrative texts (literary and non-literary, spoken and written) responsible for their temporal organization. Indeed, many discourse analysts argue that a defining characteristic of narrative discourse is its temporal organization. Labov (1972: 360) defines a minimal narrative text as 'a sequence of two clauses which are temporally ordered: that is, a change in their order will result in a change in the temporal sequence of the original semantic interpretation'. For example, the semantic interpretation of the temporal sequence, 'I punched this boy/and he punched me', will be altered if the order of the clauses is reversed: 'This boy punched me/ and I punched him'. Based on Labov's definition, a text must contain at least two such clauses (what he terms 'narrative clauses') in order to be a narrative. In other words, for Labov a defining characteristic of narrative is the existence of a partial matching between the temporal order of events in the real or a fictional world and their order of presentation in a text. Fleischman (1990, 1991) argues that included in the linguistic competence of all normal adults is a narrative norm, that is, 'an internalized set of shared conventions and assumptions about what constitutes a well-formed story' (Fleischman 1991: 78). Among these conventions are (1) that narratives refer to *specific* experiences that occurred in some real or imagined *past* world and are normally reported in tenses of the past (emphasis in text), (2) that while narratives contain both sequentially ordered events that move the narrative forward and non-sequential background material, it is the events that comprise the skeleton of a narrative and (3) that the most usual order of presentation in a narrative is one in which the order of represented events matches their order of occurrence in the real or imagined past world.[1] In this chapter, I examine some linguistic properties of narrative texts related to narrative conventions of temporality. After considering narrative texts that conform to the narrative conventions outlined above, I then go on to look at 'violations' of these norms in both literary and oral narratives.

The movement of narrative time

It is a distinguishing characteristic of narratives that they create a timeline – a narrative present – during which events of the narrative occur. Readers or listeners are aware of a narrative past, present or future, with events of the narrative present functioning to move time forward in the depicted world. Recent work in discourse semantics (for example, Dry 1983; Dowty 1986) has attempted to isolate the linguistic properties of clauses responsible for the perception of time movement in narrative discourse. Dry (1983) claims that predicates which refer to the initial and/or final endpoints of situations create this impression. The effect is illustrated in (1) below:

(1) Fred walked into the room. The janitor *sat down* on the couch.
(2) Fred walked into the room. The janitor *was sitting down* on the couch.

In (1) the event represented by the predicate 'sat down' is inter-preted as occurring later than the time of Fred's walking into the room. Because the simple past tense in English refers to the endpoint of a situation, the second sentence of (1) moves the reference time of the narrative forward. When the same predicate occurs in the past progressive (which refers to a point that is not a situation's endpoint) as in (2), its event is interpreted as contemporaneous or overlapping with the previous sentence's event. Thus, the second sentence of (2) does not have the effect of pushing the reference time of the narrative forward. This aspectual alternation between the simple past and past progressive in English interacts with predicate-type to the extent that only events (i.e. situations with natural endpoints), and not states (i.e. situations without natural endpoints), in the simple past tense will create new reference points on the narrative timeline. Using Vendler's (1967) taxonomy of predicate-types, Dry (1983) categorizes both achievements and accomplishments as events and both activities and statives as states. Within this system, achievements are defined as situations with a punctual occurrence having a natural endpoint (e.g.

reaching the top, blinking). Accomplishments also have natural endpoints but are situations of greater duration than achievements (e.g. building a house, typing a letter). Activities (e.g. running, swimming) and statives are classified as states rather than events because neither have natural endpoints, only arbitrary ones. Statives are different from activities in that there is no energy required to maintain them (e.g. knowing someone, being short, owning a car). The effect of predicate-type on the movement of narrative time is illustrated in (3) and (4) below:

(3) Fred walked into the room. Susan *got up* from her chair.
(4) Fred walked into the room. Susan *sat* in her chair.

Because the second sentence of (3) contains the achievement predicate 'got up', it refers to the endpoint of this situation and therefore is interpreted as denoting an event which occurs later than the previous sentence's event. In contrast, the second sentence of (4) contains an activity predicate (i.e. a situation without a natural endpoint) and thus the state denoted by this predicate is interpreted as overlapping with the previous sentence's event; the reference time of the narrative does not move time forward.

Dry (1983) makes the following generalization on the basis of examples such as (1)–(4): English main clause achievement and accomplishment predicates (i.e. event predicates) in simple past tense will serve to propel the reference time of a narrative forward.[2] In the following passage, for example, from D. H. Lawrence's *Sons and Lovers* (1913/1971), the italicized predicates (all achievements and accomplishments in the simple past tense) designate timeline events that function to move the reference time of the narrative forward:[3]

(5) Mrs Morel *looked down* at him. She had dreaded this baby like a catastrophe, because of her feelings for her husband. And now she *felt* strangely towards the infant. Her heart was heavy because of the child, almost as if it were unhealthy, or malformed. Yet it seemed quite well . . .
  'He looks as if he was thinking about something – quite sorrowful,' *said* Mrs Kirk. Suddenly, looking at him, the heavy feeling at the mother's heart *melted into* passionate grief. She *bowed* over him, and a few tears *shook* swiftly *out* of her very heart. The baby *lifted* his fingers.
  'My lamb!' she *cried* softly.
  And at that moment she *felt*, in some far inner place of her soul, that she and her husband were guilty.

The baby was looking up at her. It had blue eyes like her own but its look was heavy, steady, as if it had realized something that had stunned some points of its soul.

(Lawrence 1913/1971: 50)

Several sentences in the initial paragraph of this passage do not contain achievement and accomplishment predicates in simple past tense and thus do not move time forward. Rather, they represent states that obtain both before and after the timeline events of the narrative (e.g. 'Her heart was heavy because of the child', 'Yet it seemed quite well') or activities that occurred before the events of the narrative present (e.g. 'She had dreaded this baby like a catastrophe'). Likewise, the final paragraph of the passage contains an event in the past progressive (i.e. 'was looking') and a stative (i.e. 'had blue eyes') that are interpreted as simultaneous with the previously mentioned time-line event.

VIOLATION OF A NARRATIVE CONVENTION: REPETITION OF NARRATIVE EVENTS

Having identified certain narrative conventions and their linguistic reflexes, it goes without saying that such conventions can be violated in both literary and non-literary texts. In articulating the narrative conventions that are included in an adult's linguistic competence (some of these are outlined above), Fleischman (1991) is not saying that all narratives conform to these conventions. Rather, she argues that violations of these narrative conventions have the stylistic or rhetorical effects they do precisely because a narrative norm is operative:

That is, the fact that artificial narratives, in particular, exhibit such features as flashbacks, prolepses, or other violations of chronology, or repeat the same events more than once . . . the fact that certain texts foreground description rather than events . . . the fact that narratives commonly exhibit these marked features does not in-validate the notion of a narrative norm or prototype. To the contrary, without a *norm* – understood as a set of unmarked values for particular properties – the *marked* values could not produce the effects they do.

(Fleischman 1991: 79)

What I demonstrate below are the stylistic and rhetorical effects produced by the repetition of narrative events in literary texts. Such repetition undermines the narrative convention of iconicity whereby the representation of narrative events parallels their occurrence in the depicted world. That is, an event that occurs once in the narrative world is narrated several times (i.e. repeated) in the narrative text. In particular, I am concerned with the repetition of events that are initially represented by achievement and accomplishment predicates in simple past tense. What is noteworthy about these repetitions is that they do not represent the events as being anterior to the narrative present, even though the initial mention of the event indicates (through the simple past tense and achievement or accomplishment predicate-type) that the event is completed. Dry (1983) applies the terms 'given' and 'new', ordinarily used in relation to the representation of noun phrases within a discourse, to the representation of events within a discourse. For Dry (1983: 34), 'in the case of time movement, what is to be judged given or new is the information that a certain event has occurred, or a certain state come into being.' Consider, for example, the constructed discourse below:

(6) Mary finally finished her manuscript. Having finished this substantial piece of work, she felt free to move on to her long-neglected domestic tasks.

While the first sentence of this discourse conveys (through the simple past tense and accomplishment predicate-type) that its event is complete within the narrative world, the repetition of the event in a participial construction represents it as 'given' information (i.e. as having already taken place within the narrative world). That is, the second representation of the event as 'given' is coherent with the first mention which represents the event as having been completed. By contrast, the examples I discuss below are temporally incoherent to the extent that the repeated events are represented as 'new' information (i.e. as occurring for the first time in the narrative world), even though their initial mention has established the events as 'given' information.

Consider the following examples from Virginia Woolf's fictional prose:

(7) Judging the turn in her mood correctly – that she was friendly to him now – he was relieved of his egotism, and told her now how he had been thrown out of a boat when he was a baby; how his father used to fish him out with a boat hook; that was how he had learnt to swim. One of his uncles kept the light on some rock or other off the Scottish coast, he *said*. He had been there with him

84   Susan Ehrlich

in a storm. This *was said* loudly in a pause. They had to listen to him when he *said* that he had been with his uncle in a lighthouse in a storm. Ah, thought Lily Briscoe, as the conversation took this auspicious turn, and she felt Mrs Ramsay's gratitude.

(Woolf, *To the Lighthouse*, 1927/1964: 106)

(8)   'Oh, Mr Tansley,' she *said*, 'do take me to the Lighthouse with you. I should so love it.'

She was telling lies he could see. She *was saying* that she did not mean to annoy him, for some reason. She was laughing at him.

(Woolf, *To the Lighthouse*, 1927/1964: 99–100)

(9) Now it was time to move and as a woman gathers her things together, her cloak, her gloves, her opera-glasses and gets up to go out of the theatre into the street, she rose from the sofa and *went* to Peter.

And it was awfully strange, he thought, how she still had the power as she came tinkling, rustling, still had the power as she *came across* the room, to make the moon which he detested, rise at Bourton on the terrace in the summer sky.

(Woolf, *Mrs Dalloway*, 1925/1964: 55)

(10)   'No going to the Lighthouse, James,' he *said* as he stood by the window, speaking awkwardly but trying in deference to Mrs Ramsay to soften his voice into some semblance of geniality at least.

This going to the Lighthouse was a passion of his, she saw, and then as if her husband had not said enough with his caustic saying that it would not be fine tomorrow, this odious little man *went and rubbed it in* all over again.

(Woolf, *To the Lighthouse*,1927/1964: 18)

In each of these passages, the first italicized predicate serves to move the reference time of the narrative forward; that is, each of the predicates is in the simple past tense and is either an achievement or an accomplishment. In Dry's (1983) terms, the designated events become 'given' information within the discourse because it is communicated through their tense and predicate-type that they have occurred in the narrative world. The subsequent mentions of these events, however, do not represent them as 'given' information (i.e. as anterior to the narrative present), but rather as 'new' information (i.e. as occurring for the first time in the narrative world). The superficial temporal incoherence evident in these passages, then, represents a violation of the narrative norm of iconicity, a violation that I am claiming is the source of a particular stylistic and rhetorical effect.

Stylistic effect: shifts in point of view

In order to describe the function of the repetitions exemplified above, it is helpful to consider Genette's (1980) distinction between 'who sees' within a narrative and 'who speaks'. It is not necessarily the case that the consciousness whose point of view orients the events and descriptions of a narrative (i.e. who sees) is also the formal voice (i.e. who speaks) within a narrative. Indeed, in much of Virginia Woolf's prose the subjective impressions of characters emerge even though the act of telling the narrative is performed by a narrator who is distinct from the characters and occurs at a point in time after the narrated events. Auerbach (1968: 536) characterizes Woolf's style as a multi-personal representation of consciousness: 'The essential characteristic of the technique represented by Virginia Woolf is that we are given not merely one person whose consciousness (that is, the impressions it receives) is rendered but many persons, with frequent shifts from one to another.' Thus, not only is there sometimes a disjunction between the formal speaker of the text (i.e. the narrator) and the point of view through which the narrative is mediated in Woolf's prose, there are also frequent shifts in the source consciousness perceiving the events and descriptions of the narrative. My claim is that the temporal incoherence resulting from the presentation of 'given' narrative events as 'new' can be resolved if the repetition of the event is interpreted as conveying a different perspective or point of view on the event. That is, the representation of the second (or third) mention of the event as 'new' within the narrative world is coherent if the event is indeed interpreted as occurring for the first time, but from the point of view of a different source consciousness. A visual analogy is perhaps useful at this point. If narrative events are repeated within a film, one strategy for making sense of such repetition is to attribute their second occurrence to a new character or consciousness. Thus, the repetition of completed events within a narrative can result in a superficial temporal incoherence which, in its resolution, can function to create a 'new' vantage point from which 'given' events are interpreted.

Consider example (7) above. The first instance of Mr Tansley's (the referent of 'he') speech act is represented by an accomplishment predicate in the simple past tense ('he said') and serves to move the reference time of the narrative forward. Thus, the second and third mention of Mr Tansley's speech act in the simple past tense ('was said', 'he said') are temporally incoherent (at least, superficially) with the first mention to the extent that they do not represent the event as 'given' information, i.e. as being anterior to the current reference time of the narrative. This repetition shifts the perspective from which the speech act is viewed. While initially the speech act is represented from Mr Tansley's point of view, subsequent mentions invoke the perspective of some character for whom Mr Tansley's speech act is 'new' information within the narrative world. The last sentence of the passage makes clear that it is Lily Briscoe's consciousness through which the second and third mention of the speech act are mediated. Similarly, example (8) initially represents Lily Briscoe's (the referent of 'she') speech act as an accomplishment predicate in simple past tense. Thus, the speech act becomes 'given' information within the discourse. The second mention of the speech act, however, in the past progressive represents the event as ongoing. As a way of imposing coherence on what seems to be temporally incoherent, I am claiming that the reader interprets the second mention of the speech act as filtered through a different source consciousness. That is, while from one point of view the speech act is completed within the narrative world, from a different point of view (i.e. Mr Tansley's) the act is ongoing and simultaneous with thoughts about Lily Briscoe's true feelings.

Examples (9) and (10) are slightly different from (7) and (8) in that the repetition is not exact repetition: different predicates designate the second mention of the narrative events in question. In (9), Mrs Dalloway's travelling across the room is first represented by the accomplishment predicate 'go to', in simple past tense ('went to Peter') and then by the accomplishment predicate 'come across', in simple past tense ('she came across the room'). Again, I am claiming that the temporal incoherence that results from presenting a 'given' narrative event ('went to Peter') as 'new' ('she came across the room') can be resolved if the second mention of the event is interpreted as conveying a different perspective on the event. Put another way, the second mention of the event *is* 'new' within the discourse from the perspective of a new or different source consciousness. In (9), the point of view shifts from the narrator (a relatively objective vantage point) to Peter. Likewise, in example (10) the point of view shifts from the narrator to Mrs Ramsay. Like example (9), passage (10) represents 'given' information as 'new' with the repetition of a speech act designated by an accomplishment predicate in simple past tense ('went and rubbed it in'). Rather than interpreting the second mention of the event as incoherent with the first, I am claiming that readers impose a shift in point of view on the second mention of the event and impute it to a new source consciousness, that of Mrs Ramsay.[4]

Hrushovski (1982), in a general discussion of strategies or procedures for imposing coherence on superficially incoherent texts, cites 'imposing a shift of speaker' as one such strategy. He provides the following example:

(11) He opened the door. A few pieces of clothing were strewn about. He caught the fish in his net.

(Hrushovski 1982: 162)

While the first two sentences in (11) are not connected by any formal or logical means, they are readily interpreted as coherent if we assume that readers draw inferences about doors being entrances to rooms and rooms often containing clothes. According to Hrushovski, it is more difficult to interpret the third sentence of (11) as coherent with previous discourse, because fish are not normally caught with nets in rooms. At least two strategies can be used to restore coherence to this passage. A metaphorical interpretation is possible whereby the third sentence could be understood non-literally, for example, as a man entering a room and catching a thief. Alternatively, Hrushovski claims, a shift of speaker can be imposed upon the passage such that the sentence is interpreted as the man's thoughts (i.e. as a shift in point of view) as he enters the room. In a similar way, I am suggesting that the repetition of narrative events in the passages from Woolf's prose functions (along with other linguistic features) to introduce a different point of view into the discourse. Rather than interpreting the repeated events as incoherent with the representation of the original event, they are interpreted as events occurring for the first time (i.e. in the narrative present) but from the point of view of a different source consciousness. Thus, the superficial temporal incoherence that results from the repetition of *completed* events within the narrative world (representation of 'given' events as 'new') can be resolved if the repeated events are imputed to a different consciousness. This shift in point of view, of course, relies crucially on the similarity involved in repetition. The introduction of a new narrative event into the discourse would not necessarily invoke a shift in perspective; it is the repeating of 'given' events that helps to create a 'new' perspective on them.

MODE AND PLANNEDNESS

While it seems clear that the narrative conventions outlined above are operative in both oral and written narratives, it is not at all clear that the 'violations' of narrative iconicity described above would have the same stylistic or rhetorical effects in oral narratives. More specifically, the fact that literary texts are written and highly crafted may determine how such 'violations' get interpreted. In what follows, I examine the repetition of narrative events in oral narratives comparable to those instances of repetition discussed above. While oral and literary language may exhibit similar linguistic features (i.e. the repetition of narrative events), I demonstrate that differences in mode and plannedness can result in differences in the function of such linguistic features.

Mode: spoken versus written discourse

Psycho-linguistic studies investigating differences in the comprehension of spoken and written language (Olson 1977; Hildyard and Olson 1982) have suggested that reading a text may produce a bias towards what is actually said in the text, whereas listening to a text will produce a bias towards what is meant by the text. Hildyard and Olson (1982: 20) comment on the differences between the way meaning is retained in spoken and written discourse:

> In oral language, the point, intention or significance of the language, the 'speaker's meaning' is preserved in the mind of the listener; as the actual words, syntax and intonation are ephemeral, they are rapidly exchanged for those interpreted meanings which can be preserved. In written language, the words and syntax, the 'sentence meaning', is preserved by the artifact of writing, and mental recall becomes the precise reproduction of that artifact.

As regards repetition in spoken language, it has been claimed that many of its functions are related to the physical and cognitive characteristics of language production in the spoken (as opposed to the written) mode. For example, Tannen (1987, 1989) discusses the way in which repetition facilitates the production of spoken language in that it 'enables a speaker to produce fluent speech while formulating what to say next' (Tannen 1989: 48). Likewise, repetition is said to facilitate the comprehension of spoken language to the extent that it allows for the production of 'semantically less dense discourse'. In both cases, repetition provides a relief from the demands of face-to-face interaction: the speaker is provided with an opportunity to plan what she will say next while the listener's processing demands are diminished with the redundancy that accompanies repetition.

Norrick (1987: 247), writing on the function of repetition in conversation, distinguishes between 'random repetition' – instances of repetition that 'are explicable in terms of the speaker's task of production in face-to-face conversation' and 'significant repeats' – instances of repetition that perform some identifiable operation on their previous occurrence. For Norrick, random repetitions 'require no special attention by either the speaker or hearer' (246) and are 'those repetitions that we produce unintentionally, interpret subliminally' (248). Random repetitions, then, while easing the demands of face-to-face interaction, are not linguistic forms that are remembered or focused on to any great extent. In this sense, they are emblematic of spoken language as Hildyard and Olson characterize it; that is, speech is generally more 'ephemeral' than writing, with the linguistic forms of speech 'being rapidly exchanged for those interpreted meanings which can be preserved'. Clearly, then, some instances of repetition in spoken language are more closely tied to the demands of the oral medium than others. And, while it may share some functions with oral repetition, repetition in most genres of written, planned discourse is not likely to be random repetition or repetition that results from the physical and cognitive characteristics of the spoken medium. Indeed, Norrick (1987: 248) claims that random repetitions 'are those which careful speakers and writers edit out when they have a chance to pre-plan their discourse'.

Plannedness: unplanned versus planned discourse

Ochs (1979: 55) defines unplanned discourse as 'discourse that lacks forethought and organization preparation' and planned discourse as 'discourse that has been thought out and organized (designed) prior to its expression'. There is, of course, no one-to-one correspondence between unplanned and spoken discourse, on the one hand, and between planned and written discourse, on the other. While speech is more likely than writing to be unplanned, there are genres of spoken language that are relatively planned (e.g. a formal speech) and genres of written language that are relatively unplanned (e.g. casual letter writing). Literary discourse constitutes an extreme point on the planned/unplanned discourse continuum, a point that Ochs (1979: 55) characterizes in the following way: 'verbal behavior in which every idea and every lexical item and every structure in which the idea is to be expressed is considered and designed in advance.' It is precisely because literary texts are highly crafted and planned that readers of literature undoubtedly approach them with the expectation that their linguistic forms will be extremely significant. Thus, not only will there be no instances of random repetition in literary texts, from the reader's point of view there will be no instances of repetition without specifiable semantic effect, given the expectation that 'every lexical item and every structure . . . is considered and designed in advance'.

Violation of a narrative convention: repetition of narrative events

Given the difference between highly crafted, literary texts and spoken, unplanned texts, one would expect a difference in the way that the so-called violation of narrative iconicity (discussed above) is interpreted. Because literary texts are highly crafted, readers assume that their linguistic forms (e.g. repetition of narrative events) have been carefully considered and designed in advance, and are not affected by the demands of face-to-face interaction. If readers assume that repetition in these texts is not meant merely to provide speakers with planning time nor listeners with redundant information, then they will search for other interpretations to explain its occurrence. For example, as demonstrated above, they may seek to resolve incoherence by interpreting the repetition of narrative events as indicating a 'new' perspective on 'given' narrative material. By contrast, the repetition of events within an oral, unplanned narrative will be less readily interpreted as signalling a shift in point of view, given the other functions of repetition in spoken language, i.e. facilitating the production and comprehension of speech.

As illustrated in the following example (from Polanyi 1982: 161), shifts in point of view in spoken, unplanned discourse tend to be more linguistically overt:

(12) And my grandfather says now I'm going to stick the broom under the couch. I'm going to pull it out and you start hitting. He's telling my father youse start hitting the rat with the hammer. You squash him, right?

Polanyi (1982: 161) claims that the repetition of what the grandfather says above gives us two views of the same event, 'one distanced somewhat (in the narrator's diction) and one much more intimate (in the grandfather's voice and thus from within his world)'. While repetition is involved in the signalling of this shift in point of view, the crucial element to my mind is the change in diction that accompanies the repetition. If this speech event were repeated without the word choice that approximates the grandfather's style of speech (i.e. if the shift in perspective were less linguistically overt), it would be less readily interpreted as reflecting the grandfather's point of view, given the other functions of repetition in spoken language. In passage (13) from Johnstone (1990), there are several instances of repetition of a narrative event:

(13) So we went across as soon as the traffic cleared,
and we're headed up there towards that diamond,
and it's about . . . maybe . . . mile . . . two miles . . . north of Twenty-four on Aboite Center
and this guy's following us see,
as we're going up there this little hill right there . . .
at Ranch Eggs uh . . .
We're going up this hill,
and this guy's right on my tail . . .
And Lisa was with me,
and she said 'That guy is right on your tail!' (imitating female voice).

('You Gotta Do Something', Johnstone 1990: 24–6)

The event of going up the hill is repeated in this example: it appears first as 'as we're going up there this little hill right there' and then as 'We're going up this hill'. Notice that this repetition of a narrative event does not invoke a shift in point of view. By contrast, the repetition of 'this guy's right on my tail' does. However, like in example (12) this shift of speaker is achieved in a linguistically overt way. The second instance of 'this guy's right on my tail' is direct discourse imputed explicitly to Lisa by the quotative 'she said'. In addition, Lisa's voice is imitated by the narrator.

CONCLUSION

Because of the other functions associated with repetition in spoken discourse, the mere repetition of a narrative event in spoken language is not in itself enough to introduce a different point of view into the discourse. In both (12) and (13), we see shifts in point of view being achieved in much more linguistically overt ways, that is, the diction or voice quality of the new 'speaker' is represented. On the other hand, the repetition of a narrative event in literary texts can invoke a shift in perspective, due to the significance attached to each and every structure in highly crafted, literary texts. So significant are linguistic structures in literary contexts that readers are driven to make sense of them, often in spite of a superficial lack of coherence. And as we have seen, such attempts to restore coherence to superficially incoherent texts can be the source of stylistic and rhetorical effects.[5]

SUGGESTIONS FOR FURTHER WORK

1 Both Labov and Fleischman define a narrative in terms of a partial matching between events in the real or depicted world and their order of presentation in a text. The following article from the *New York Times* describes temporal events, yet there seems to be no match between the order of events as they occurred and their order of presentation here. For Labov and Fleischman, then, this would not constitute a narrative. Do you think their criterion for narrativity yields the correct results? In other words, is this text perceived as a narrative or not? If events were re-ordered so that they matched their actual order of occurrence, would the text be perceived as a narrative? Is this article typical of journalistic discourse in its non-narrative format? Explain.

Jean-Pierre Getti, the lower court judge who brought the charges against Mr Touvier, lamented the appeals court's ruling but noted that 'never before has France engaged in such a debate, in such a serious reflection about Vichy and the notion of crimes against humanity'.

Newspapers and magazines have covered the Touvier case in great detail, often providing long historical accounts and documents detailing Vichy's anti-Jewish posture. Television stations have held prime-time debates about what happened under Vichy.

Two French lawyers *caused a stir* by refusing to appear before the three judges who handled the Touvier case. A manifesto signed by 188 well-known artists, writers and intellectuals *accused* the three judges – Jean-Pierre Henne, Yves Chagny and Jean-Paul Dupertuys – of falsifying history.

In the Norman town of Pressagny-l'Orgueilleux, Mayor Jean-Marie Malafosse *canceled* the traditional May 8 commemorative ceremonies, arguing that the court's decision was 'a victory for those whom we thought until now were the losers of the last war'.

(from 'Rulings Jar France into Reliving its Anti-Jewish Role in Nazi-Era Policies', *New York Times*, 10 May 1992)

2 Consider the following passage from Hemingway's short story 'A Clean, Well-Lighted Place' (1927/1964). Determine which of the predicates will move time forward within the narrative world and which of the predicates constitutes background material (non-temporal-advancing material), according to Dry's (1983) generalization regarding time movement. What function does the non-temporal-advancing linguistic material have in this passage? Do you see any problems for Dry's condition on time movement in this

passage? Do all sentences that move the reference time of the narrative forward contain achievement or accomplishment predicates in simple past tense? Explain.

It was late and every one had left the café except an old man who sat in the shadow the leaves of the tree made against the electric light. In the day time the street was dusty, but at night the dew settled the dust and the old man liked to sit late because he was deaf and now at night it was quiet and he felt the difference. The two waiters inside the café knew that the old man was a little drunk, and while he was a good client they knew that if he became too drunk he would leave without paying, so they kept watch on him.

'Last week he tried to commit suicide,' one waiter said.

'Why?'

'He was in despair.'

'What about?'

'Nothing.'

'How do you know it was nothing?'

'He has plenty of money.'

They sat together at a table that was close against the wall near the door of the café and looked at the terrace where the tables were all empty except where the old man sat in the shadow of the leaves of the tree that moved slightly in the wind. A girl and a soldier went by in the street. The street light shone on the brass number on his collar. The girl wore no head covering and hurried beside him.

'The guard will pick him up,' one waiter said.

'What does it matter if he gets what he's after?'

'He had better get off the street now. The guard will get him. They went by five minutes ago.'

The old man sitting in the shadow rapped on his saucer with his glass. The younger waiter went over to him.

'What do you want?'

The old man looked at him. 'Another brandy,' he said.

'You'll be drunk,' the waiter said. The old man looked at him. The waiter went away.

(Hemingway 1927/1964: 29)

3 This chapter describes passages in which an event that occurred once in the narrative world is narrated several times (i.e. repeated). A different type of 'violation' of the narrative convention of iconicity is one where events that occurred several or many times are narrated only once. Consider the opening of D. H. Lawrence's *The Rainbow* (1915/1981); the many activities of the Brangwen men over

the years are narrated only once. What are the effects of this 'violation' of narrative iconicity in the context of *The Rainbow?*

4 The following passage from Virginia Woolf's short story 'Together and Apart' (1943/1972) displays repetition of a speech act. Consider this repetition. Is it similar in its function to the instances of repetition discussed in this chapter? Explain. What other linguistic devices might contribute to the shift in point of view? Think here about the differences between direct and indirect discourse.

No! That was the danger – she must not sink into torpidity – not at her age. 'On Stanley, on,' she said to herself, and asked him:

'Do you know Canterbury yourself?'

Did he know Canterbury! Mr Serle smiled, thinking how absurd a question it was – how little she knew.

(Woolf 1972: 137–8)

NOTES

1 These narrative conventions are said to characterize the Western narrative tradition, broadly construed.

2 Dry (1983) points out exceptions to this generalization. First, certain adverbials indicate that a state has just come into being and thus sentences containing such adverbials will create the illusion of time movement. Second, under certain conditions, subordinate clauses, reduced clauses and participials can trigger a perception of temporal movement.

3 The sentence 'And now she felt strangely towards the infant' does not have an accomplishment or achievement predicate. However, the presence of the adverbial 'now' indicates that this activity has just begun. The initial point of the activity is referred to and, hence, the sentence creates the illusion of time movement.

4 Repetition of narrative events is just one linguistic device by which shifts in point of view are signalled. (See Banfield 1982 and Ehrlich 1990 for more exhaustive accounts of the linguistic reflexes of literary point of view.) In these passages, then, there may be other linguistic features contributing to the shifts in question. For example, in passage (9) the presence of the verb 'come', denoting the second occurrence of the event, helps to invoke the perspective of the individual located at the goal of the motion (Fillmore 1983), that is, Peter. In passage (10), the description of Mr Tansley as an 'odious little man' also helps to invoke Mrs Ramsay's point of view as it is clear from the content of the narrative that such a description can only be attributed to Mrs Ramsay.

5 An earlier version of this chapter was presented at the First Conference of the International Association of Literary Semantics, Canterbury, England in August 1992. I acknowledge with thanks permission granted by Ablex Publishing Corporation to reprint portions of my chapter 'Repetition and Point of View in Represented Speech and Thought' (Ehrlich 1994).

REFERENCES

Auerbach, E. (1968) *Mimesis*, Princeton: Princeton University Press.

Banfield, A. (1982) *Unspeakable Sentences*, Boston: Routledge and Kegan Paul.

Dowty, D. (1986) 'The Effects of Aspectual Class on the Temporal Structure of Discourse: Semantics or Pragmatics?', *Linguistics and Philosophy* 9: 37–61.

Dry, H. (1983) 'The Movement of Narrative Time', *Journal of Literary Semantics* 12: 19–53.

Ehrlich, S. (1990) *Point of View: A Linguistic Analysis of Literary Style*, London: Routledge.

—— (1994) 'Repetition and Point of View in Represented Speech and Thought', in B. Johnstone (ed.) *Repetition in Discourse*, Norwood, New Jersey: Ablex.

Fillmore, C. (1983) 'How to Know Whether You're Coming or Going', in G. Rauh (ed.) *Essays on Deixis*, Tübingen: Gunter Narr Verlag.

Fleischman, S. (1990) *Tense and Narrativity*, Austin: University of Texas Press.

—— (1991) 'Toward a Theory of Tense – Aspect in Narrative Discourse', in J. Gvozdanovic, T. Janssen and O. Dahl (eds) *The Function of Tense in Texts*, Amsterdam: North-Holland.

Genette, G. (1980) *Narrative Discourse*, Ithaca: Cornell University Press.

Hemingway, E. (1927/1964) 'A Clean, Well-Lighted Place', in *The Snows of Kilimanjaro and Other Stories*, New York: Charles Scribner's Sons.

Hildyard, A. and Olson, D. (1982) 'On the Comprehension and Memory of Oral vs. Written Discourse', in D. Tannen (ed.) *Spoken and Written Language*, Norwood, New Jersey: Ablex.

Hrushovski, B. (1982) 'Integrational Semantics', in H. Byrnes (ed.) *Contemporary Perceptions of Language: Interdisciplinary Dimensions*, Washington, DC: Georgetown University Press.

Johnstone, B. (1990) *Stories, Community and Place*, Bloomington: Indiana University Press.

Labov, W. (1972) *Language in the Inner City*, Philadelphia: University of Pennsylvania Press.

Lawrence, D. H. (1913/1971) *Sons and Lovers*, Harmondsworth: Penguin.

—— (1915/1981) *The Rainbow*, Harmondsworth: Penguin.

Norrick, N. (1987) 'Functions of Repetition in Conversation', *Text* 7: 245–64.

Ochs, E. (1979) 'Planned and Unplanned Discourse', in T. Givon (ed.) *Discourse and Syntax*, New York: Academic Press.

Olson, D. (1977) 'From Utterance to Text: The Bias of Language in Speech and Writing', *Harvard Educational Review* 47: 257–81.

Polanyi, L. (1982) 'Literary Complexity in Everyday Storytelling', in D. Tannen (ed.) *Spoken and Written Language*, Norwood, New Jersey: Ablex.

Tannen, D. (1987) 'Repetition in Conversation: Towards a Poetics of Talk', *Language* 63: 574–605.

—— (1989) *Talking Voices: Repetition, Dialogue, and Imagery in Conversational Discourse*, Cambridge: Cambridge University Press.

Vendler, Z. (1967) *Linguistics in Philosophy*, Ithaca: Cornell University Press.

Woolf, V. (1925/1964) *Mrs Dalloway*, Harmondsworth: Penguin.

—— (1927/1964) *To the Lighthouse*, Harmondsworth: Penguin.

—— (1943/1972) 'Together and Apart', in *A Haunted House and Other Short Stories*, New York: Harcourt, Brace and World.

6   Free indirect discourse in Doris Lessing's 'One off the Short List'

A case of designed ambiguity

Helen Aristar Dry

EDITOR'S PREFACE

Doris Lessing's 'One off the Short List' (1958/1992) is a short story 'about a journalist who forces sex on a woman who does not want him and afterwards makes the humiliating discovery that he and his sexual attentions are of minimal importance to the woman's scheme of things. Though the subject is what Germaine Greer has characterized as "petty rape", in [the story the woman], without stooping to conscious retaliation, [affirms her] moral and intellectual superiority over a cocksure and intellectually manipulative male' (Harvey 1993: 66).

With such a male protagonist, the reader of 'One off the Short List' is likely to dismiss him right from the beginning as a cad. But, in fact, Doris Lessing makes us at least to some extent empathize with Graham Spence. And she achieves this by giving us *inside views* of the character. In other words, we get into his head, we hear what he thinks. The language she uses in order to present her character's thoughts is commonly referred to as *free indirect discourse* (FID). In her chapter, Helen Aristar Dry provides a thorough discussion of the intricacies of this method of speech and thought presentation which plays such a prominent role in modern narrative studies.

Aristar Dry shows how, largely as a result of her use of FID, Lessing succeeds in making us sympathize with Graham Spence's problems as a failed writer and share his insights into his own deficiencies. We realize that he suffers from an inferiority complex and that he makes up for it by seducing successful women. We begin to see him not only as the predator but also as the victim of a competitive, aggressive society.

There is thus an ambiguity in his character which is kept alive by

Lessing's use of FID. For FID is an inherently unstable and ambiguous category, and often it is not clear whose voice we hear, the narrator's or the character's. In particular, sentences interspersed between clear indicators of FID can be read as reflecting either the narrator's point of view or the character's point of view or both. Aristar Dry distinguishes between two types of narrative ambiguity:

(a) is the information communicated accurate?
(b) if it is accurate (because there is, for instance, independent evidence for it in another part of the story), is the character aware of it?

Here the reader has to decide, and Aristar Dry shows that the way we read these passages influences our interpretation of the story and especially our understanding of the extent to which Graham Spence is aware of his own motives.

J. J. W.

In modern novels and short stories, we often encounter passages which represent a character's words or thoughts but which are not enclosed in quotation marks or otherwise set off from the rest of the narrative. For example, in Doris Lessing's 'One off the Short List' (1958/1992), we follow Graham Spence's thoughts as he plots his seduction of Barbara Coles:

(1) Now, a problem. He wanted to be closer to her, but she was fitted into a damned silly little chair that had arms. If he were to sit by her on the floor? – but no, for him, the big bulky reassuring man, there could be no casual gestures, no informal postures. Suppose I scoop her out of the chair on to the bed? He drank his coffee as he plotted. Yes, he'd carry her to the bed, but not yet.

(1992: 26)

It is sometimes said that there are two ways to present the thoughts or speech of a character: *direct discourse* (DD), in which the character's exact words are presented in quotation marks; and *indirect discourse* (ID), in which someone else (often the narrator) summarizes the character's thoughts or remarks. But if authors were indeed confined to these two styles, we should find the first two sentences above phrased as either:

Direct discourse: Graham thought, 'Now, a problem. I want to be closer to her, but she is fitted into a damned silly little chair that has arms.'

or:

> *Indirect discourse*: Graham recognized that he had a problem. He wanted to be closer to her but he saw that she was fitted into a chair that had arms.

In passage (1) above, however, we have neither direct nor indirect discourse, but something in between: 'Now, a problem' sounds like Graham's own words. But the next sentence 'He wanted to be closer to her' seems to be the narrator talking *about* Graham until we reach the phrase 'a damned silly little chair'. This phrase again sounds like Graham expressing irritation at the obstacles keeping him from Barbara. Thus Lessing's paragraph weaves some of the words of a character into text attributed to the narrator; and the result is a specific style of speech and thought representation which is usually called *free indirect discourse* (abbreviated as FID).[1]

Free indirect discourse is a relatively new technique in English, having come into prominence only at the beginning of the nineteenth century, with the novels of Jane Austen. But now it is common in English narratives, in part because it can be used to create both empathy and ambiguity.[2] And narrative ambiguity – uncertainty about who is telling the tale or how completely we should believe the account – is a hallmark of twentieth-century fiction. For example, Doris Lessing's 'One off the Short List', from which our first quotation was taken, employs FID to create narrative ambiguity at the same time as it fosters empathy for the character whose voice we hear. Lessing's story relates a seduction attempt: Graham Spence, an unsuccessful writer, tries to seduce Barbara Coles, a successful scene designer, as a way of compensating for his own professional inadequacy. The story is ambiguous in a number of ways – not least of which is whether we should call the attempt a success or a failure. Barbara does, in fact, go to bed with Graham – but she does so merely to get rid of him. No sexual conquest is involved, since she is never deceived by his wiles and her acquiescence merely indicates her indifference to the values that motivate Graham.

We do not know, however, to what extent Graham himself is aware of his own motives; and this is the deeper ambiguity in the story. Graham seems manipulative and power-hungry, but in some sense he is a victim as well as a predator. And his glimmerings of self-knowledge give us a sense that he himself suffers, thus evoking a (perhaps unwilling) sympathy. As we shall see, Lessing's use of free indirect discourse initially contributes to narrative ambiguity; but the ambiguous passages, like the other passages of FID in the story, help to generate empathy, because they encourage us to withhold judgement of Graham until we have learned to see through his eyes.

FREE INDIRECT DISCOURSE

Free indirect discourse is called 'free' because it is not tied to a conventional introductory phrase like 'he said' or 'she exclaimed'. But it is also 'free' in that it allows variation. Like direct and indirect discourse, free indirect discourse is a style which can be used to represent either verbalized thoughts or spoken words. But FID allows an author considerable freedom in choosing how many of the character's words to use and how precisely to represent them. Thus it is partly responsible for the fact that there can be many textual gradations between unequivocal representation of the character's voice and uninterrupted narrative exposition. (See Rimmon-Kenan 1983: 109–10 for discussion and examples.)

In the single paragraph given as (1) above, for example, there are four styles of thought representation:

(2) (a) The narrator's summary of the character's thoughts: 'he plotted'.
(b) A few of the character's words interpolated into the narrator's report: '. . . a damned silly little chair that had arms'.
(c) The character's sentences transposed to third person: 'If he were to sit by her on the floor? – but no.'
(d) The character's sentences in his or her exact words: 'Suppose I scoop her out of the chair on to the bed?'

Example (a) is the narrator's summary, and example (d) is what is called 'free *direct* discourse', since it retains the direct discourse pronouns and verb tenses.[3] But (b) and (c) are both FID although they differ in the number of character's words represented. Other variations are possible as well, some of them so unobtrusive as to foster uncertainty about the source of the passage.

The linguistic features of FID

To define FID precisely, we should look at the most obvious examples of FID, passages like (2c) above. Such passages combine some of the linguistic features of direct discourse with those of indirect discourse, as we can observe by comparing sentences (3), (4) and (5) below. These sentences illustrate the direct, indirect and free indirect discourse forms of the same passage:

(3) *Direct discourse*: Sue exclaimed, 'But you promised to stay here with Mother tomorrow! What am I going to do?'

(4) *Indirect discourse*: Sue exclaimed that he had promised to stay there with her mother the next day. She asked what she was going to do.

(5) *Free indirect discourse*: Sue was angry. But he had promised to stay here with Mother tomorrow! What was she going to do?

To see that sentence (5) combines specific linguistic features of direct and indirect discourse, let us compare the linguistic characteristics of these two styles. In Figure 6.1, sentences (3) and (4) are aligned, one above the other, to highlight eight major differences between the direct and indirect discourse forms:

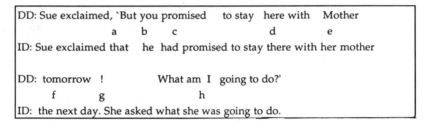

Figure 6.1 Differences between direct and indirect discourse

Direct and indirect discourse exhibit the following stylistic contrasts (the alphabetization is keyed to that in Figure 6.1):

(a) In direct discourse, the speaker's words are separated from the verb of saying or thinking by a comma and are put into quotation marks. In indirect discourse these punctuation marks are replaced by 'that'.

In direct discourse, words like 'now', 'here', 'I' and 'you' refer to the time, place and participants of the initial speech act. Such words are called orientational words or *deictics* (from the Greek word meaning 'to point'). And in indirect discourse, they become re-oriented to the situation of the new speaker, i.e. the person quoting Sue in (4) above. So:

(b) 'You' becomes 'he' in the indirect discourse of (4) above. And the original speaker Sue, who is referred to as 'I' in direct discourse, is referred to as 'she' in indirect discourse.

(c) Past tense verbs like 'promised' become past perfect ('had promised') in indirect discourse. This is called the 'backshifting' of tenses, and it shifts each direct discourse tense into its indirect discourse equivalent. Thus present tense ('What *am* I') also becomes past ('What *was* she').

(d) 'Here' becomes 'there' in indirect discourse.

(f) 'Tomorrow' becomes 'the next day' in indirect discourse.

And the expressive constructions preserved by direct discourse – such as hesitations, exclamations, repetitions and incomplete syntax – must be changed or omitted in indirect discourse. Thus:

(e) The speaker's address term 'Mother' becomes 'her mother' in indirect discourse.

(g) The exclamation point and any other punctuation marks showing the speaker's emotion are omitted.

And, finally:

(h) Direct questions, in which the verb precedes the subject, are changed in indirect discourse so that the subject precedes the verb; and the question mark is omitted. Figure 6.2 illustrates this reordering:

---

verb + subj.

DD: She asked, 'What **am**   I   going to do?'

ID: She asked what **she**   **was** going to do.

subj. + verb

Figure 6.2 Subject–verb ordering in questions

Now, as we have seen, these linguistic features are blended in free indirect discourse so that our sentence (3) becomes (5):

(5) *Free indirect discourse*: Sue was angry. But he had promised to stay here with Mother tomorrow! What was she going to do?

The way FID blends direct and indirect discourse features is shown in Figure 6.3, which aligns sentences (3), (4) and (5) to highlight the shared features. A letter placed above the FID version indicates a feature that (5) shares with the direct discourse sentence; lettering below the FID sentence indicates a feature shared with the indirect discourse version. A letter in parentheses identifies a feature unique to FID:

DD: Sue exclaimed, `But you promised to stay here with Mother	
(a) d e	
FID: Sue was angry. But he had promised to stay here with Mother	
(a) b c	
ID: Sue exclaimed that he had promised to stay there with her mother	
DD: tomorrow ! What am I going to do with her?'	
f g h	
FID: tomorrow ! What was she going to do with her?	
ID: the next day. She asked what she was going to do with her.	

Figure 6.3 Direct, indirect and free indirect discourse

FID is introduced only by a reference to the character's internal state (a), not by the conjunction 'that' or an attributive phrase. Like indirect discourse, it shifts first and second person pronouns (e.g. 'I', 'you') into the third person (b), and it backshifts verb tenses (c).[4] Like direct discourse, on the other hand, it retains deictic time and place words oriented towards the original speaker (d, f), direct questions (h), and the expressiveness of the speaker's words, e.g. her names for others ('Mother' in e) and the exclamation point that shows her emotion (g).

The effects of FID

Comparing (4) and (5) above, we can see that our sense of immediacy, or closeness to the character, increases with the increasing use of the character's own words. This is one of the primary effects of FID: it gives the reader a sense of being 'inside' the character's mind. And this in itself creates a certain amount of empathy. For, as one critic has said, a 'sustained inside view leads the reader to hope for good fortune for the character with whom he travels, quite independently of the [personality traits] revealed' (Booth 1961: 245–6).

To feel the empathy produced by an 'inside view', of course, we must know that it is the character whose voice we hear. But FID can also create ambiguity; and narrative ambiguity is often dependent on uncertainty whether the narrator or the character is the source of the passage. Both effects can be achieved at the same time by interweaving sentences having almost no features of FID into passages which are clearly marked as FID. It is the information in the unmarked sentences that can be attributed either to the narrator or the character. If the narrator is reliable and the character is not, this may leave us not knowing whether the information communicated is true or false. Or if we know that the information is credible (perhaps because it is verified elsewhere in the story), we may not know whether or not the character is aware of the facts presented. In this way – as 'One off the Short List' demonstrates – two types of uncertainty can be created, each with its own effects on our understanding of the story.

EMPATHY AND AMBIGUITY IN 'ONE OFF THE SHORT LIST'

Ambiguity is apparent early in 'One off the Short List', in the description of Graham's second sighting of Barbara Coles. He sees her first before she becomes famous, and he thinks her expression is sullen and her hairstyle gauche:

(6) But her eyes were all right, he remembered: large, and solidly green, square-looking because of some trick of the flesh at their corners. *Emerald-like eyes in the face of a schoolgirl or a young schoolmistress who was watching her lover flirt and would later sulk about it . . . . She was a stage decorator, a designer, something on those lines.*

(1992: 9; emphases added)

In this representation of Graham's memories, the italicized portions are marked as FID by the incomplete sentence ('Emerald-like eyes . . .') and the partial repetition of 'a stage decorator, a designer, something on those lines'. But the second meeting, after she becomes 'one of the "names" of the theatre', is narrated in a way that leaves us unable to attribute the value judgements involved:

(7) One night he saw her across the room at a party. She was talking with a well-known actor. Her yellow hair was still done on one side, but now it looked sophisticated.

(1992: 9)

The sentence 'Her yellow hair was still done on one side, but now it looked sophisticated' could be either Graham's voice or the narrator's, since it does not contain any of the linguistic markers of FID discussed above. If it is Graham's voice, we can conclude that her hair is exactly the same but now Graham finds it attractive. If it is the narrator's voice, we may conclude that her hair is still done on the side, but now it is styled in a way which anyone would call sophisticated. In the first instance we have pigeonholed Graham as someone who is attracted, not by Barbara, but by her success. In the second case, this part of Graham's character is left undetermined. We only know that, after she fails to remember him, he suddenly uses of her the 'private erotic formula: *Yes, that one*' which places her on the list of women he intends to seduce.

At paragraph 8, the topic changes to Graham's twenty-year marriage, and the ambiguities increase. The passage gives us many of Graham's thoughts in sentences of unequivocal FID. But other, less distinctive sentences leave us uncertain whether all of this rueful description is his:

(8)   His [marriage] had run true to form even to the serious love affair with the young girl for whose sake he had almost divorced his wife – yet at the last moment had changed his mind, letting the girl down so that he must have her for always (not unpleasurably) on his conscience. It was with humiliation that he had understood that this drama was not at all the unique thing he had imagined. It was nothing more than the experience of everyone in his circle. *And presumably in everybody else's circle too?*

Anyway, round about the tenth year of his marriage he had seen a good many things clearly . . . . He understood he was not going to make it, that he had become – *not a hack, no one could call him that* – but a member of that army of people who live by their wits on the fringes of the arts . . . . *Yes, that's what he had become, an impresario of other people's talent.* These two moments of clarity, about his marriage and about his talent, had roughly coincided; and (perhaps not by chance) had coincided with his wife's decision to leave him for a man younger than himself who had a future, she said, as a playwright. *Well, he had talked her out of it. For her part, she had to understand he was not going to be the T.S. Eliot or Graham Greene of our time – but after all, how many were? She must finally understand this, for he could no longer bear her awful bitterness.*

(1992: 10–11; emphases added)

The italicized phrases above (e.g. 'but after all, how many were?', 'Yes, that's what he had become', and 'Well, he had talked her out of it') clearly represent FID. Notice that in these phrases we have a direct question ('how many were?') as well as expressive words like 'yes' and 'well', in which we hear Graham's tone of weary resignation.

But the whole passage does not exhibit such features, so we are not sure whether all of it represents Graham's own analysis. Who, for example, is the source of the two parenthetical remarks? Does Graham have enough self-awareness to recognize that it is 'not unpleasurable' to have a woman on his conscience – i.e. that the power to disappoint a woman gratifies his ego?

And does he have the perception to recognize that his two sudden insights occur 'not by chance'? Recall that Graham recognizes the ordinariness of his emotional life and of his talent at exactly the time that his wife threatens to leave him:

(9) These two moments of clarity . . . had roughly coincided; and (perhaps not by chance) had coincided with his wife's decision to leave him.

(1992: 11)

This is a significant conjunction of events, because it shows how important female support is to Graham's self-esteem. Without a woman, his illusions about his own 'specialness' collapse. But we cannot be sure that Graham himself is aware of this, because we have no linguistic indications that sentence (9) is FID.

This ambiguity is maintained in the assessment of Graham's current relationships with women:

(10) The formula: *Yes, that one* no longer implied a necessarily sexual relationship. In its more mature form, it was far from being something he was ashamed of. On the contrary, it expressed a humorous respect for what he was, for his real talents and flair, which had turned out to be not artistic after all, but to do with emotional life, hard-earned experience. It expressed an ironical dignity, a proving to himself not only: I can be honest about myself, but also: I have earned the best in *that* field whenever I want it.

(1992: 11)

By the time we have finished the story, we will know that this claim to maturity is invalid; it reflects Graham's self-deception, and therefore paragraph (10) must reflect Graham's voice. However, when we encounter this passage in the eleventh paragraph of the story, we do not know Graham well enough to be sure that this is not an accurate description. And there are not enough linguistic indicators of FID to identify the words as Graham's. It is true that the passage ends with a direct quotation 'I can be honest about myself.' But in the preceding sentences only the repetition ('for what he was, for his real talents') and the expressive 'after all' hint at Graham as the source.

This paragraph then exemplifies one kind of narrative ambiguity: it may or may not offer accurate information. And the parenthetical statements in (8) exemplify another kind of ambiguity: they present accurate observations but leave us uncertain whether the point-of-view character perceives or acknowledges their truth. In both cases, ambiguity arises because the relevant sentences are interspersed among sentences of clear FID but do not themselves contain salient linguistic markers of a character's voice. In both cases, too, the effect is to leave us uncertain about aspects of Graham's character – e.g. whether he has, in sexual matters, either 'maturity' or insight.

Why might the author wish us to read the opening pages uncertain of the depth of Graham's insight into himself? There might, of course, be a number of reasons. One possibility is verisimilitude: we come to understand this character in the gradual way that we come to know an acquaintance: significant details pass unremarked at the outset of the acquaintance; but, later, after a pattern of speech and action has been established they 'fall into place' as meaningful indicators of character.

Another reason might be that Lessing wishes us to reserve judgement about Graham Spence, lest we dismiss him immediately as a cad and miss the wider implications of his behaviour. This is in keeping with the use of FID elsewhere in the story. Elsewhere, FID generates sympathy for Graham by letting us know of an inner life which does not necessarily show in his acts.

For example, FID is often used to convey the suffering attendant on his professional failures and social embarrassments. When Graham is assigned to conduct a radio interview with Barbara, he picks her up at the theatre and there observes a professional camaraderie that leaves him stricken. His anguish is presented in FID:

(11)   Suddenly Graham couldn't stand it. He understood he was shaken to his depths . . . . His eyes were filled with tears . . . . *That group of people there – working, joking, arguing, yes, that's what he hadn't known for years. What bound them was the democracy of respect for each other's work, a confidence in themselves and in each other. They looked like people banded together against a world which they – no, not despised, but which they measured, understood, and would fight to the death, out of respect for what they stood for, for what it stood for . . . .* It was then, with the tears drying on his eyelids, which felt old and ironic, that he decided he would sleep with Barbara Coles.
(1992: 14–15; emphases added)

The italicized sentences above are marked as FID by the inter-rupted syntax ('That group of people there – working, joking'), the expressive repetitions, discourse particles ('yes', 'no'), and emphatic stress ('for what *they* stood for, for what *it* stood for'). Only after these sentences of FID does the narrator inform us of Graham's decision to sleep with Barbara. This decision makes an entirely different impression after the FID than it might have before: having heard Graham's suffering in his voice, we realize that his need for sexual dominance arises from the pain of failure, loss and envy.

Even after we see Graham at his worst, insisting on an expensive restaurant to show off and delaying dinner in order to make Barbara tipsy, we can empathize with his professional loss because we are privy to his thoughts:

(12) But he understood he had been stupid. *He had forgotten himself at twenty – or, for that matter, at thirty; forgotten one could live inside an idea, a set of ideas, with enthusiasm . . . . But at least he now had the key; he knew what to do.* At the end of not more than half an hour, they were again two professionals, talking about ideas they shared, for he remembered caring about all this himself once. *When? How many years ago was it that he had been able to care?*
(1992: 22; emphases added)

The FID sentences in italics above echo Graham's voice in the interrupted syntax ('at twenty – or, for that matter, at thirty'), the repetitions ('an idea, a set of ideas'), and the direct questions at the end. So even his scheme to use ideas as 'the key' to seducing Barbara does not efface the poignancy of his final question to himself.

Later, after his self-respect is bolstered by a collegial talk with Barbara, Graham's desire for conquest wanes. And, once again, this clue to the privation that drives him is presented in FID:

(13) *It would all be easy.* They worked out five or six questions, over coffee, and took a taxi through rain to the studios. He noted that the cold necessity to have her, to beat her down, had left him . . . . *This comradeship was extraordinarily pleasant. It was balm to the wound he had not known he carried until that evening,* when he had had to accept the justice of the word 'journalist'. He felt he could talk forever about *the state of the theatre, its finances, the stupidity of the government, the philistinism of . . .*
(1992: 23; emphases added)

In the backshifted 'will' of 'It would all be easy', we hear Graham's voice, just as we do in the deictic 'this comradeship', the expressive 'extraordinarily', and the rhythms of the final list, with its suggestion that these topics are merely representative of the many discussed. Such passages of clear FID are useful because they prevent us from judging Graham the way we might if we saw his actions only from the outside. We have only to imagine how these scenes would be narrated by Barbara Coles to realize how much these inner views of Graham add to the complexity of the story. Without them, we would lose all knowledge of Graham's occasional bursts of fellow-feeling, of his more generous impulses, and of his inner humiliation. Without the empathy they foster we might dismiss Graham before realizing that he himself is a victim of the masculine gender role he attempts to epitomize.

Graham needs sexual dominance to compensate for a sense of professional failure. But the idea that a man's worth is determined either by his professional success or by his success with women is not original with Graham. Rather it is an unmistakable part of the male burden in traditional society. In the story, this is underscored by Jack Kennaway, whose boasting of an affair with Barbara suggests how widespread is the association of masculinity with sexual power. Furthermore, the part played by Graham's wife suggests how import-ant professional achievement can be to the female assessment of male value. Graham's wife makes sacrifices to allow him to write and, after his second novel fails, develops an 'awful bitterness' and threatens to leave him for a younger man who has 'a future' as a playwright. Through her, we see that Graham's boorishness is not his own entirely but arises as part of an oppressive cycle: Graham preys on women but is himself the victim of societal demands – enforced, in part, by women.

In order to contextualize Graham's posturings against a societal definition of masculinity, however, we must withhold judgement of him long enough to assimilate his struggles. As readers, we will never attain this more complex vision if we dismiss Graham in the first few paragraphs as an egotistical lecher. Apportioning blame so swiftly, we may never look beyond his individual failings to the failings of society.

For this reason the first few pages do not allow us to decide unequivocally either that the perceptive observations are *not* Graham's or that the reprehensible opinions *are*. And, as we have seen, Lessing's use of FID makes a major contribution to this designed uncertainty. Indeed, in 'One off the Short List', the interweaving of FID into the narrator's text functions economically to control the reader's distance from the main character at the same time as it conveys the events of the story primarily from his perspective. This combination of narrative ambiguity and poignant 'inside views' encourages us to withhold condemnation until we can arrive at a more empathetic, and therefore more insightful, evaluation of Graham Spence.

SUGGESTIONS FOR FURTHER WORK

1 In the passage below, taken from Jane Austen's *Emma* (1816/1923), the heroine Emma reproaches herself for improperly encouraging Harriet Smith, a low-born protégée who has had the audacity to fall in love with Mr Knightley, the man that Emma herself loves:

> To understand . . . her own heart was [Emma's] first endeavour . . . . *Oh! had she never brought Harriet forward! Had she left her where she ought, and where he had told her she ought!* . . . . *How Harriet could ever have had the presumption to raise her thoughts to Mr Knightley!* – *How she could dare to fancy herself the chosen of such a man till actually assured of it!* – *But Harriet was less humble . . . than formerly . . . – She had seemed more sensible of Mr. Elton's being to stoop in marrying her, than she now seemed of Mr Knightley's.* – *Alas! was not that her own doing too? Who had been at pains to give Harriet notions of self-consequence but herself?*
>
> (Austen 1816/1923: 412–14; emphases added)

(a) Identify the linguistic features of FID which are present in this passage. First describe the feature in general terms, then give an example, as in the following:

   Direct question: 'Who had been at pains to give Harriet notions of self-consequence but herself?'

(b) Turn the italicized sentences of FID above 'back' into direct discourse. Your passage might begin:

   Emma reproached herself, thinking, 'Oh, had I never brought Harriet forward!'

2 Below is a paragraph from 'One off the Short List' which presents Graham's reaction to Barbara's eyes.

   She smiled, from a cool distance. He saw, in the small light from the ceiling, her extraordinary eyes. 'Green' eyes are hazel, are brown with green flecks, are even blue. Eyes are chequered, flawed, changing. Hers were solid green, but really, he had never seen anything like them before. They were like very deep water. They were like – well, emeralds: or the absolute clarity of green in the depths of a tree in summer. And now, as she smiled almost perpendicularly up at him, he saw a darkness come over them. Darkness swallowed the clear green.

   (1992: 25)

(a) Underline the parts of the passage which seem to be free indirect discourse. Then put double-underlining beneath the parts that seem to be free *direct* discourse. (Remember that free direct discourse retains the tense and pronouns of direct discourse; so it looks exactly like direct discourse without quotation marks.)

(b) Now re-write the paragraph using only direct discourse. Is it possible to translate the last sentence into direct discourse? Why or why not?

3 Re-write the last three paragraphs of 'One off the Short List', narrating the return to the theatre as Barbara Coles might have told it. If you can, represent her thoughts using FID. How does this shift in point of view alter the reader's impression of the final scene?

4 It has sometimes been suggested that FID interrupts the action less than either direct or indirect discourse. That is, since the character's words or thoughts are presented in third person, they are more easily interwoven into a third-person account of the action. Test this theory by re-writing the following passage using either direct or indirect discourse for Graham's thoughts:

She looked abstracted. Graham was on the whole flattered by this: it probably meant she was at ease in his presence. He realised he was a little tight and rather tired. Of course, she was tired too; that was why she was vague. He remembered that earlier that evening he had lost a chance by not using her tiredness. Well now, if he were intelligent . . . . She was about to pour coffee. He firmly took the coffee-pot out of her hand, and nodded at a chair. Smiling, she obeyed him. 'That's better,' he said. He poured coffee, poured brandy, and pulled the table towards her. She watched him. Then he took her hand, kissed it, patted it, laid it down gently. Yes, he thought, I did that well.

(1992: 25–6)

5 The passage below, in which Graham Spence plots to accompany Barbara home, contains some FID woven into a description of the action. What makes you sure that the last sentence is Graham's? Why must the next-to-last sentence be the narrator's?

'I can drive you home and you can give me a drink. I have to go past you.'

'Where do you live?'

'Wimbledon.' He lived, in fact, at Highgate; but she lived in Fulham. He was taking another chance, but by the time she found out, they would be in a position to laugh over his ruse.

(1992: 23)

6 Below are two passages of represented speech. The first is from Virginia Woolf's *To the Lighthouse* (1927) and presents Mrs Ramsay's reluctant invitation to a guest:

So [Mrs Ramsay] turned with a sigh and said, 'Would it bore you to come with me, Mr Tansley?' She had a dull errand in the town; she had a letter or two to write; she would be ten minutes perhaps; she would put on her hat.

(Woolf 1927: 18)

The second is from George Eliot's *Middlemarch*:

Mr Tucker . . . was invaluable in their walk . . . being able to answer all Dorothea's questions about the villagers and the other parishioners. Everybody, he assured her, was well off in Lowick: not a cottager in those double cottages at a low rent but kept a pig, and the strips of garden at the back were well tended. The small boys wore excellent corduroy, the girls went out as tidy servants, or did a little straw-plaiting at home: no looms here, no Dissent; and though the public disposition was rather towards laying by money than towards spirituality, there was not much vice.

(Eliot 1871–2/1963: 102)

In each passage above, underline the portions which seem to present the speech of a character using free indirect discourse style. Which passage seems closer to the character's own words and which seems closer to a narrator's summary? Why?

NOTES

1 The style is also called *narrated monologue* and *erlebte Rede* (experienced speech).
2 These two effects of FID were identified by the critic Dorrit Cohn in an article entitled 'Narrated Monologue: Definition of a Fictional Style' (Cohn 1966).
3 Some critics make even more precise terminological distinctions, differentiating, for example, between FIT (free indirect thought) and FIS (free indirect speech), as well as between FT (free thought) and FS (free speech). See for example Short (1982: 184) and also Simpson and Montgomery (this volume). For our purposes, however, DD, ID and FID will be sufficient, since we are discussing linguistic styles; and the same styles are used to represent both speech and thought.
4 The backshifting of tenses has interesting results when the direct discourse tense is future, as in 'you *will come* to a bad end'. A backshifted 'will' becomes 'would', as in 'he *would come* to a bad end'. But 'would' occurs in independent clauses only in three circumstances:

(a) following a conditional clause, as in 'If he went, he *would enjoy* himself';

(b) referring to a habitual event, as in 'Every few days, he *would go* to the store';
(c) in FID, as in 'She *would be* back. She must be. How could he live without her?'

So when you find 'would' in an independent clause which is neither conditional nor habitual you have a reliable clue that the passage is FID.

REFERENCES

Austen, J. (1816/1923) *Emma*, in R. W. Chapman (ed.) *The Novels of Jane Austen*, Oxford: Oxford University Press.

Booth, W. (1961) *The Rhetoric of Fiction*, Chicago: The University of Chicago Press.

Cohn, D. (1966) 'Narrated Monologue: Definition of a Fictional Style', *Comparative Literature* 28: 97–112.

Eliot, George (1871–2/1963) *Middlemarch*, Harmondsworth: Penguin.

Harvey, S. (1993) 'Doris Lessing's "One off the Short List" and Leo Bellingham's "In for the Kill"', *Critical Survey* 5: 66–76.

Lessing, D. (1958/1992) 'One off the Short List', in *A Man and Two Women*, London: Paladin.

Rimmon-Kenan, S. (1983) *Narrative Fiction: Contemporary Poetics*, London: Methuen.

Short, M. H. (1982) 'Stylistics and the Teaching of Literature: With an Example from James Joyce's *A Portrait of the Artist as a Young Man*', in R. Carter (ed.) *Language and Literature: An Introductory Reader in Stylistics*, London: Routledge & Kegan Paul.

Woolf, V. (1927) *To the Lighthouse*, New York: Harcourt Brace Jovanovich.

7 Language and perspective in Katherine Mansfield's 'Prelude'

David A. Lee

EDITOR'S PREFACE

Katherine Mansfield's 'Prelude' (1918/1948) is the story of a family moving into a new house. Its most remarkable feature, according to Tomalin (1988: 162), is that it is 'written in a series of short sections without explanatory or linking passages; the reader is simply plunged directly into one fresh scene, one character's thoughts, after another'.

Such a story inevitably brings up the question of point of view or perspective, both in the sense of visual perspective (who sees? or, more accurately, through whose eyes does the reader experience the fictional world?) and of ideological perspective (what attitudes, beliefs, values and norms colour or inform our experience of the fictional world?). Both concepts of point of view are inextricably interwoven, since no visual perception is ever pure or unmediated by the human mind.

In literature (unlike in film) it is language which helps us to decide whether represented perceptions are more compatible with the narrator's orientation or a particular character's orientation. David Lee therefore analyses the beginning of 'Prelude' and shows how Mansfield's linguistic choices take us beyond the visual perception of a detached observer–narrator to interpretation and evaluation. Whose interpretation and evaluation it is is subject to ambiguity and change: sometimes there is an orientation towards the mother's perspective, emphasizing her detachment from the children; but mostly the orientation is towards the children's perspective, suggesting their feelings of anxiety or their freshness of vision.

'Prelude to what?' D. H. Lawrence asked when he heard of Katherine Mansfield's story (Tomalin 1988: 161). In the hands of David Lee, the story also becomes a prelude to a serious study of perception and interpretation, of perspective and point of view.

J. J. W.

The notion of 'point of view' or 'perspective' is one of the most frequently invoked concepts in stylistic analysis (Booth 1961). A distinction is often drawn between the point of view of the narrator and that of a character, for example, or between the perspective of one character and that of another. Writers themselves use the notion, sometimes structuring their work in such a way as to present their material from different viewpoints, sometimes interweaving different perceptions within a chapter, within a paragraph, within a sentence even. But what is 'perspective'? The term is obviously derived from the field of visual perception. Are we then employing the term purely metaphorically when we refer to 'perspective' in literature?

I will take Katherine Mansfield's short story 'Prelude' (1918/1948) as the main focus for discussion of these questions. Let me start, however, with a brief illustration from another century of the importance of perspective in a work of literature: Jane Austen's *Pride and Prejudice* (1813/1970). The central focus of *Pride and Prejudice* is on the way in which Elizabeth's perception of Darcy changes in the course of the novel – a theme which raises general questions about the kind of values that human beings employ in judging others and the nature of the evidence on which such values are based. On their first meeting Elizabeth sees Darcy as an arrogant, conceited snob and subsequent experiences confirm this impression. By the end of the novel, however, her perception of him has changed dramatically, so much so that she falls in love and marries him. Now in speaking of Elizabeth's 'perceptions' in these terms, we are clearly referring to certain general judgements that she has formed, not to the process of 'vision' in the literal sense. We all form judgements of this kind in relation to people that we know. They are presumably instantiated in our brains in the form of some kind of mental structure, which is connected to memories associated with the individuals to whom the judgements relate. In other words, when we say that Elizabeth 'sees' Darcy in a particular way, we are reporting the nature of a mental construct that bears only a tenuous relation with the process of 'seeing'. To that extent the term is metaphorical.

Yet this way of thinking about the process of understanding a person or a situation is strongly 'motivated' in the sense of Lakoff (1987: 91).[1] In the first place, the process of visual perception is inextricably interwoven with the process of interpretation. Our brains work on the raw data provided by the visual apparatus to produce mental constructs. For example, when I look out of the window of the room where I am writing this, I see a tree. Yet this statement is true only at a rather abstract level. The signals that impinge on my retina constitute a

complex set of visual information that change their character constantly from one moment to another as the eye scans across different
parts of the object. It is my brain that converts this kaleidoscopic
information into a mental construct that we call 'a tree'. On some
occasions the brain may fail to make sense of the incoming data or it
may construct the 'wrong' interpretation. For a few moments, perhaps,
I see a person standing under the tree, only to realize a moment later
that it is an effect of light. These observations show how closely the
process of perception is bound up with the process of interpretation.
In many respects 'seeing' *is* interpreting.

There is one other aspect of the relationship between understanding and seeing that is particularly relevant to the analysis of literature.
When we see an object, we see it from a particular vantage point. This
normally means that we do not see the whole of the object. Someone
else viewing the same object from a different viewpoint will receive a
quite different set of visual signals. In some cases this may not matter.
But on occasions, it can make a crucial difference. I may think that
this person coming towards me looks quite harmless, whereas he is in
fact holding a knife behind his back. This is an informal example of
a crucial aspect of Einstein's theory of relativity – the viewpoint of the
observer is a vital ingredient in the way the observer sees and interprets
a situation.

Now this point about the 'relativity' inherent in the process of
seeing can be applied directly to the process whereby we construct
meaning in a more general sense. One reason why Elizabeth has a
different 'view' of Darcy from that of his friend Bingley is that she is
working from a different set of experiences. Her knowledge of Darcy
is based on meeting him in a very restricted range of settings (such as
society balls), whereas Bingley has known him for a long time as a close
friend. In other words, when we apply the notion of 'perspective' to
the process of understanding in the general sense of the term, the
analogue to the literal concept of 'vantage point' is the set of
experiences that we bring to the interpretation of any situation. Moore
and Carling (1982: 11) have called this our 'knowledge base'. They
have argued that it is misleading to think of meaning as something
that is 'carried' from speaker to hearer (or from writer to reader) by
language. Rather, meaning is a product of the interaction between
language and knowledge base. Since we each bring a unique set of
experiences to the interpretation of any situation, the possibility is
always present that different individuals will produce different interpretations of what is in a sense 'the same situation'. Thus, there is a
striking parallel between this view of the process of interpretation and

the process of perception. Just as our vantage point can have a crucial influence on the nature of our perceptions in the literal sense, so the experiences, assumptions and expectations that we bring to the process of interpretation can have a profound effect on the output of the interpretive process. Metaphorically speaking, this mental baggage constitutes the 'position' from which we view the world and make judgements about it.[2]

Let me now consider how some of these intricate relationships between seeing and understanding, between 'position' and interpretation, can be traced in certain key passages in 'Prelude'. We will focus on the role of language in the mediation of perspective in both the literal and metaphorical sense. The story opens as follows:

> There was not an inch of room for Lottie and Kezia in the buggy. When Pat swung them on top of the luggage they wobbled; the grandmother's lap was full and Linda Burnell could not possibly have held a lump of a child on hers for any distance.
>
> (1948: 11)

The 'position' in which these sentences place a reader is very similar to the one we would occupy if we were suddenly deposited on the lawn in front of the house where the buggy is waiting (as we might be by the opening sequence of a film, for example). Yet the fact that the scene is presented through language means that there are certain differences between the reader's experience and that of the detached 'observer' in the literal sense of this word. If we were actually viewing the scene, we would see an older woman and a younger woman sitting in a buggy piled high with goods and chattels and we would see the driver perch two little girls on top, where they wobble dangerously. We would see all kinds of details that are not specified in the written text – the state of the weather, the kind of clothes being worn, the nature of the luggage, the colour of the buggy and so on. It might be wrong to assume that features of this kind form *no* part of the experience of reading the text, for it may be that readers construct some of these details as part of the process of reading. But we can be reasonably sure that they are much less fully specified in reading a book than in viewing a scene (or watching a film) and there must be considerable variation from one reader to another with respect to such specification. There are also certain pieces of information that would be immediately obvious to the viewer that emerge only gradually for the reader – the fact that Lottie and Kezia are young children, for example. On the other hand, the text produces a richer reading in some respects. We know the names of some of the participants:

Lottie, Kezia, Pat, Linda Burnell. (If we were watching a film, this information would normally be conveyed through speech.) And we know or can deduce something of the relationships involved – we know that the older woman is a grandmother, for example, from which we may deduce that Lottie and Kezia are her granddaughters. And we may also infer that Linda Burnell is her daughter and the children's mother, though this is certainly not made explicit in the text at this point. Thus, there is a strong metaphorical element in the suggestion that the text places us as detached 'observers'. In many ways, the experience of reading the text is very different from that of viewing the scene.

Let me consider now a more subtle example of this general point – one that differentiates the reading experience quite significantly from the viewing experience. This has to do with the italicized clause in the sentence 'The grandmother's lap was full and *Linda Burnell could not possibly have held a lump of a child on hers for any distance.*' This clause can plausibly be interpreted as an example of what Hough (1970: 204) calls 'coloured narrative', which he defines as 'narrative or reflection or observation more or less deeply coloured by a particular character's point of view'. In this case, the text seems to indicate a reading in which Linda Burnell has said something like 'I cannot possibly hold a lump of a child on my lap for any distance.' A transformed version of this appears in the text, with the name 'Linda Burnell' substituted for the first-person pronoun and a change in the tense of the verb such that 'cannot hold' becomes 'could not have held'. These changes are required by the fact that the narrative voice here is characterized by the use of third-person forms and by past tenses. But the question arises: how do we know that this clause has a different status from the one that precedes it ('The grandmother's lap was full')? How do we know that it is not simply a straightforward narrator comment? The key phrase, clearly, is 'lump of a child'. As speakers of English, we know a good deal about the socio-linguistics of this phrase. For one thing, we know that it belongs to a casual, informal register of the language. We also know that it is an expression that an adult might use when having to lift or carry a particularly heavy child. In speech act terms we know that it is a form of complaint and that its illocutionary force is close to insult. In other words, the pragmatics of the phrase make it much more compatible with Linda's orientation to the general situation here than with that of the narrator, who is adopting a neutral stance, reporting events perceived mainly through the visual medium. Thus, a full interpretation of the phrase depends on quite sophisticated socio-linguistic knowledge, with respect to the kinds of contexts in which a phrase of this kind occurs and the kinds of interpersonal relationships that it signals.

It is an interesting question (one that we cannot pursue here) as to whether there is any analogue to 'coloured narrative' in visual perception. Linguistic forms and structures carry with them a whole set of social, pragmatic and semantic connotations (a kind of historical 'baggage'), bringing with them into the text all kinds of indirect meanings and associations from their discursive history. In a sense, phenomena that we observe may also carry certain special meanings or be interpreted in specific ways depending on the 'viewpoint' of the observer (in the metaphorical sense). But it is doubtful whether the process of vision as such is characterized by elements that correspond closely to the kind of discursive complexity, the shift from one way of speaking to another, that we find in texts.[3] One of the crucial properties of linguistic structure is that it is inextricably bound up with social structures, social processes. In order to comprehend the full significance of this observation, we need to break away from the traditional idea that a language is a single, homogeneous, unitary entity. Rather, texts need to be seen as a kind of patchwork cobbled together out of different pieces, different 'chunks' deriving from a wide range of social and historical origins. Particular meanings and forms carry with them a rich set of connotations related to their social origins – connotations which have profound implications for the way in which we read texts.[4]

One other aspect of these opening sentences requires comment. It is interesting to see here four different ways of referring to people: (a) first name only ('Lottie', 'Kezia', 'Pat'); (b) first and second name ('Linda Burnell'); (c) a referring expression ('the grandmother'); (d) pronouns ('they', 'them', etc.). Pronouns are governed largely by textual factors in that they are typically used to refer to entities that have been mentioned in previous discourse. But the contrasts between the other three modes of reference have socio-linguistic significance and they position a reader quite differently in relation to the characters concerned. Various factors are involved in these patterns. The use of first name for the driver is a reflex of the general convention in operation at the time of these events for the use of this style in referring to servants. In the case of Lottie and Kezia the same style is motivated partly by the fact that they are children (alternatively, we might say that this is part of the semiotic process signalling to the reader that they are children) but it also positions the reader as someone who is in an intimate relationship with them and who perhaps feels sympathy and affection for them. By contrast, the use of the first and second name in reference to Linda Burnell is an indicator of distance. There is, moreover, a certain ambiguity here concerning the question of whether this distancing effect is a reflex of the narrator's perspective or whether it relates to that of the children. In the course of the story, it becomes clear that Linda does not have a close relationship with Lottie and Kezia and that most of the love and attention that they enjoy comes from their grandmother.

Similar ambiguities surround the term 'the grandmother', given that there are a number of alternatives that might have been employed: 'Granny', 'Mrs Fairweather', 'Linda's mother' and so on. Is this a reflex of the relatively detached narrator perspective, functioning simply to communicate to the reader information about some of the family relationships here? Is it a reflex of the children's perspective, filtered through the narrator voice? Lottie and Kezia are, after all, in the habit of thinking of her as their 'grandmother' (rather than as 'Mrs Fairweather' or 'Linda's mother') and they normally address her as 'my granma'. Or is it a reflex of Linda's perspective? As the story unfolds, we realize that it is the grandmother rather than Linda herself who deals with most of the practical aspects of running the household, as well as looking after the children. In other words, Linda and her husband Stanley tend to see her as someone who fills a particular role in the household – that of 'grandmother', with all the duties that this entails in their view – rather than as an individual in her own right.

The relationship between vision and perception (in the extended sense) forms one of the central themes of 'Prelude'. As a further example, consider the passage that follows the opening sentences cited above:

> Isabel, very superior, was perched beside the new handy-man on the driver's seat. Holdalls, bags and boxes were piled upon the floor. 'These are absolute necessities that I will not let out of my sight for one instant', said Linda Burnell, her voice trembling with fatigue and excitement.
>
> Lottie and Kezia stood on the patch of lawn just inside the gate all ready for the fray in their coats with brass anchor buttons and little round caps with battleship ribbons. Hand in hand they stared with round solemn eyes, first at the absolute necessities and then at their mother.
>
> (1948: 11)

Here, we will focus on the phrases 'with round solemn eyes' and 'absolute necessities', both of which mediate complex perspectives. The general viewing position is still that of someone standing nearby, contemplating the preparations for the journey, experiencing the scene primarily in visual terms. But the phrase 'round solemn eyes' goes beyond the visual. It is one of our beliefs about the world that people's inner states can be 'read' in their eyes, in particular that emotions such as anxiety and surprise often cause the eyes to appear 'rounder' than normal. Therefore, to say that the children contemplated the scene with 'round eyes' suggests something of their perspective. A 'detached' observer noticing this feature of the visual scene and placing it in the context of other clues (the fact that the children are standing 'Hand in hand') might well see the scene in their terms, understand something of the anxiety that they feel in what is for them an unsettling experience, of moving away from the familiar into the unknown. The predication of 'solemn' of 'eyes' produces a similar effect but in a slightly different way. In literal terms, eyes do not have the property of 'solemnity' in the same sense that they possess the property of 'roundness'. Whereas roundness is merely an *indicator* of an inner state, solemnity *is* such a state. In a sense, therefore, there is an incongruity in using this adjective to denote a property of a physical entity such as a pair of eyes. Yet we experience no more difficulty in interpreting the phrase 'solemn eyes' than we do in interpreting 'round eyes'. It is part of a large set of such phrases which derive from (and propagate) the belief that 'the eyes are containers for the emotions' (Lakoff and Johnson 1980: 50) – 'sad eyes', 'happy eyes', 'angry eyes', etc. Again, however, it should be emphasized that these phrases are interpretable only in relation to a knowledge base that contains such a belief, that interpretation is not purely a matter of reading off the meanings of individual words but of bringing language into interaction with a knowledge base of a particular kind.

The phrase 'absolute necessities' also has interesting resonances for the question of perspective. This is another example of 'coloured narrative' in the sense that it is ostensibly part of the narrator voice – the voice that is reporting this scene primarily in visual terms – but is in fact taken from Linda's comment reported in the previous paragraph. This phrase therefore begins as an expression of Linda's perspective, a judgement of hers on one aspect of the general scene. On its second appearance in the text, however, another ambiguity arises. Is this sentence to be interpreted as 'They stared at the luggage which I as narrator have just heard Linda Burnell describe as *absolute necessities*' or is it to be interpreted as 'They stared at the luggage which they had just heard their mother describe as *absolute necessities*'? If we read it in the latter way, then this inevitably draws attention to the impact that their mother's statement may have had on them. In uttering these words, the mother has in effect identified the luggage as more important to her than the children themselves and we might infer that such a remark would heighten their feelings of anxiety and rejection. Such a perception might in turn provoke in a reader certain feelings of sympathy and pity for the children. In other words the phrase here resonates with three different perspectives, three different sets of judgements: those of Linda, the children and the reader.

Lottie and Kezia are eventually left behind in the care of a neighbour, waiting for the storeman to collect them. Later they wander back to their old house – another experience that is reported in highly visual terms:

> The Venetian blind was pulled down but not drawn close. Long pencil rays of sunlight shone through and the wavy shadow of a bush outside danced on the gold lines. Now it was still, now it began to flutter again and now it came almost as far as her feet.
>
> (1948: 14)

Of particular interest is a small incident when Lottie goes to the dining-room window, which has a square of coloured glass at each corner, one blue, one yellow. Kezia looks through the blue glass and sees 'a blue lawn with blue arum lilies' and then looks through the yellow glass seeing 'a yellow lawn with yellow lilies and a yellow fence' (14). Two themes are interwoven here. There is something of the child's freshness of vision and fascination with the unusual. There is also a hint of an idea discussed earlier – the notion that the vantage point of the observer is a crucial factor in our perception of the world. Our perceptions (in the sense of interpretations or understandings) are consequently provisional, subject to revision in the light of further experiences. The issue is posed explicitly in the following passage:

> As she looked a little Chinese Lottie came out on to the lawn and began to dust the tables and chairs with a corner of her pinafore. Was that really Lottie? Kezia was not quite sure until she had looked through the ordinary window.
>
> (1948: 14)

This small incident ties together precisely the problematic nature of vision in the narrow sense and interpretation in the extended sense.

If space permitted, we might explore further the way in which the issues indicated above work themselves out in the course of the story. What is so remarkable about 'Prelude' is the subtle way in which themes that are central to human experience are developed in the context of a situation that is apparently so banal. From the opening sentences surprisingly complex issues arise in relation to the nature of perspective. This poses the essential problem of the process of making sense of the world. Given the way in which seeing is a function of the vantage point of the observer, to what extent are our perceptions and our judgements reliable, to what extent does our view differ from that of others? All the characters illustrate the theme in some way. But there is a particular fascination here with the children's perceptions. Their freshness of vision, their wonder at the world around them, their curiosity, their search for understanding are perfectly encapsulated in Kezia's question to the storeman as they drive through a luminous night to the new home. 'Do stars ever blow about?', she asks; 'Not to notice', he replies (17).

SUGGESTIONS FOR FURTHER WORK

1 Consider the following (abbreviated) passage from William Golding's novel *The Inheritors* (1955/1961):

A stick rose upright and there was a lump of bone in the middle . . . . The stick began to grow shorter at both ends. Then it shot out to full length again.
    The tree by Lok's ear acquired a voice. 'Clop!'
    His ears twitched and he turned to the tree. By his face there had grown a twig: a twig that smelt of other, and of goose, and of the bitter berries that Lok's stomach told him he must not eat.
    (Golding 1961: 106)

The perceived event here is the drawing of a bow and the firing of an arrow. If we take it that these sentences represent the perspective of a particular observer, how does this perspective differ from our own? (The concept of 'perspective' here is intended to include the concept of 'knowledge base', as discussed in the chapter.) Why might it be significant that this observer (a) uses words like 'stick' and 'twig' rather than 'bow' and 'arrow'? (b) uses intransitive constructions like 'rose upright' and 'grow shorter' rather than transitive structures such as 'lifted the bow' and 'drew the bow'? (c) believes that his stomach 'tells' him not to do things?

2 Consider the passage below from a Sherlock Holmes story by Conan Doyle ('The Adventure of the Norwood Builder'). Holmes is talking to Dr Watson. Why is the passage an example of coloured narrative? What particular features of the text show that it is coloured narrative?

Finally, having drawn every other cover and picked up no scent, I tried my luck with the housekeeper. Mrs Lexington is her name, a little, dark, silent person, with suspicious and sidelong eyes. She could tell us something if she would – I am convinced of it. But she was as close as wax. Yes, she had let Mr McFarlane in at half-past nine. She wished her hand had withered before she had done so. She had gone to bed at half-past ten. Her room was at the other end of the house and she could hear nothing of what passed. Mr McFarlane had left his hat and, to the best of her belief, his stick in the hall. She had been awakened by the alarm of fire. Her poor, dear master had certainly been murdered. Had he any enemies? Well, every man had enemies, but Mr Oldacre kept himself very much to himself.

(Doyle 1928: 598)

3 Consider the following incident in E. M. Forster's novel *A Passage to India* (1924/1974), set in India during the period of British colonization. Ronny, a British administrator with racist attitudes, knows that his mother, Mrs Moore, and his fiancée, Adela, are visiting a local college. When he arrives there to take them home, he is shocked to find Adela sitting in the courtyard chatting with two Indians, Dr Aziz and Professor Godbole. The headmaster of the college, Fielding, is showing Mrs Moore around the buildings but the others had decided to stay behind to rest. On Fielding's return, Ronny reproaches him saying: 'I think perhaps you oughtn't to have left Miss Quested alone' and a little later: 'I don't like to see an English girl left smoking with two Indians' (Forster 1974: 76). Are the two statements (a) 'Fielding left Adela alone' and (b) 'Fielding left Adela' true or false? Could they be *both* true *and* false? How do the general concepts of perspective and ideology relate to this question?

4 A permanent European presence in Australia was first established in 1788. Until recently, this phenomenon was referred to in Australia and elsewhere as 'European settlement' but more recently some Australians, particularly Aboriginal people, refer to it as 'European invasion'. In what way does the choice between these terms relate to contrasting perspectives on the phenomenon?

5 Consider some of the following metaphors from Lakoff and Johnson (1980):

ARGUMENTS ARE BUILDINGS; UNDERSTANDING IS SEEING; EMOTIONAL EFFECT IS PHYSICAL CONTACT; THEORIES ARE BUILDINGS; SIGNIFICANT IS BIG; SEEING IS TOUCHING; IDEAS ARE FOOD; IDEAS ARE PEOPLE; IDEAS ARE PLANTS; THE

EYES ARE CONTAINERS FOR THE EMOTIONS; IDEAS ARE PRODUCTS; IDEAS ARE
COMMODITIES; PHYSICAL AND EMOTIONAL STATES ARE ENTITIES WITHIN A
PERSON; LIFE IS A CONTAINER.

Give some examples of ways of speaking that illustrate these
metaphors. For example, when we say 'That's not clear' to express
the meaning that we have not understood something, we are using
the metaphor 'Understanding is seeing'. Do you think all languages
use the same set of metaphors or do you think there might be cross-
linguistic (and therefore cross-cultural) differences in this respect?

6 To illustrate the fact that meaning is a product of an interaction
between language and knowledge base, consider what the following
sentence might mean to you out of context: 'The haystack was
important because the cloth ripped'. Would it mean more to you
if you were thinking about one of the following situations: washing
clothes, launching a ship, typing a letter, a parachute jump, a
football game? Which one? What about 'The journey was not
delayed because the bottle shattered'? (The examples are taken
from Bransford and Johnson 1972.) Have you ever had difficulty
understanding something that someone has said because of some
discrepancy in your mutual knowledge or mutual focus of interest
at that moment?

7 Below is the opening sentence of Jane Austen's novel *Emma*:

Emma Woodhouse, handsome, clever, and rich, with a comfortable
home and happy disposition, seemed to unite some of the best
blessings of existence; and had lived nearly twenty-one years in the
world with very little to distress or vex her.

(Austen 1816/1972: 37)

Which word here indicates that some of these judgements concerning Emma might be those of an observer other than the
narrator. What is the effect of the construction of such an observer?

8 'Australia was discovered by James Cook.' In what sense is this
statement both true and false?

NOTES

1 Lakoff's (1987) discussion of metaphor, following on from Lakoff and
Johnson (1980), raises some difficult issues. In principle, the concept of
'metaphor' applies when talk about one domain of experience is
structured in terms of a different domain. The issue arising here is: do
the processes of understanding and seeing in fact constitute substantially
different domains?

2 Much of this mental 'baggage' is, of course, derived from the process of socialization. It consists in the beliefs, assumptions and attitudes that are an integral part of our native culture, defined in terms of such concepts as class, gender, age, ethnicity and so on.

3 The film medium is another matter. Film-makers can create visual analogues of discursive mixture, by superimposing or juxtaposing images from different social or historical contexts, for example.

4 This view of language is developed at length in Bakhtin (1981). For discussion, see Lee (1992: 50–1).

REFERENCES

Austen, J. (1813/1970) *Pride and Prejudice*, London: Oxford University Press.
—— (1816/1972) *Emma*, Harmondsworth: Penguin.
Bakhtin, M. M. (1981) 'Discourse in the Novel', in M. Holquist (ed.) *The Dialogic Imagination*, Austin: University of Texas Press.
Booth, W. (1961) *The Rhetoric of Fiction*, Chicago: University of Chicago Press.
Bransford, J. D. and Johnson, M. K. (1972) 'Contextual Prerequisites for Understanding', *Journal of Verbal Learning and Verbal Behavior* 11: 717–26.
Doyle, A. C. (1928) *Sherlock Holmes: The Complete Short Stories*, London: John Murray.
Forster, E. M. (1924/1974) *A Passage to India*, Harmondsworth: Penguin.
Golding, W. (1955/1961) *The Inheritors*, London: Faber and Faber.
Hough, G. (1970) 'Narrative and Dialogue in Jane Austen', *The Critical Quarterly* 12: 201–29.
Lakoff, G. (1987) *Women, Fire and Dangerous Things: What Categories Reveal about the Mind*, Chicago: University of Chicago Press.
Lakoff, G. and Johnson, M. (1980) *Metaphors We Live By*, Chicago: University of Chicago Press.
Lee, D. A. (1992) *Competing Discourses*, London: Longman.
Mansfield, K. (1918/1948) 'Prelude', in *Collected Stories of Katherine Mansfield*, London: Constable.
Moore, T. and Carling, C. (1982) *Understanding Language: Towards a Post-Chomskyan Linguistics*, London: Macmillan.
Tomalin, C. (1988) *Katherine Mansfield: A Secret Life*, Harmondsworth: Penguin.

8 Discourse style makes viewpoint
The example of Carver's narrator in 'Cathedral'

Michael Toolan

EDITOR'S PREFACE

The narrator of 'Cathedral' (1981/1989) is a typical Carver character, lonely and alienated, self-centred and callous. He spends the evening drinking with his wife and her blind friend Robert, and when his wife falls asleep, the narrator and the blind man watch (the narrator watches, the blind man listens to) a programme on television about cathedrals. As the narrator feels unable to describe to Robert what a cathedral is like, he draws one for Robert with the latter holding his hand in order to share the experience. This unexpected moment of physical touch and communication leads the narrator to a final, though inarticulated, insight into the meaning of life.

In this chapter Michael Toolan develops the notion of perspective or viewpoint as a set of beliefs and attitudes, which was adumbrated by David Lee in the previous chapter, and shows how the narrator's lexical and grammatical choices set forth his detached and hostile views, his stereotyping and prejudiced judgements. He focuses mostly on a number of pragmatic features of language. He looks at deixis, arguing that the very first words of the story ('This blind man') have what he calls a 'reverse-deictic' or distancing effect: the narrator does not want to get too closely involved with the blind man, he prefers to keep him at a distance. Next, Toolan examines what the narrator takes for granted (presuppositions) and what he implies (implicatures), and analyses how these implicit meanings characterize the narrator's stereotyped way of thinking. He also examines the narrator's naming practices: for example, why does the narrator generally choose to refer to his wife and to her friend by generic noun phrase (my wife, the blind man) rather than by proper name?

Toolan asks the reader to consider and discuss the effects of these, and many others, of the narrator's lexicogrammatical choices. Since the whole chapter is built around a series of exercises, it was deemed inappropriate to add a further set of exercises. This explains why the present chapter is the only one in the book without a *Suggestions for Further Work* section.

J. J. W.

This chapter focuses on some of the language effects in a short story achieved by the use of certain words, phrases, and verbal stagings of the situation, and the absence of other, 'expectable' locutions. The story in question is told in the first person, so the viewpoint revealed or implied by all the language choices discussed can be fairly attributed to the story's narrator. This is why I suggest, in the chapter's title, that the style of a discourse can set forth the viewpoint, the values and attitudinal individuality, of that text's speaker.

I want to begin with an exercise, in which you, the reader, put yourself in an authorial-cum-narratorial position. Specifically, I would like you to write the beginning of a story, one in which you will figure as both narrator and participant. What follows is the essential information you will need to complete this writing assignment.

(Imagine) you are male, white, American, aged around 30, able-bodied, married, without children.

Your wife has an old friend, a blind person, whom she met when she worked for him one summer ten years ago (long before she met you). They became firm friends. Although he moved to a distant town, he was someone she could confide in, and they kept in touch by sending each other messages on audiocassettes.

This friend's wife has recently died. And since he is visiting his in-laws, who live in Connecticut, 'just' five hours away from your town by train, the friend has telephoned your wife and arranged to visit you both, and spend the night.

That is the material with which I would like you to write the beginning of a story. Treat the information as *setting the scene* for the story; in other words, the above are not events in the story you're going to tell, but the orientational background for the significant happening that you intend to narrate. As for your addressee, imagine you are telling the story to someone you don't know well, but a social equal, and someone you are able to be fairly informal with (perhaps someone you have got into conversation with in a bar or café). In a dozen or so fairly simple sentences in the past tense, write out this scene-setting introduction to your story, sticking closely to the information supplied in the previous paragraph. If this is an in-class assignment, you could work in small groups, to produce a single shared story-opening; or compare and contrast individual story-openings, when completed, in small groups.

When you have completed this writing assignment, turn to the appendix to this chapter (page 137), where you will find another version of this story-opening; this is the one that appears in Raymond Carver's story, 'Cathedral'. Now itemize, as best you can, the main differences between the way you told the story-opening, and the way your alter ego, Carver's narrator, told it. Of course I cannot second-guess the specifics of your version and its contrasts with the 'Cathedral' opening. But at the very least I hope that the exercise so far has established one of the basic assumptions of stylistic analysis: choices and differences. Even with quite specific information and instructions – as supplied above – writers (you, or Raymond Carver) have umpteen choices as to how to conceive and cast their material, and the choices reflect and create differences of effect, emphasis and interpretation. Stylistics tries to dwell, in a quite focused way, on the specifics of textual choices and their consequences.

1

Let us review a few of Carver's narrator's choices. He begins by saying:

> This blind man, an old friend of my wife's, he was on his way to spend the night.
>
> (1989: 356)

Why does he choose to say the blind man 'was on his way to' spend the night? What difference does that choice make?

We often use the construction 'on one's way to' figuratively, as in 'she is on her way to becoming Frankfurt's leading psychiatrist'. But here the usage is literal – the blind man really is travelling towards the couple – and it also has the effect of bringing us readers to the very 'edge', the about-to-begin imminence, of the story of the visit. It is a simple but effective way for the story-teller both to get the story under way and immediately to create a notional span of time (the vague but delimited span of time between the beginning of the friend's journey and his actual arrival at the couple's house) which the teller can use in the immediately following paragraphs to fill in relevant back-ground. The effect is therefore different (you, as writer–reader, must decide whether, in the circumstances, it is 'better') from both the simple past tense version of the sentence, using 'came':

This blind man, an old friend of my wife's, he came to spend the night

or the past progressive version, using 'was coming':

This blind man, an old friend of my wife's, he was coming to spend the night.

The simple past version doesn't enable the teller to generate any sense of 'imminence': the whole visit is already over and done with. The progressive version does convey the sense of 'in the process of happening' – but only in a general way. 'On his way to' is closer to the progressive in meaning, but in addition dramatically focused on the 'immediately about to happen'.

2

'This blind man', the story-teller begins, not 'a blind man', 'a friend', 'an old friend of my wife's', 'this man called Robert', or any other formulation. At least two questions are triggered by this: why 'this', not 'a' or, possibly, 'the'; and why the early mention of the 'blindness'?

In fact the first two phrases of the story, describing the visitor, encode and rank a collection of 'charged' or evaluative characteristics, and it is useful to contemplate alternative formulations of those same characteristics:

This man, a blind old friend of my wife's, he was . . .
This old friend of my wife's, a blind man, (he) was . . .
An old friend of my wife's, who was blind, he was . . .
A blind old friend of my wife's was . . .

Some alternative versions make less of the blindness, or of the person's gender. But you cannot, without distortion, get away from the narrator's assertion that the individual is specifically his wife's friend; now just how strongly and contrastively the teller wants to imply that the man is not *his* friend is something we can only infer at this point, although the covert hint is soon enlarged upon in subsequent paragraphs. Besides, we have the 'this' to guide us.

The word 'this' is what linguists call a deictic expression (deictic is the adjective, deixis is the noun; both are related to the 'dex' part of the word 'index', and like 'index' have to do with singling things out by pointing to them). When a speaker uses a deictic expression, the expression 'points' to a person, place or time *from* the assumed place and time which that speaker occupies. You have to know or assume just where and when a speaker is positioned, in order to make sense of any deictic expressions they use. Core deictic expressions are the personal pronouns (especially 'I/me' and 'you'), 'here', 'there', 'this', 'that', 'now', 'then', 'today', 'tomorrow', 'yesterday' and even the verbs 'come' and 'go'. They tend to come in pairs, with one term implying 'close to speaker', the other implying 'distant from speaker'.

To give you an example of how you have to know a speaker and their spatio-temporal location in order to make sense of deictic expressions, imagine finding a slip of paper between the next two pages of this book (this – deictic! – book you are currently reading) on which is written, in a hand you do not recognize, 'Hey, gorgeous! Come and have tea with me tomorrow.' Who, specifically, has written this note: to whom does the text's deictic word, 'me', refer? And is it addressed specifically to you (one *is* gorgeous, certainly, but nevertheless . . .)? And how is the date 'today', relative to that which the writer deictically refers to as 'tomorrow'? So many deictic indeterminacies! If only the writer had written 'Hey, gorgeous Pat! Come and have tea with me, Kim, on Tuesday 11 May.'

To get back to 'this blind man', what we can say is that the use of the deictic word 'this' has the effect of pointing to the man as if he were close to the narrator and, possibly, close to the reader. But in fact this is a story opening and we have no prior acquaintance with the blind man; besides, from other evidence in the sentence and the paragraph we can see that the man is not physically close to the narrator, nor emotionally close. One intertextual analogy to the usage here, I would suggest, is a somewhat comparable usage in jokes and stories:

> This Englishman, Irishman, and Scotsman are painting this enormous bridge.
>
> I was just walking along the street when this police car screeches to a halt beside me.

In examples like these, two effects seem to be sought for: (a) the addressee is projected into an experience of the story-events by having particular participants pushed, by the teller, into the foreground of the addressee's attention; (b) intimations of teller–addressee solidarity, a co-opting of the addressee as in sympathy with the teller and distanced from or even opposed to the denoted participant. The latter amounts to a reverse-deictic effect: someone or something is both foregrounded and regarded with detachment – sometimes even with disfavour – at the same time, as when one disgustedly lifts a banana-skin off the piano keyboard and holds it up and asks 'Who left *this* here?'

Whatever is hinted at by the reverse-deictic use in 'this blind man' is amply enlarged by the use of the distancing definite article in sentence 3, quoted below:

His wife had died. So he was visiting *the* dead wife's relatives in Connecticut.

(1989: 356)

Not that using the more natural 'his' would entirely solve the problem: 'So he was visiting his dead wife's relatives'. The 'the' is jarring in its detachedness, especially coming after mention of 'his wife'; but any mental correction from 'the' to 'his' only makes clearer to us, as readers, that there is something egregious and inappropriate about the redundant and graceless mention of the relatives as belonging to 'the dead wife'. (And is there any connection between this and the use of the cohesive conjunction 'so', rather than, say, the more 'general purpose' connector 'and'; or is such a suspicion a 'considering too nearly'?) Why, we should be wondering at some level, could not the narrator have simply stated:

His wife had died. So he was visiting her relatives in Connecticut.

This would have been a more natural way of putting things. And yet the narrator has evidently gone out of his way to express things differently, with a detachment close to antipathy – and almost as if he thought we might have forgotten that the man's wife was dead, had he not reiterated the fact in this way.

3

This last feature of some of the narrator's odd or jarring contributions is one of the most interesting, and persists through much of the story. At numerous moments the narrator, on the basis of quite warped or blinkered assessments of what are relevant or likely expectations – thus, concomitantly, ill-judged assessments of what his addressee would expect – unwittingly reveals his prejudices, hostilities and insecurities concerning his subject-matter. Such 'showings' are particularly interesting to identify, since they have to do with presupposition and implicature in discourse, rather than anything that is overtly and directly stated.

Let us take one example. Before the visitor arrives, the husband quips that maybe he could take the blind man bowling. His wife asks him to show a little compassion:

'Goddamn it, his wife's just died! Don't you understand that? The man's lost his wife!'

I didn't answer. She'd told me a little about the blind man's wife.
Her name was Beulah. Beulah! That's a name for a colored woman.
'Was his wife a Negro?' I asked.
'Are you crazy?' my wife said. 'Have you just flipped or some-
thing?' She picked up a potato. I saw it hit the floor, then roll under
the stove. 'What's wrong with you?' she said. 'Are you drunk?'
'I'm just asking,' I said.

(1989: 359)

Here, as elsewhere in the story, what is jarring in the man's question
'Was his wife a Negro?' – so jarring as to prompt the wife's outburst
in response – is the occurrence of just this question here. The husband
learns (and reports) that the woman's name is Beulah (we thus learn
the name of the blind man's wife, from the narrator, and have it
evaluated by the narrator, long before we discover the name of the
blind man himself). He reacts to the name in a way that, from the
exclamation point, we can infer is disapprobatory or scornful; and
then appends his own stereotyping generic comment. This gives rise
to his question 'Was his wife a Negro?', which, although relevant to
his own line of thought (a line of thought which dwells on appear-
ances and categories: the woman's name, her ethnicity), has slight
relevance to his wife's reminders, which were to do with the blind man
himself. In the specific context of the conversation between the
husband and wife, how relevant is it whether Beulah was, or was not,
black? Clearly, not at all. And yet, as revealed, the question is relevant
to the husband's way of thinking – a way characterized by stereotypes
and ignorance and negative presumptions.

Another of many examples of this, both comic and pathetic, occurs
in the way the husband now proceeds to sketch out the life Beulah
and the blind man had together, before she succumbed to cancer. He
summarizes:

They'd married, lived and worked together, slept together – had
sex, sure – and then the blind man had to bury her.

(1989: 360)

Again what jars is what the husband assumes to be in need of telling,
on the presupposition that if he had not done so, we addressees might
have assumed otherwise. Thus he judges that he needs to tell us that
Beulah and Robert 'slept together – had sex, sure –', believing that we
wouldn't have expected such normal human behaviour from a couple
that included a blind person. What the narrator does here is typical
of what he does frequently in the story; and it may be characteristic of

the narrators of Carver's acclaimed and allegedly 'minimalist' fiction: characters' values and preoccupations and kinds of hurt are not declared directly in what they say and do, but only indirectly, via what is presupposed by what they say and do.

4

Let us look again at the phrasing 'This blind man, an old friend of my wife's', since the order of words in phrases, and the order of phrases in sentences, commonly reflects an implicit evaluative ranking. Just as there may be considerable difference in meaning between 'an old blind friend' and 'a blind old friend' (the former is advanced in age, the latter may not be), so there are glaring differences in implication between:

This blind man, an old friend of my wife's

and, say:

This old friend of my wife's, a blind man.

The former quite clearly implies that the individual's maleness and, especially, his blindness are more important characteristics – in the speaker's view – than the fact that he is an old friend of the speaker's wife.

5

The first sentence exhibits use of what is sometimes called a 'resumptive pronoun'. In standard written English, it is ungrammatical to append a subject or object pronoun to an already-supplied noun phrase; pronouns in English typically are 'economical' free-standing substitutes for other nominal expressions, thus not to be used together with the replaced form: that would be an extravagance, not an economy. On the other hand just this resumptive use of pronouns is common, like the use of 'this' noted earlier, in partisan jokes and stories. And at the very least, the use here clearly signals narratorial informality, colloquialism, and vernacular casualness. It is a marker of orality rather than written-ness.

6

How do we know, as we do know, that the blind man is going to spend the night *with the narrator and his wife* – when the opening sentence only states that the blind man was 'on his way to spend the night'?

Here, as in many other points in the story, the reader has to make a reasonable inference, in order to make the text fully coherent. After all, in a sense, we are all always on our way to 'spending the night'. Here, reflecting his general colloquial informality, the narrator doesn't spell out the contextually inferable fact that it was at the home of the speaker of the utterance 'on his way to spend the night' that the blind man was going to spend the night.

At the same time, perhaps the omission is not entirely accidental: just how participatorily active in the arrangement of this visit – as this narrator tells it – are the narrator and his wife? Look again at the relevant sentences:

> He called my wife from his in-laws'. Arrangements were made. He would come by train, a five-hour trip, and my wife would meet him at the station.
>
> (1989: 356)

It is the blind man who acts, involving the wife in his plans; certainly, there is no mention of the husband here.

7

The burden of this chapter has been that – potentially, at least – every single language-choice made by the author of 'Cathedral' is important and makes a difference. With that in mind, assess how your version of the story-opening expresses the information which, in the Carver version, is cast thus:

> They made tapes and mailed them back and forth.

And now comment on any differences of meaning or evaluation there could be between the above sentence and the following one:

> They made tapes and mailed them to each other.

8

The husband–narrator, from the beginning of this story and through-out, refers to his spouse as 'my wife', and their guest as 'the blind man'. The narrator thus never introduces his co-protagonists, nor does he denote them by their proper names. What kind of attitudes might one suspect of a speaker who never denotes their spouse, in a story, by name, and who invariably uses the formulation 'my wife'?

9

In view of the speaker's seeming reluctance to name his wife or (with only very particular exceptions) the blind man, what sense can we make of his interjection in the following sentence, in the course of his rehearsal of his wife's earlier life with her first husband, a military officer?

> Her officer – why should he have a name? he was the childhood sweetheart, and what more does he want? – came home from somewhere, found her, and called the ambulance.
>
> (1989: 358)

10 Turns of phrase

(a) In the second paragraph of the story we are told how the blind man, on the last day she worked for him, asked if he could touch the wife's face. The text continues: 'She agreed to this' (357). What construction might the narrator be suspected of putting on this incident, by the narrator's choice of these words?

(b) Similarly, consider some of the word choices in the following section, and how they disclose the husband's implicit suspicions of and lack of respect for his wife:

> So okay. *I'm saying* that at the end of the summer she let the blind man run his hands over her face, said goodbye to him, married her childhood *etc.*, who was now a commissioned officer, and she moved away from Seattle. *But* they'd kept in touch, she and the blind man. She made the first contact after a year or so.
>
> (1989: 357; emphases added)

(c) Now consider these lines from the middle of the story, where the husband reports the 'getting re-acquainted' conversation between his wife and the blind man:

> They talked of things that had happened to them – to them! – these past ten years. I waited in vain to hear my name on my wife's sweet lips: 'And then my dear husband came into my life' – something like that. But I heard nothing of the sort. More talk of Robert. Robert had done a little of everything, it seemed, a regular blind jack-of-all-trades.
>
> (1989: 364–5)

> What emotions in the husband, not fully declared or acknowledged, do some of the turns of phrase here point to?

11

Besides the idea that 'style creates viewpoint', it is also clear that, in some circumstances, content creates viewpoint. This is what I conclude from my experiences when asking my own students to create a story-opening for the 'blind man' story, using the information supplied at the opening of this chapter. Rather to my surprise, a number of these students commented on how the information that the narrator and his wife are aged about 30 and 'without children' was, for them, a strong signal of dysfunction and 'trouble'. These students took the information as a 'warrant' for starting the story as one in which the couple are at odds with each other in some way.

Do you agree with those students? Is the inference they drew, that to be married without children suggests some problem in a partnership, a culturally-specific one? Should I have left out the information that the couple had no children? A seemingly slight piece of orientational material, particularly when compounded with the idea that the visitor is *her* friend but not *his*, makes a considerable difference to the kinds of stories students began to construct.

12

This chapter only scratches the surface, or rather the opening paragraphs, of Carver's powerful story; in actuality the story is saturated with resonant linguistic choices on every line. And the discussion here has only begun to display some of the issues that the story is about. My chief hope at this stage is that you will feel prompted – will be able – to get hold of the story and read it through.

If you do so, this final exercise will make sense! The task, first, is to think about the following set of English pronouns:

nothing, everything, something, anything

and to jot down a few ideas about how they are used, and particularly how they are used in everyday situations such as conversation. What do they mean, what uses are they put to?

Then I would urge you to scan the entire 'Cathedral' story, noting all the uses of these words in the narration, or in characters' speech. The prominence of these pronouns, in the story, does not seem to me incidental; but if that's the case, then what effects are they intended to project? As two examples among many, notice how the narrator closes the discussion of cathedrals by saying 'The truth is, cathedrals don't mean anything special to me. Nothing. Cathedrals. They're something to look at on late-night TV. That's all they are' (372). And consider also the story's end, where the narrator keeps his eyes closed ('I thought it was something I ought to do' 375) rather than opening them to look at the picture he has drawn:

> My eyes were still closed. I was in my house. I knew that. But I didn't feel like I was inside anything.
> 'It's really something,' I said.
>
> (1989: 375)

To repeat, it may be appropriate to argue that several distinct effects are created by the prominent use of the 'something, nothing, etc.' pronouns at major points in the narrative. But one way to pursue the topic would be to relate these pronouns' use to the suggestion, proposed by education theorist Basil Bernstein, that a contrast exists between a more restricted and a more elaborated way of using language description and self-expression, with the restricted 'code' sometimes being associated with disempowerment, marginalization, and inarticulacy, by comparison with the elaborated code. For a brief discussion of this topic, see Fowler (1977: 115 ff.).

APPENDIX

> This blind man, an old friend of my wife's, he was on his way to spend the night. His wife had died. So he was visiting the dead wife's relatives in Connecticut. He called my wife from his in-laws'. Arrangements were made. He would come by train, a five-hour trip, and my wife would meet him at the station. She hadn't seen him since she worked for him one summer in Seattle ten years ago. But she and the blind man had kept in touch. They made tapes and mailed them back and forth. I wasn't enthusiastic about his visit. He was no one I knew. And his being blind bothered me. My idea of blindness came from the movies. In the movies, the blind moved slowly and never laughed. Sometimes they were led by seeing-eye dogs. A blind man in my house was not something I looked forward to.
>
> (Carver 1981/1989: 356)

REFERENCES

Carver, R. (1981/1989) 'Cathedral', in *Where I'm Calling From: New and Selected Stories*, New York: Vintage Books: 356–75.
Fowler, R. (1977) *Linguistics and the Novel*, London: Methuen.

9 Language, literature and film

The stylistics of Bernard MacLaverty's *Cal*

Paul Simpson and Martin Montgomery

EDITOR'S PREFACE

What artifices does a writer use to persuade readers to co-operate in creating a fictional world peopled by characters who foist their views and ideas, indeed their whole life stories upon them? Paul Simpson and Martin Montgomery offer a plausible answer to this ever recurring question by presenting a stylistic model of narrative rhetoric. To prove the feasibility of their model, they apply it to Bernard MacLaverty's successful novel *Cal* (1983/1984), comparing their findings with an analysis of the later film version of the story.

For a story teller to tamper with linear time and disrupt the temporal order of events is no doubt the most natural thing to do. So, once a story gets told, it is not likely to become a straightforward account of past events in strict chronological order. Therefore, Simpson and Montgomery make the elementary distinction between *plot* and *discourse*: the plot then is the basic story-line in which events happen in the order in which they happened; it is the crude material which the writer moulds into an artistic narrative design: the discourse. Thus, the discourse may show all kinds of narrative devices such as flashbacks, flashforwards, extension or compression of narrational time, reiteration of the same event, and other rhetorical mechanisms which are of course all designed to encourage the reader's active participation in creating the fictional world. (As Paul Simpson writes elsewhere, it is a bit unfortunate that there is such a puzzling proliferation of terms to indicate this primary distinction. In the order of plot/discourse, he mentions as examples: diegesis/narrative, *fabula/sjuzhet*, *histoire/discours* and story/discourse (Simpson 1993: 45). See also Wales 1989: 355–7.)

After its transformation into discourse, the story has assumed a sense of artistic coherence and, unlike plot, no longer lends itself to a simple summary. These elements of organization and arrangement come under *textual structure*, the first of the six narrative categories of Simpson and Montgomery's model.

One of the questions readers almost instinctively ask when they read a novel is where and when it is set, because they know that factors such as socio-historical and linguistic setting have effects on or, reversely, are a projection of character and events. Therefore, *cultural context* and *linguistic code* jointly form the second narrative component.

The interest of readers may also be roused when they recognize, actively or passively, other texts or images which fit into the cultural code of a novel's discourse and therefore prompt signification. This so-called intertextuality is included in the third narrative category of the schema, designated as *intertext(s)*.

Henry James's dictum, 'What is character but the determination of incident? What is incident but the illustration of character?' (*Prefaces*, 1909) 'ties in with the fourth narrative component, which is labelled as *characterization: action and events*, thus indicating that character, actions and events are strongly interdependent.

While interpreting this interfusion of character and action, the reader will wonder, 'Who tells all this and from what perspective or point of view is it seen, experienced or assessed?' Simpson and Montgomery relate this fundamental question in literary criticism to the fifth element of their model: *focalization*. This term has the advantage of being conveniently connected with a verb, namely *to focalize*, and two other nouns: the *focalizer* and the *focalized*, the former being the one who experiences and the latter denoting who or what is being experienced. This wealth of interrelated terms facilitates the investigation of point of view, to which the reader has been introduced in the previous chapters.

The narration of action and characterization is not only dependent on the above stylistic devices but also on a medium: language, drawings, film, and so on. Accordingly *textual medium* is the sixth and last signifying segment in this narrative schema, which enables Simpson and Montgomery to shift to the film version of *Cal*, and to point out how this change in medium significantly affects particular issues of narration and consequently the construction of character.

Finally, it is of paramount importance for us to note that in specifying the narrative components of their model, the authors of this chapter have, of necessity, taken them in isolation, but it must be recognized that they have only done so to show how these separate components ultimately synthesize into an intellectual and artistic whole.

P. V.

INTRODUCTION

This chapter has two main aims. The first is to present a stylistic model of narrative communication. The second is to offer, within the parameters of our narrative model, a detailed stylistic analysis of both the novel and film versions of Bernard MacLaverty's story *Cal* (1983/ 1984). We intend to demonstrate how practical narrative analysis can yield useful insights into the development of plot and characterization in fiction. We are also suggesting that our model is both replicable and transferable in so far as it can be extended and applied to narrative texts other than those used in the present study.

MacLaverty's novel was published in 1983. A tale of forbidden love across Northern Ireland's sectarian divide, it tells of the ill-fated relationship between the eponymous protagonist, Cal, and Marcella Morton, the widow of a policeman in whose murder Cal has been involved. Pat O'Connor's film, with John Lynch and Helen Mirren in the central roles, was released in 1984, only a year after the publication of the novel. Favourable public and critical response has ensured continued wide circulation of both versions of the story.

Given the nature of the present study, it would be helpful if our readers had some knowledge of *Cal*. For those who don't, we will provide appropriate contextual information on both film and novel wherever possible throughout our study.

STYLISTICS AND NARRATIVE

What elements make up a narrative? Providing an answer to this question has become one of the central challenges for a stylistics of prose fiction. Much work in modern narrative stylistics seeks to isolate the various units which combine to form a novel or short story and to explain how these narrative units are interconnected. Having identified the basic units in this way, the next task is to specify which type of stylistic model is best suited to the study of which particular unit.

This is the kind of procedure which we intend to adopt in our own study. The first step involves locating our analysis within a broader narrative framework, so, to this effect, we begin by proposing a basic model of narrative structure (see Figure 9.1).[1]

This model is designed to identify and sort out the various elements which together comprise a fully-formed, holistic narrative. By offering a set of six basic reference points, it should also help organize narrative analysis into clearly demarcated areas of study. Shortly, we will suggest which stylistic 'toolkit' is best equipped to handle which component

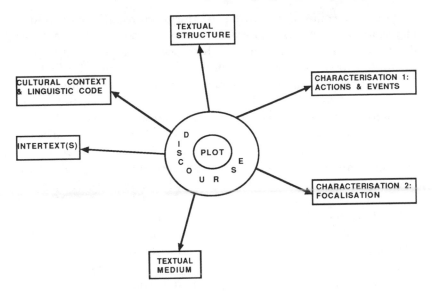

Figure 9.1 A stylistic model of narrative structure

on the schema, but first, some explanation of the schema itself is in order.

In keeping with much work in stylistics and narratology, we have retained the primary distinction between narrative *plot* and narrative *discourse*. The term *plot* is generally understood to refer to the basic story-line of a narrative; in other words, the sequence of elemental, chronologically-ordered events which generate a narrative. Narrative *discourse*, by contrast, encompasses the manner or means by which the plot is narrated. Narrative discourse, for example, is often characterized by stylistic devices such as flashback, prevision and repetition – devices which all disrupt the basic chronology of a story. So, where plot represents the abstract story-line of a narrative, discourse is the actual text which is produced by a writer.

When mapped on to *Cal*, the importance of the plot/discourse distinction should become clear. In terms of plot, two key narrative events may be abstracted from the story. The first is the murder of the policeman, Robert Morton, by Cal and Crilly; the second the relationship which unfolds between Cal and Marcella Morton. The chronology of these two events is straightforward: the second event occurs one year after the first. However, this 'real' sequence of events is subverted in the discourse of both novel and film texts. In the novel, the developing relationship between Marcella and Cal is narrated first, while a full account of the murder of Morton, through the technique of flashback, is offered mid-way through the novel. The narrative discourse of the novel thus effectively reverses the chronology of plot. In the film text, chronology is similarly manipulated. The first few images of the film minimally sketch the murder scene with neither killers nor victim identified. After the opening credits, the action jumps forward one year to the unfolding relationship between Cal and Marcella. However, during the critical love-making scene towards the end of the film, Cal re-lives, in flashback, his involvement in the murder of Morton. Not only is this re-enactment more graphic than that of the opening scene, but some of its more grisly images are repeated over and over in counterpoint with the sexual act between Cal and Marcella. In terms of the plot/discourse contrast, where the murder of Morton is a narrative event that happens only *once* at the level of plot, it is narrated *several times* in the discourse of the film.

Beyond the plot/discourse distinction, there remains a further six narrative categories on our narrative model. The boxed components studded around the schema constitute the basic units of analysis in narrative description. Although there will be substantial areas of overlap between these units, they nonetheless offer useful reference points for stylistic analyses of prose fiction.

The first of the six categories is *textual structure*. This accounts for the way individual narrative units are arranged and organized in a story. A study of textual structure may focus on large-scale elements of plot as well as more localized features of the story's organization. We have already pointed out at some length the ways in which the textual structure of both the novel and film versions of *Cal* re-orientates and disrupts the sequence of narrative events at the level of plot. A range of stylistic models are available for the analysis of different levels of textual structure in a narrative, of which the frameworks of *cohesion*, *coherence* and *natural narrative* have proved especially popular among stylisticians.[2]

Cultural context and *linguistic code* jointly express the historical, cultural and linguistic setting which frames a narrative. Cultural context, more specifically, locates the narrative in time and place and identifies the socio-cultural backcloth which informs it. The variety of language which reflects this cultural context is the linguistic code. In *Cal*, the cultural context is obviously that of Northern Ireland and its 'troubles'; a context as sadly relevant now as it was in the period in the early 1980s when *Cal* is set. The 'romance' elements of the narrative unfold against the backdrop of Northern Ireland's divided society, and the development of the relationship between Cal and Marcella is inextricably linked with the opposing factions of Loyalism and Nationalism. The juxtaposition of characters like Dunlop and Skeffington, whose language reflects the rhetoric of these opposing factions, reinforces political divisions: the morose, entrenched Ulster-Scot contrasted to the cunning Republican ideologue. Further reinforcement of the context and code which frames the story is derived from the local television news reports which are inserted throughout the narrative. Much of the dialogue of both film and novel is acted out against these surreal (though accurate) litanies of day-to-day carnage in the Province of Northern Ireland.[3]

As narratives do not exist in literary, social and historical vacuums, they often echo and allude to other texts, images and voices. We reserve the term *intertextuality*, our third narrative component, to refer to this type of 'allusion' in fiction. For instance, there is a very clear intertextual reference to a painting by Grunewald, the sixteenth-century painter best known for his depictions of the crucified Christ. Perhaps the most famous of these paintings is described in detail in the novel and given momentary visual prominence in the film. Closely identified with Marcella its role is curious: it seems to suggest an analogy between herself and the Christ's mother, Mary. If so, then further parallels might be suggested between the figure of Christ and her dead husband, Morton, or even Cal himself.

As the three remaining categories on the schema will receive more detailed attention in the sections which follow, we shall offer only shorter definitions here. The first of the two *characterization* components describes how character, actions and events intersect. It also accounts for the ways in which the events of narrative are connected with what a character does, thinks and says. The second category of narrative characterization, *focalization*, concerns the relationship between a character's viewpoint and mode of narration. It explains, for instance, whether a narrative is first person or third person, or whether the events of the story are viewed from the perspective of a particular character or from that of an omniscient narrator. *Textual medium*, the sixth and final component on the schema, is simply the physical channel of communication through which a story is narrated. Two common narrative media are film and novel, although a variety of other types are available such as ballet, musical or strip cartoon. We are now in a position to provide a more detailed application of the narrative model to *Cal*, beginning with the first of the two *characterization* components.

CHARACTERIZATION AND TRANSITIVITY

The title of the novel places one of its characters centre-stage from the outset so that when we meet the pronoun 'he' in the opening sentence we naturally assume that its referent must be Cal:

(1) *He* stood at the back gateway of the abattoir, *his* hands thrust into *his* pockets, *his* stomach rigid with the ache of want.

(1984: 1; our emphasis)

Indeed, 'he', referring back to Cal, continues as the most common subject of the remaining clauses of this paragraph and into the beginning of the next:

(2) Men in white coats and baseball caps whistled and shouted as they moved between the hanging carcasses. (3) *He* couldn't see *his* father, yet *he* did not want to venture in. (4) *He* knew the sweet warm nauseating smell of the place and *he* had had no breakfast. (5) Nor had *he* smoked *his* first cigarette of the day. (6) Smells were always so much more intense then. (7) At intervals the crack of the humane killer echoed round the glass roof. (8) Queuing beasts bellowed in the distance as if they knew.

(9) *He* saw the Preacher standing waiting with his glass.

(1984:1)

Thus, Cal as the referent of the pronoun 'he' in sentences 1, 3, 4, 5 and 9 dominates the paragraph: so much so, that it is easy to read the references to sounds and sights in the remaining sentences as descriptions of what Cal can hear and see. Much of the rest of the novel is like this with Cal's actions or sensations strongly thematized.

It is on this basis that we recognize Cal as the central character in the fiction: but what kind of character is he? Despite his central position, the overwhelming impression that readers gain from the novel is one of inactivity. As regards the two central events in the novel, Cal is a reluctant accomplice to the murder of Morton and uncertain in his wooing of Marcella. However, the impression of inertia or inactivity goes far beyond these two events and is widespread throughout the novel. We can, indeed, show how it is woven into the fabric of the text by looking at some of the characteristic transitivity choices as they involve Cal.

Transitivity relations in the English clause (as presented in Halliday 1985) can be understood in terms of the kind of relationship encoded by the verb and the accompanying participant roles – basically, transitivity is that domain of the linguistic system that expresses 'who (or what) does what to whom (or what)'. Four fundamental types of process may be distinguished:[4]

	Material:	He struck the match.
	Mental:	He studied her face.
TRANSITIVITY	*Verbal*:	'Fondling', he said.
	Relational:	His nails had become soft. His face was the colour of wax.

Each type of process has associated with it a different set of participant roles. Material action processes (realized by verbs such as 'break', 'grab', 'hit', 'scratch') are associated with participant roles such as an AGENT (someone or something to perform the action), and an AFFECTED (ENTITY) (someone or something on the receiving end of the action). Thus:

the big one	grabbed	Cal
AGENT	PROCESS	AFFECTED

Mental processes (realized by verbs such as 'see', 'notice', 'scrutinize', 'look', 'know') are associated with inherent roles such as SENSER (the one who performs the act of 'seeing', or 'noticing') and PHENOMENON (whatever is seen or noticed by the SENSER), as in examples such as the following:

Cal	saw	that she wore no stockings
SENSER	PROCESS	PHENOMENON

he	noticed	that he was crying
SENSER	PROCESS	PHENOMENON

he	imagined	her as the Sleeping Beauty
SENSER	PROCESS	PHENOMENON

In any full account of transitivity it is important to describe all the roles associated with the complete range of choices of process-type. However, in the case of Cal it is sufficient to look at these two process types to be able to show significant patterns at work. With regard to material action processes we find patterns such as the following:

AGENT	MATERIAL ACTION PROCESS	AFFECTED
Cal	turned, closed, shook, raised,	his face, his eyes, his hands, his legs, etc.

Thus we find examples throughout the book such as the following:

he turned his face away

(1984: 8)

he put his head forward

(10)

Cal took out one hand (to hold his cigarette)

(12)

he closed his eyes and leaned his head against the brick wall

(13)

he shook his head

(13)

Cal closed his eyes

(15)

he swung his legs off the bed

(20)

he raised his head off the pillow

(29)

Cal . . . threaded his fingers into his hair

(37)

Cal pushed his aching back into the upholstery

(60)

he curled his tongue

(86)

he scrubbed his teeth with toothpaste

(98)

Although Cal does appear in the grammatical role of AGENT, the constructions are typically reflexive in the sense that he – or part of his body – turns out to be the AFFECTED. Contrast this kind of pattern with the following examples involving Crilly, the more dedicated IRA activist:

Crilly edged him into a cubicle
Crilly grabbed Smicker by the shoulders
He handed two photographs . . . to Cal
Crilly then lifted the boy bodily off the lavatory seat

(19)

As an AGENT Crilly typically takes some other entity, often human, as AFFECTED. A similar claim can also be made about Marcella, as we can see from examples such as the following:

Marcella lifted Lucy and hugged her

(120)

She would touch his arm as she made a point and when he cracked
a joke she would punch him playfully on the shoulder

(123)

She took his face between her hands and kissed him affectionately
on the mouth

(133)

Thus it is perfectly common when Marcella occurs as an AGENT for her
to take another character (her child, Lucy, or Cal himself in the
examples above) as AFFECTED.

If Cal typically takes some part of his own body as AFFECTED, it is not
unusual for these parts themselves to behave involuntarily in their own
right, as in:

his stomach tightened

(11)

his legs were shaking

(20)

his hand was shaking badly

(88)

The particular pattern of choices constructed around Cal, and the
difference between these choices and those that relate to other
characters, contribute to the sense of him as inactive. In addition,
however, there is a further pattern, more semantic in tendency, which
plays an important role in defining him. It may be illustrated by the
following examples:

he tried to guess her age
    but couldn't

(12)

he moved his mouth to smile back
    but the muscles of his face would not respond properly

(13)

he was worried
    but he didn't say so

(30)

one evening he stood watching for her
    but she did not come out

(41)

In each case the simple pattern of co-ordination connects a positive
and a negative assertion in such a way that the second clause,
introduced by 'but', involves some kind of reversal of the expectations

set up by the first. The first clause seems to project a further event which gets denied or deferred by the second. All of this helps to contribute to a sense of Cal as a character whose agency is severely circumscribed. His actions tend not to affect others; he behaves involuntarily; and his intentions are defeated.

There is, however, another area of the transitivity system that is important not just for the way in which the character of Cal is created but also for the whole way in which the fiction is narrated – a dimension to be further developed in the next section. Most of the mental processes in the novel are attributed to Cal. Even in the examples of semantic reversal given above many of the cases involve mental processes:

> he tried to recall the woman's face
>   but could not
>
> (13)
>
> he didn't want to watch
>   but he felt compelled to
>
> (86)
>
> He thought of borrowing the torch that sat on the shelf
>   but realized that if he could see the house anyone in the house
>   could see him
>
> (90)

Part of Cal's position as the central figure in the novel is that we are given repeated access to the contents of his consciousness. In this way (as we shall see in more detail below) he becomes the reflector or focalizer of the fiction: much of what takes place in the novel is filtered to us in varying degrees through his consciousness. Marcella, for instance, is often presented to us literally 'through Cal's eyes'. Cal, however, is not a neutral or transparent focalizer. The manner in which he focalizes is precisely nuanced to reveal aspects of his character – especially in terms of his relationship to Marcella:

> Beneath the stuff of her blouse he could see a faint laciness where her body touched it on the inside
>
> (16)
>
> Cal saw as she crouched that she wore no stockings
>
> (25)
>
> Between her mantilla and the back of her dress he could see the slope of her neck and the pin-holes of her pores and the slight down of hair that furred her spine
>
> (38)

This is more than the use of one character to tell us about another. Cal here is revealed in his relationship to Marcella as an uncomfortable voyeur. He observes her from a hidden vantage point without being observed in return; and, in observing her, his attention often lingers in a fetishistic fashion on a fragment of clothing or elements of her appearance. It is not just that Cal is a character–narrator who discloses to us what is going on in the fiction. The manner of disclosure reveals to us further aspects of his character.

CHARACTERIZATION AND FOCALIZATION

The term *focalization*, which was sketched informally towards the end of the previous section, refers to the 'point of view' or 'angle of telling' that is adopted in a narrative. Point of view may be that of an omniscient narrator outside the story or that of a character participating within the story. Should a narrative exhibit the second type of focalization, then the character whose point of view is represented is called the *reflector* of fiction. Although a third person narrative, *Cal* exhibits sustained focalization from the perspective of its central character. In other words, Cal is consistently the reflector of fiction: events are described from his viewing position and mediated through his consciousness. To give a clearer picture of how this technique works, it will be worth examining the episode where Cal has just begun work on Morton's farm:

(1) All that week Dunlop gave him a lift to and from town, morning and evening. Several times Cal *saw* the yellow Anglia pass in the opposite direction and *followed it with his eyes*. During the day he occasionally *saw* Marcella's child playing in the back garden or *heard* her prattling from another room when he was standing having a cup of tea in the kitchen. He also *heard* again the stomach-churning bubble of coughing from somewhere in the house.

(1984: 69; our emphasis)

These mental process verbs, as was demonstrated in the previous section, function to underscore Cal's self-reflective inertia. The fact that these processes also exclusively express human *perceptions* serves notice that events are being mediated through the perceptual domain of a single character. Indeed, the extensive use of verbs of seeing and hearing illustrates how the narrative focalization here is unequivocally locked within the parameters of Cal's consciousness.

There are often clear stylistic indices which signal whether the viewing position in a narrative is that of a particular character or of a narrator external to the story. As we have seen, mental processes of perception are one such index. Another is the system of *deixis* in language. Deixis is the grammar of 'directionality' and *deictics* are 'pointing' words which indicate the position of the speaker relative to what is said. Some deictic words, like 'bring', 'come' and 'here', suggest proximity, while others, such as 'take', 'go' and 'there', suggest distance. Thus, where 'Come here' signals motion *towards* the speaking source, 'Go there' indicates motion *away* from the speaking source. In fiction, deictics are often a strong indicator that focalization is being conducted through a reflector. Consider this scene, where Cal is waiting outside the library for Marcella, and look out for the deictic word in the opening sentence.

(2) She came out, putting on a cream-coloured mac, wrinkling her face against the rain. Then she ran with a stiff-legged awkwardness towards the end of Main Street. Cal followed her, walking with long strides. She went into the car park outside the Control Zone and got into a yellow Anglia. As she drove past him he could not see her face because of the misted windows and the flapping windscreen wipers.

(1984: 16)

The use of 'came' signals that events are described from Cal's perceptual vantage point. It is also worth noting how a simple transposition of this deictic to its more remote counterpart 'went' radically transforms the viewing position: the reflector would now have to be positioned *inside* not outside the library. The reflector's point of view is sustained even after Marcella emerges from the library. The deictic word in 'She *went* into the car park' now suggests she is moving away from the speaking source. An additional point of view marker occurs in the type of construction that came under scrutiny in the previous section: 'As she drove past him he [Cal] *could not see* her face'. Although this suggests that Cal makes an attempt to see Marcella's face, his limited perspective prohibits the full revelation that omniscient narration could claim.

Perhaps the most important index of narrative focalization in fiction is the means by which the speech and thought of characters is presented.[5] A complex array of modes are available for representing speech and thought, and the selection of one mode in favour of another may have a number of stylistic functions. It may, inter alia, mark a subtle shift in perspective, determine a greater or lesser degree of empathy with a particular character or create ironic distance between narrator and character. As the speech and thought model receives treatment in other chapters in this volume, a simplified account should suffice here.

The standard techniques for representing speech and thought are through the *Direct* and *Indirect* modes:

Direct Modes:

Direct Speech: 'I know these tricks of yours!' she said.
Direct Thought: 'Does she still love me?' he wondered.

Indirect Modes:

Indirect Speech: She said that she knew those tricks of his.
Indirect Thought: He wondered if she still loved him.

The operations which transform the Direct modes into their Indirect equivalents are as follows. The first is to bring the quoted material in inverted commas under the control of the reporting clause. The second is to convert all the deictic words, tense forms and pronouns to more remote or distant counterparts. So, the deictic word 'these' becomes 'those', while present tense 'know' and 'love' become past tense 'knew' and 'loved'. Pronouns are similarly transformed: first and second person 'I', 'yours' and 'me' become the third person forms 'she', 'his' and 'him' respectively.

A further transformation may be performed on these standard modes of speech and thought presentation. By removing their reporting clauses (and, if desired, any inverted commas that are present), they can be converted into 'Free' forms. Here again are the Direct and Indirect modes, this time stripped of their reporting clauses:

Free Direct Modes:

Free Direct Speech: 'I know these tricks of yours!'
Free Direct Thought: Does she still love me?

Free Indirect Modes:

Free Indirect Speech: She knew those tricks of his!
Free Indirect Thought: Did she still love him?

Perhaps the best way of conceptualizing the distinctions between, on the one hand, the Free and Standard modes and, on the other, the Direct and Indirect modes, is to imagine two continua cutting across each other. Figure 9.2 illustrates how the Free/Standard cline intersects the Direct/Indirect cline, with the four resulting modes lying in the quadrants created by the intersection.

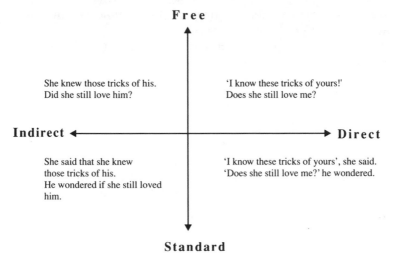

Figure 9.2 Modes of speech and thought presentation

The Free Indirect quadrant incorporates perhaps the most intriguing of all the techniques of speech and thought presentation, yielding some of the most sophisticated and elusive forms available for narrative fiction. The stylistic richness of this quadrant cannot be fully assessed here, but some measure of its subtlety can be gained when we examine the deployment of its two modes in *Cal.*

Given his status as reflector of fiction, it is not surprising that privileged access to Cal's thoughts is sustained throughout the narrative. What is more significant is that Free Indirect Thought is the preferred technique of presentation, often being used to create abrupt transitions from narrative description into the active mind of the central character. The second sentence in the following sequence illustrates this:

(3)   Cal lay on the bed smoking. What did Crilly want?

(1984: 18)

Where a Direct form would retain the present tense ('What *does* Crilly want?') the use of past tense 'did' signals that this sequence is unequivocally in the *Indirect* mode. However, this indirection is offset by the immediacy which is created as the Free form dispenses with the reporting clause characteristic of Standard modes.

Here now is a longer sequence from the novel displaying some more Free Indirect Thought:

(4) The man was now almost level with the car. Cal turned his head away, pretending to look for something in the back seat. Where the fuck was Crilly? Was he choosing a wine? The man stopped patiently for his dog again then moved off into the pool of the next street light.

(1984: 61)

Again, narrative description is brought up short with the sequence: 'Where the fuck was Crilly? Was he choosing a wine?' Unlike the Direct types of presentation, the past tense forms and third person pronouns of Free Indirect Thought often make this mode difficult to separate out from the narrative framework that surrounds it. A common effect (and this passage is no exception) is that the narrator's and character's voices seem to merge, so much so that it can be difficult to tell them apart. It is for this reason that Free Indirect Thought is sometimes referred to as the 'dual voice'.

Like its counterpart in the thought paradigm, the use of Free Indirect Speech has implications for characterization and focalization. Because it presents the discourse of characters at one remove from the immediacy of Direct Speech, Free Indirect Speech operates often as an ironizing device or distancing technique. The deployment of this mode in *Cal* is interesting, especially when it is used to report the speech of Marcella. The passage which follows is part of a conversation between her and Cal. However, in order to illustrate better how Free Indirect Speech is constructed and its often dramatic stylistic force when employed, we have decided to present it to you first in the Standard Direct mode:

(5a) Marcella told him something of her upbringing in Portstewart.
    'I am of an Italian family, the D'Agostinos who have a café business on the sea-front – cream walls with quadrants gouged in soft plaster,' she said.
    'They sent me to the nuns at Portstewart Convent for my education, a great Elsinore of a place built on a cliff overlooking the Atlantic,' she continued.
    'As a matter of fact,' she added, 'Lucy and I have just been to Rome in the summer for a holiday. It wasn't really a holiday, but something to get my mind off what happened here. Have you heard about the awful thing they did to my husband?'
    Cal nodded.

The present tense forms, reporting clauses, inverted commas and first person pronouns signal that Marcella's speech is unambiguously in the Standard Direct Speech mode. In this format, the actual words spoken by Marcella are represented and her discourse consequently has the feel of a highly personalized, almost ostentatious piece of self-disclosure. Now, in order to convert this reported speech to the Free Indirect mode, two steps need to be taken. The first is to make the report *Indirect* by altering pronouns and tense forms to their more distant counterparts. Thus, '*I am* of an Italian family' becomes '*She was* of an Italian family', while '*Have you* heard about the awful thing' converts to '*Had he* heard about the awful thing'. The second step is to render the report *Free* by stripping away all its reporting clauses. So, 'she said', 'she continued' and 'she added' all disappear to leave the report in a Free, albeit Indirect, form. This is, in fact, the very form which is preferred in the novel. Readers may care to examine the stylistic differences between it and the direct speech version of 5a:

(5b)   Marcella told him something of her upbringing in Portstewart. She was of an Italian family, the D'Agostinos who had a café business on the sea-front – cream walls with quadrants gouged in soft plaster. They had sent her to the nuns at Portstewart Convent for her education, a great Elsinore of a place built on a cliff overlooking the Atlantic. As a matter of fact, she and Lucy had just been to Rome in the summer for a holiday. It wasn't really a holiday, but something to get her mind off what had happened here. Had he heard about the awful thing they had done to her husband? Cal nodded.

(1984: 99–100)

In evidence here is the kind of stylistic 'double-take' that often characterizes the Free Indirect mode. The immediacy engendered by the removal of the reporting clauses is counterbalanced by the displacement of the characters' voice which is created through remote tense forms and pronouns. So, even though the 'excess baggage' of reporting clauses is dispensed with, the narrator (or reflector?) still presides over the character's words, bringing the report into line with the narrative framework that surrounds it. It is a common feature of Free Indirect Speech that although a character is allowed to 'hold the floor', there remains an often ironic distance from the actual words spoken. In contrast with the kind of narrative proximity which characterizes Cal, Marcella is often portrayed at a remove, becoming very much 'the other' in terms of the discourse of the novel. The manner by which this and other aspects of focalization are translated into the film text will be one of the issues addressed in the next section.

TEXTUAL MEDIUM AND NARRATION: FILM AND PROSE FICTION[6]

The translation of story materials from one medium to another raises interesting questions about the similarities and differences that hold between the media. At one level, of course, film and prose are very different, with film constructed in images and prose in words. This very fundamental difference has repercussions for the whole process of narration discussed above. Some would argue that film is a 'non-narrated medium': that prose narrative tells a story, in various voices, whereas film narrative shows it directly. However, even though film only rarely uses the voice of an audible narrator, it still depends on a complex set of conventions to underpin the process of narration. Such conventions, for instance, help make intelligible the transition from one shot to another as part of an unfolding sequence. They also bear comparison with prose narrative devices such as those associated with point of view.

One important filmic convention for managing the transition from one shot to another in a coherent fashion is the use of the look or the gaze. Thus, if in one shot we (as viewers) see a character gazing out of frame, we then routinely interpret the next shot (whenever possible) as depicting what that character could see from the position s/he occupies. Whilst this is not by any means the only way of managing the transition from one shot to another, it is symptomatic of how mainstream cinema unfolds an intelligible narrative for an audience. In many ways, the camera operates within narrative scenes somewhere between the eye of a character and the eye of a detached observer, occasionally adopting quite specifically the point of view of one of the participants, and broadly showing us events as if from a human standpoint within the scene that it observes. The camera, however, is not just anthropomorphic. It can be seen, as Mulvey (1975) argues, as voyeuristic: it indulges the male gaze while depicting women as the object of male desire.

In this respect *Cal*, the novel, poses an interesting task to the film-maker. Consider again, for instance, one of the passages discussed in the previous section:

(2) She came out, putting on a cream-coloured mac, wrinkling her face against the rain. Then she ran with a stiff-legged awkwardness towards the end of Main Street. Cal followed her, walking with long strides. She went into the car park outside the Control Zone and got into a yellow Anglia. As she drove past him he could not

see her face because of the misted windows and the flapping windscreen wipers.

(1984: 16)

Various deictic cues ('came out', 'went into') and the characteristic 'he *could not see* her face' focalize the passage from Cal's perspective. In the film version the deictic cues are observed faithfully. The sequence begins with a medium shot on Cal's watching face. The next shot encompasses both Cal and Marcella as he watches her emerge from the library. In the next, Marcella moves towards the camera with Cal following surreptitiously. Figure 9.3 gives the sequence as it appears in the film.

In all of this Marcella is unaware of being observed and as such it conforms to other voyeuristic patterns of observation which we can discern in both the film and the book. In the feminist critique of mainstream film-making, however, this pattern is associated with male dominance and female subordination. It is interesting, therefore, to note that in the film this voyeuristic pattern is progressively challenged as the film develops. Several sequences depict Cal watching Marcella – clearly with sexual interest – but the film 'catches him out' doing so, often in ways not provided for by the prose text. Consider, for instance, the following passage describing Cal in the library:

(6)   The floor was covered in large green carpet tiles. One at Cal's foot had a grey coin of recent chewing-gum stuck to it. Through the open shelves he could see Marcella coming – at least he could see her legs. She walked into the shelved alcove next to him and he looked at her heels. She was again wearing Scholls. She rose on her toes to reach a shelf and he could see the arched insoles of her dark stockings. She came round the corner to his alcove. 'Hello.' She smiled, seeing him, and his insides went to water. 'Hi.' He stood up, the magazine flopping in his hand.

She had unloaded her pile of books except one, which she held flat to her breast. She turned sideways to Cal, scanning the shelf. The profile of her breast had become a plateau touched at its tip by the book. Cal wanted to close his eyes. To make a shutter image of it.

(1984: 71)

In the film the scene unfolds with a shot sequence as follows:

(1) a long shot of Marcella entering a library alcove carrying books;
(2a) a medium shot of Cal standing at magazine rack leafing through a magazine and glancing sideways out of frame repeatedly;

Figure 9.3 Line drawings of three stills from *Cal*

(2b) the camera pans to follow him as he moves behind shelves in the alcove where he proceeds to look between a gap in the stacked books towards camera;

(3) a shot from Cal's position through a gap in the books observing Marcella from behind in adjacent alcove;

(4) a shot from Marcella's alcove showing Cal peering towards camera from between books;

(5) a shot from Cal's point of view, again framed by books, which pans downwards to follow Marcella's actions as she bends to reshelve books;

(6) a shot from Marcella's alcove showing Cal peering towards camera from between books, as in (4) above;

(7) a shot from Cal's point of view, again showing Marcella who rises and turns towards camera, smiles directly at camera in recognition, saying 'Oh. Hello';

(8) a shot from Marcella's alcove showing Cal peering between the books towards camera; he starts guiltily and moves to meet Marcella around the corner of the alcove.

The film in effect gives Marcella at this moment a much more positive role in spotting Cal while he peers at her, and in returning his look directly, though without disapproval. In this way it undermines any dominance that might accrue to Cal as the unseen watcher. Indeed, one whole extended episode of voyeurism from the book, in which Cal observes Marcella in her bathroom ('The fact that she was totally unaware of his spying presence made him shake' 91), does not survive the translation into film. Instead, two new episodes are substituted, in each of which Cal watches Marcella, only for him to be noticed doing so. In one of these Cal looks down on Marcella from a rooftop as she is about to get into a car and drive way. She, looking up, is seen to notice him. The next shot, from her position, shows an empty space on the roof where Cal had previously stood, implying embarrassment on his part.

CONCLUSION

These last observations on narration in the film and prose versions of *Cal* help to demonstrate an important aspect of the model which was outlined at the beginning of this chapter. The model helps to distinguish between separate dimensions of a narrative text and provides analytical tools for observing and thinking about the way in which these separate dimensions work. Now, it might seem that this way of proceeding breaks a text down into separate properties in a fragmentary and reductive fashion, so that we end up only able to see the parts and not the whole. We would contend, however, that the opposite is in fact the case: that it helps our understanding of the whole text if we can distinguish clearly, as we consider it, between the separate dimensions which make it up. At the same time, what emerges clearly as we use this model is the interconnected nature of the separate components. Thus, focalization is an important dimension of narration – of the telling of the tale. But we saw also how, in the case of *Cal*, the manner of the focalization overlapped with issues of character, in as much as the central focalizer, Cal himself, has a particular way of focalizing which is congruent with other aspects of his character. When we turn to issues of medium, the connectedness of dimensions is reinforced. The changes in medium affect issues of narration, such as the interplay of modes of speech and thought presentation as well as the availability of interior, mental processes to narration. We saw also that analogous modes of focalization in the two media don't work in precisely the same way; subtle changes in focalization brought about in the translation from one medium to another have significant consequences for how the character is constructed for the viewing and reading audience.

In addition, and perhaps most significantly, we have attempted to show ways in which quite precise features of textual organization are related to the broader categories of the model. Thus, aspects of deixis and also considerations of speech and thought presentation have been shown to be important to the realization of focalization. And aspects of transitivity, for example, have illuminated the textual realization of character. What our model offers, therefore, is an approach that is both holistic and particular. We would not necessarily argue for its total integrity: like most such constructs it remains to some extent provisional and open to modification in the light of the texts to which it is applied. But we do believe that it helps to enhance our understanding of how a fictional text works. We hope that we have at least begun this process in the case of *Cal.*

SUGGESTIONS FOR FURTHER WORK

1 The following extract comprises a conversation between Cal and his
    father, Shamie. It takes place in the abattoir where Shamie works.

> Shamie looked at him and said,
> 'Put my jacket on or you'll freeze.'

Cal shivered as he put the jacket on, not used to the cold silk of the lining next to his skin. He cradled his mug of tea in both
(5) hands for the warmth, sitting on the bottom of the bed.

'You're very quiet these days, Cal. Is anything wrong?'

'No.'

'You go to that room of yours all the time. We don't talk anymore.'

'If I had a job it might be different.'

(10) 'You should never have left the abattoir.'

'The smell made me want to throw up all the time.'

'You'd have got used to that.'

Cal said nothing. They'd had this conversation many times before, but never had it been spoken quietly. Shamie went on,
(15) 'I mean, do you know how embarrassing it was for me? I moved heaven and earth to get you in there. There's few enough Catholics. God knows. And you go and jack it in before the week's out. You should have seen the look Mr Loudan gave me.'

'Crilly's a Catholic.'

(20) 'Crilly's not my son. But I'll say this for him, he does your job a damned sight better than you ever did.'

Cal saw the tumble of purple and green steaming innards fall from the raised carcass and subside on the ground at his feet, the
(24) nervous flick and jig of movement in them. He could see them still.

(1984: 31–2)

(a) Identify the dominant mode of speech presentation in this passage. It may help to refer to the model on p. 152 asking the question which quadrant would most of the dialogue fall into?

(b) Transpose the dialogue in the passage into each of the three remaining modes of speech presentation. You may find transpositions to some modes easy and others difficult. If so, why?

(c) Can you prepare a screenplay for this dialogue? What obstacles are there in filming the entire passage, including the sequence from lines 22 to 24? How would you surmount them? Try to compare your version with the film version.

2 This passage is from the episode in the novel where Cal and his accomplice Crilly rob an off-licence. (In the film version of this scene, the off-licence is replaced by a cinema.) Cal is waiting in the 'getaway car':

Cal turned up the collar of his coat. Crilly stood on tiptoe, looking over the dulled and lettered half of the door. Cal saw him flip up

the hood of his anorak and pull his scarf over his mouth. He pushed the door open with his foot and stepped in. The door swung shut after him on its spring but in the instant that it was
(5) open, as if it was the shutter of a camera, Cal saw two women customers look up in fright. Fourteen, fifteen, sixteen. He knew that to count accurate seconds he should say one thousand and seventeen, one thousand and eighteen. A man came round the corner and began walking towards the car. Was it the law? . . . The
(10) man was now almost level with the car. Cal turned his head away, pretending to look for something in the back seat. Where the fuck was Crilly? Was he choosing a wine? The man stopped patiently for his dog again then moved off into the pool of the next street light.

(1984: 61)

(a) Identify the reflector of fiction in this passage using the following stylistic criteria:

• deictics
• mental processes (especially verbs of perception)
• modes of thought presentation

(b) In terms of filming this passage, what can be done about the sequence from lines 12 to 13? How could you compensate for this piece of text in a film version? Again, try to compare your own interpretation with that of the film.

NOTES

1 This narrative model has resonances with other models in stylistics and narratology. One of the closest is Gerard Genette's typology (1980), although there are still substantial points of departure between the two approaches. While there is not the space here to elaborate on the major differences between the two, Simpson (forthcoming) outlines the theoretical rationale of the present model.

2 This aspect of narrative is the primary focus of attention in the following representative studies: Toolan (1988), Montgomery *et al.* (1992: 177–83), Simpson (1992), Stubbs (1982).

3 In a pedagogical context, the provision of adequate information on context and code can be a daunting challenge. It is impossible to produce an exhaustive account of the complexities of any society in conflict, especially that of Northern Ireland, nor is it easy to decide what information is necessary for the appreciation of a text and what is not. The problem is likely to be aggravated, moreover, in classrooms where the participants' culture is alien to that of Northern Ireland.

For those who wish to use our chapter as a teaching package and who may be approaching the text without much background knowledge, we have prepared a checklist of contextual notes on Northern Ireland which

162   *Paul Simpson and Martin Montgomery*

can be found in an appendix to this chapter. It should be especially helpful to those unfamiliar with the background to the conflict, the references in the novel to geographical regions, and the names of security forces, terrorists and political parties.

4 For more complete and complex treatments of transitivity see Fawcett (1980) and Halliday (1985). Detailed applications of the transitivity model can be found in Montgomery (1986) and Simpson (1993: 86–118). See also Mills (this volume).

5 Speech and thought presentation and point of view are two topics which have received a great deal of attention in stylistics. For speech and thought presentation see: Leech and Short (1981), Simpson (1993: 11–45). These are generally more sophisticated treatments than that offered here. Point of view is dealt with extensively in Fowler (1986), Simpson (1993) and Montgomery *et al.* (1992: 177–201). See also the chapters by Ehrlich, Aristar Dry, Lee and Toolan in this volume.

6 The standard introductory text on film theory is Bordwell and Thompson (1990). With respect to the material covered in this section, two other useful texts are Bordwell (1985) and Branigan (1984).

REFERENCES

Bordwell, D. (1985) *Narration in the Fiction Film*, London: Methuen.
Bordwell, D. and Thompson, K. (1990) *Film Art: An Introduction* (Third Edition), New York: McGraw-Hill.
Branigan, E. (1984) *Point of View in the Cinema*, New York: Mouton.
Fawcett, R. (1980) *Cognitive Linguistics and Social Interaction*, Heidelberg: Julius Groos.
Fowler, R. (1986) *Linguistic Criticism*, Oxford: Oxford University Press.
Genette, G. (1980) *Narrative Discourse*, New York: Cornell University Press.
Halliday, M. A. K. (1985) *An Introduction to Functional Grammar*, London: Edward Arnold.
Leech, G. N. and Short, M. (1981) *Style in Fiction*, London: Longman.
MacLaverty, B. (1983/1984) *Cal*, London: Penguin Books.
Montgomery, M. (1986) *An Introduction to Language and Society*, London: Methuen.
Montgomery, M., Durant, A., Fabb, N., Furniss, T. and Mills, S. (1992) *Ways of Reading*, London: Routledge.
Mulvey, L. (1975) 'Visual Pleasure and Narrative Cinema', *Screen* 16, 3: 6– 10; reprinted in T. Bennett, S. Boyd-Bowman, C. Mercer and J. Wollacott (eds) (1989) *Popular Television and Film*, London: Open University Press and BFI.
Simpson, P. (1992) 'Teaching Stylistics: Cohesion and Narrative Structure in a Short Story by Ernest Hemingway', *Language and Literature* 1, 1: 47–67.
—— (1993) *Language, Ideology and Point of View*, London: Routledge.
—— (forthcoming) '"Nothing New Under the Sun": Can Stylistics be Radical?'
Stubbs, M. (1982) 'Stir Until the Plot Thickens', in R. A. Carter and D. Burton (eds) *Literary Text and Language Study*, London: Arnold: 57–85.
Toolan, M. (1988) *Narrative: A Critical Linguistic Introduction*, London: Routledge.
Wales, K. (1989) *A Dictionary of Stylistics*, London: Longman.
Wichert, S. (1991) *Northern Ireland Since 1945*, London: Longman.

APPENDIX

Cultural context and linguistic code: *Cal*

Formation of Northern Ireland (NI)

State formed in June 1921. Partition of Ireland by Anglo-Irish Treaty produced Northern Ireland (six counties) and an independent Irish Free State (twenty-six counties). Free State now more popularly known as Eire or Irish Republic. Northern Ireland's devolved Parliament was suspended in 1972 and replaced by direct rule from Westminster which has continued to date.

Demography

Two main communities: Roman Catholic and Protestant. Protestant group comprises Presbyterians (largest group), Methodists and Anglicans. Balance of power now estimated at 55 per cent to 45 per cent in favour of Protestants, having remained constant for many years at 65 per cent to 35 per cent. West of Province mainly Catholic; east mostly Protestant. *Cal* set in rural West; near Magherafelt in County Londonderry.

Few other ethnic groups in NI, though some of Italian, Chinese and Indian background involved in retail and catering businesses. (NB: Marcella's family background.) Complex relationship between class and religion where 'political and religious sectarianism prevented the formation of an effective working-class party, which may have cut across the denominational divide on economic and social issues' (Wichert 1991: 35).

Economy and society

Industrialized in east of Ulster: shipbuilding and related heavy industry. Textile industry (linen); agriculture; service industries; tourism impoverished by conflict. Health generally poorer than British average. Education is: (1) normally segregated on religious grounds, (2) of a relatively high standard in British terms.

Language spoken

A variety of English referred to as (northern) *Hiberno English* (substantially different from southern Irish varieties). Two main subvarieties are *Ulster-Scots* (especially in counties Antrim and Down) and *Mid-Ulster* (in remaining areas). There are also the distinct urban vernaculars of Belfast and (London)derry. *Irish Gaelic* taught in Catholic schools. Increasingly popularized in some Republican areas (see interchanges between Cal and Skeffington).

The 'Troubles'

Civil Rights Movement begun by Nationalists in late 1969 to campaign against discrimination and 'gerrymandering' in elections; polarized society created conditions which led to emergence of IRA and Loyalist paramilitaries; British Army still used as police force. Current death toll: 3,111 at December 1993 (in a country with a population of only 1.5 million); including well over 100 children and infants; 65 per cent of deaths are civilian, the rest security forces. Worst carnage (so far) in 1972, with 467 deaths.

Main political parties

Unionist: Ulster Unionist Party (UUP); Democratic Unionist Party (DUP). Nationalist: Social Democratic and Labour Party (SDLP); Sinn Fein. Others: Alliance Party; Democratic Left/Workers Party.

Security forces

Royal Ulster Constabulary (RUC) is the regular police force; Ulster Defence Regiment (UDR) has been assimilated into the regular British Army since publication of *Cal.*

Terrorist organizations

Republican: Irish Republican Army. Provisional wing of IRA ('provos') (official wing of IRA ('stickies')) have renounced campaign of violence in favour of constitutional politics; Irish National Liberation Army (INLA). Loyalist: Ulster Volunteer Force (UVF); Ulster Freedom Fighters (UFF); Ulster Defence Association (UDA).

10 Virginia Woolf's 'Old Mrs Grey'

Issues of genre

Irene R. Fairley

EDITOR'S PREFACE

At the age of 59, Virginia Woolf committed suicide by drowning herself in the river Ouse. This biographical fact gives added poignancy to her literary essay 'Old Mrs Grey', in which she sketches the portrait of a 92-year-old woman who prays to God to end her suffering and to 'let [her] pass'. In her own life, Virginia Woolf exerted the right to choose for herself the moment of her death.

Virginia Woolf wrote a number of highly poetic and lyrical novels which diverge radically from the norms and conventions of the genre, and which often frustrate the reader's search for interpretive schemata. Similarly, her literary essays deconstruct and problematize culturally fixed notions of the essay genre. In this chapter, Irene R. Fairley shows how Woolf's use of literary devices gives 'Old Mrs Grey' a narrative feel. Fairley discusses a wide range of these devices, including methods of narration (omniscient narration, alternation between narrative and dialogue, interior monologue), shifts of style, textual cohesion, figurative language, ellipsis and ambiguity.

Woolf uses these literary techniques in order to provoke and shock her readers, to impose her vision upon them, instead of trying to convince them by means of rational arguments. Her logic is a logic of emotion, of images, rather than of reason. The result is an overlapping of literary and persuasive aims and styles, combined with an expressiveness that is due to the autobiographical nature of the incident. For Virginia, together with her husband Leonard, had actually visited Mrs Grey, and this is the source of the intense emotion that she feels about the old woman.

In the final part of her chapter, Fairley compares the literary essay with Virginia Woolf's diary entry about the visit to Mrs Grey, thus exploring the continuities between a literary and a non-literary genre, and at the same time giving us a fascinating insight into the process by which a creative writer turns a personal experience into a public work of art.

J. J. W.

Categories of genre are culturally defined and acquired; they provide readers with a mechanism of pre-reading. For instance, from my title and the context of this book you may already have expectations of a discussion at second remove: Fairley looking at Woolf looking at Mrs Grey. You may also expect an approach that is analytical, a focus on language and style, and an educational aim. This volume, then, contextualizes your reading, arousing expectations according to its genre.[1] Considerations of genre influence the reading of Woolf's text. Because it appears in a collection of her essays *The Death of the Moth and Other Essays* (1942), rather than a collection of short fiction, we begin reading with a particular outlook, based on our experience with essays in general, and perhaps even with Woolf's essays in particular. Most readers are more familiar with her fiction, so I will not assume previous familiarity with the essays in the discussion that follows.

What general features are suggested by the category of essays? That essays are well formed, non-fictional writing. That they have clearly delineated structure, such as a beginning, middle and end; or introduction, body and conclusion. That they have a discernible purpose or theme – so that parts are tied together in a logical relationship. These are the kinds of structures that you have probably encountered as guidelines for exercises in composition classes. Of course, there will be still other anticipations, such as that the writing will be grammatical, that the title will signal a relationship to the thematic content of the essay, that the author will not purposely thwart our reading, and so on. There are also considerations of sub-types or features within genres. Essay is indeed a broad category – we need to make adjustments when we move in our reading to technical, religious or autobiographical essays, because aims and also style features (such as choice of vocabulary, sentence structure, organization) will certainly vary.[2] Here we will be looking at the literary essay, with its further distinction between the formal essay and the informal or familiar essay that tends to be more intimate in both topic and approach. We will explore what a literary essay entails in the case of Woolf's 'Old Mrs Grey'.

Let us consider Woolf's essay (reproduced in the appendix for reference) to see how she meets or frustrates expectations. Consider the opening paragraph. In an essay so brief, we would expect the opening to rapidly introduce the subject providing background or perhaps indicating purpose. But the first paragraph moves slowly, from a vague time (as in the opening of a fairy tale) to an expansive bucolic landscape in England, 'now' (an unspecified present). A set of lexical items combine to suggest a scene: fields, hills, space unlimited, untrodden grass, wild birds flying. The paragraph concludes with the clause, 'hills whose smooth uprise continues that wild flight'. In a broad stroke, Woolf paints a scene. But because of the title the reader expects Mrs Grey to appear. While there is human presence, it takes a curiously impersonal form: 'the busiest, most contented'. With the main noun missing, modifiers may be upgraded to represent people, a plural being signalled by the nearby referent 'they'. They are busy but they 'suddenly' drop what they hold – surprisingly Woolf suggests it 'may be the week's washing'. 'Aha,' the reader might think, 'here comes Mrs Grey.' But instead enters Mrs Peel. With two surnames now indicating gender, we may expect a gendered discourse. Does the earlier pronoun 'they' refer then to women, and the washing of intimate garments suggest women working? Yet we are informed there is 'no work at all, but boundless rest'.

This first paragraph is enigmatic and frustrates a reader's expectation of a clear opening. Why are we introduced to Mrs Peel, the possible recipient of laundry, while actors remain unidentified? Other puzzles occur in the form of odd expressions, such as 'Sheets and pyjamas crumble and dissolve in their hands'. Because of a beautiful day? Because of a scene of hills and birds flying? The syntax is also problematic: why two occurrences of 'even' in the first sentence? Or the odd sequential causals 'because, though'? And the last sentence is not a complete sentence but a series of nominal expressions. An odd paragraph. On a first reading we would have to suspend closure, skim past all of these puzzles, led forward by a search for the discourse topic or theme suggested by Woolf's title.

Woolf comes through in the second paragraph where she connects 'all this' to Mrs Grey by means of 'however'. A passive construction arranges sentence parts to provide the transition from outside to inside, and concludes with the woman's point of view: 'could be seen from Mrs Grey's corner'. The logic that prevails is a movement from those generalized people of the first paragraph to Mrs Grey, from 'space unlimited' to an interior, and even more specifically, to her corner. Reversal of expectations is signalled by the causal adversative 'however'. Despite the sunshine outside, there is 'a fire burning in the grate'.

Woolf's choice of the passive modal 'could be seen' becomes even more clearly motivated given the third paragraph's focus on the woman's vision. What is she looking at? What did she see? Through a series of qualifications Woolf moves to the aged woman's limited vision and then finally to the woman's pain: 'And now at the age of ninety-two they saw nothing but a zigzag of pain wriggling across the door'. The prominence of the modifier 'Old' in the title now clicks into place, providing a possible schema for reading: an essay describing Mrs Grey's old age.

This third paragraph, another curious passage, resembles a short story more than the main body of an essay. Woolf captures the reader's interest by means of striking images, novel expressions, and by giving her essay a narrative feel. If we hardly noticed the past progressive tense of 'there was a fire burning in the grate' (paragraph 2), we cannot miss the narrative effect of the progressive, 'looking'. Woolf has gradually introduced a fictional world – the world according to Mrs Grey. Mrs Grey opens the paragraph and remains the focus, becoming, in effect, the main character. With one exception towards the end of the paragraph, sentences have subjects directly related to Mrs Grey or her body parts, especially eyes. By referring to Mrs Grey predominantly in the subject position, Woolf's narrative perspective creates empathy. Gradually, the narrator's voice comes to resemble that familiar omniscient third-person narrator of fiction.

Much as in a short story, we get to know Mrs Grey as the subject – but is she also an actor, in the sense of an initiator of actions? At first we might think, 'Yes, she is looking.' But Woolf negates that possibility: 'Her eyes had ceased to focus themselves; it may be that they had lost the power' and 'They could see, but without looking.' Semantically, Woolf has cast Mrs Grey as an experiencer rather than an agent, and goes a step further, turning the woman into a patient who is acted upon. First Mrs Grey sees 'nothing but a zigzag of pain', then the pain jerks her body as if she were a marionette. Next her body is described as being 'wrapped round the pain' much the way laundry (a sheet) hangs 'over a wire'. Finally, we understand the wire to be controlled by 'a cruel invisible hand', an antagonist of sorts that Woolf has subtly introduced. When we read, 'She flung out a foot, a hand. Then it stopped. She sat still for a moment', we understand the responses as involuntary. With age and sickness Mrs Grey has lost control of actions. Woolf closes this long third paragraph with a pause, 'She sat still for a moment.' The third paragraph, the longest in the essay, brings the reader to the essay's mid-point.

Woolf stops the 'action' to provide a glimpse of the past. The first two relatively long sentences in paragraph 4 express her youthful activity from age 10 to 25: 'running in and out of a cottage with eleven brothers and sisters'. The narrator's report of Mrs Grey's thoughts (which we might trace back to the description in paragraph 3 of what Mrs Grey saw) resembles literary devices that create the impression of seeing into a character's mind. The paragraph itself is brief and Woolf closes the reverie quite abruptly: 'The line jerked.' Mrs Grey 'was thrown forward in her chair'. So, too, the reader is moved forward.

Further enhancing the impression of a story, the fifth paragraph reports direct speech. Concretizing her loneliness, Mrs Grey laments her loss of a net of close relations, the result of the deaths of all of her siblings, her husband, and even her daughter, 'All dead'. In what resembles an internal monologue, thoughts represented in the form of speech, Mrs Grey complains, 'But I go on. Every morning I pray God to let me pass.'

In these two brief paragraphs, 4 and 5, Woolf sketches in a sense of the woman's past and her feelings. Then Woolf returns to narrative: 'The morning spread seven foot by four green and sunny. Like a fling of grain the birds settled on the land.' Words in paragraph 6 echo with items introduced in the first two paragraphs, such as the size of the front door, the sunshine, the birds. Such lexical echoes become repeated motifs that tie paragraphs together. We are also reminded of the controlling, invisible hand introduced in paragraph 3, now described as 'the tormenting hand'. As the paragraph closes, a reader may wonder whether the same hand controls both birds and Mrs Grey.

Mrs Grey's speech again structures the seventh paragraph, creating a pattern of narrative comment in the third person alternating with dialogue in the first person. This alternation provides a structure and rhythm for the section that begins with paragraph 4 and continues to the essay's conclusion in paragraph 11. While we 'hear' only one voice, the alternating creates an impression of a reported conversation. As in paragraph 5, Mrs Grey's speech in paragraph 7, as well as in 10, has a high degree of repetition. Simple parallelisms, sentences with repetition and only slight variation, demonstrate by their form and content Mrs Grey's assessment: 'I'm an ignorant old woman. I can't read or write.'

At paragraph 8 the introductory 'So' signals a subtle change introducing the narrator's commentary as an openly evaluative stance, one that is heightened by means of figurative language. The doorway image that has served as a reminder of the sunny day outside comes to represent youth or the active life: there is the life outside, then the life inside; life focused on activity versus the life of intellect (contemplation, reading). If life is an open book, where light shifts from one page to the other, Mrs Grey cannot participate in the second stage because she cannot read or write. Unlike the author, Mrs Grey has no access to literature – to the 'voices that have argued, sung, talked for hundreds of years'. The narrator's rhetorically complex language contrasts with Mrs Grey's unschooled speech. Figurative language here enhances the effect of a fictional discourse, as the reader must work through metaphor to arrive at meaning.

The single sentence that is paragraph 9 serves as a transition by way of recalling the tormenting pain that is Mrs Grey's life, much the way the two final sentences of paragraph 4 lead to her speech, here too as if the pain or tormenting hand controls the narrative as well as Mrs Grey. The third and final speech in paragraph 10 provides still another glimpse of her present life, this time revealing how it is punctuated by weekly visits from the parish doctor. As in the previous instances, her speech features oppositional structure, signalled by 'but' and 'yet'. It is, however, more direct as euphemisms such as 'let me pass' culminate in 'I don't seem able to die'.

From Mrs Grey's pronouncement, Woolf moves rapidly to the conclusion, another 'So' providing logical connection to the preceding paragraph, and possibly extending reference to all previous text. As we might anticipate in an essay's conclusion, we find a move to the general: from individual to humanity; from Mrs Grey's aged body to 'the body'; from her limbs to 'the eyes' and 'the ears'. Through an abstractive process, Mrs Grey's situation becomes representative. Also signalling a move from the specific instance to the general case, definite 'the' becomes finally indefinite 'a' ('a rook on a barn door'). Encompassing generalizations include the reader, too, as Woolf shifts from the more neutral third-person perspective to a first-person plural pronoun. First she embraces the reader in the inclusive category 'we – humanity' and then she moves to the unqualified 'We'. Presumably, the final 'we' includes everyone, writer and audience, along with the doctors.

But what is the effect of such a move on the reader? It is doubtful that anyone who stops to think about it would want to be identified as actively inflicting or prolonging pain. Woolf develops this role, moving from the first sentence with 'insist that the body shall still cling' to the next sentence with 'put out the eyes and the ears'. Finally, we become associated with an image of crucifixion comparing the extending of Mrs Grey's life to a 'rook' (large blackbird or crow) that 'we pinion' to a barn door. An especially cruel image closes the essay: 'a rook that still lives, even with a nail through it'. What a curiously harsh and accusatory ending. We, as part of humanity, are held responsible for Mrs Grey's dilemma – continuing to live in pain when she would die. The suddenness of Woolf's move and the intensity of her conclusion are startling.

We may well ask now, what is Woolf's purpose? Is she promoting euthanasia or the individual's right to choose? Is she suggesting that we withhold treatment, or administer hemlock rather than tea or medicine? But if her point is to reverse the conventional ethic of medical treatment, she has not developed it, or provided the kind of support we would expect to lead us logically to such a conclusion. Instead, Woolf's argument is semantic; it depends on impressive language and is essentially vague. Woolf doesn't explore the ethical issues she raises; her logic is implicit rather than explicit. There are 'inductive leaps' at the beginning and at the end, from a sample of one to the universal. An unstated premise could be construed; for instance, Mrs Grey's pain is worse than death, or death is preferable to a life of recurrent pain. But given the lack of clear steps and support, a reader may well question the appropriateness of the final leap, or judge as false analogy Woolf's comparison of Mrs Grey suffering to a bird that has been nailed to a barn door (an act that suggests deliberate cruelty). The image may not be valid logically, but it works on an emotional level, it has shock value. Woolf's unpredictable ending makes us *feel* – whether sadness, sympathy, guilt, fear or anger is surely an individual matter. Indeed, Woolf's aim seems to be to provoke. She carries us off into the world of Mrs Grey only to drop us down finally in the midst of a moral dilemma.

We need not judge Woolf here for logical failures or omissions; the essay, after all, lacks altogether the kind of formal scientific or even exploratory framework that might lead us to expect paragraphs with thesis statements that get elaborated and supported. While she raises questions about assumptions, with respect to treatment for instance, that most readers would regard as true, Woolf doesn't spend time exploring those beliefs, proving them wrong, or searching for new answers. She sets out only to make us see a problem. Accepted beliefs are comforting and questioning them is upsetting; readers might be resistant. So Woolf chooses to be indirect, to take the reader by surprise. She takes the literary route, shaping an essay to arrest our attention and affect our emotions. Since Woolf's purpose is not to use words for precision but to use them to stir the imagination, figurative language is pervasive. Furthermore, we cannot strip Woolf's essay of its metaphors. To a large extent they carry the meaning, but they are also crucial to the essay's structure and its aesthetic dimension.

The essay's uniqueness signals its predominantly literary aim, but we also find persuasive intent. Woolf leads us to a concluding 'lesson'. This literary essay entertains while it educates, has an aesthetic and affective function. A persuasive secondary aim is often present in literary discourse, as in fables that convey a moral. We detect persuasion in Woolf's use of analogy, figurative language and emotional appeal rather than logical proof, and in her move to the inclusive first person 'we' as she closes. Woolf enlists comparison, contrast, repetition and surprise to convince the reader, and she makes ample use of 'purr' and 'snarl' words that call up positive or negative associations and are commonly found in persuasive discourse. Most texts will have overlapping discourse aims and therefore styles; persuasion may make use of literary techniques, while literature may incorporate persuasive devices (Kinneavy 1971: 60).

Many of the essay's features are obviously literary, and some even fictional, such as the use of a narrative (however simple the story line), and the controlling perspective of an omniscient narrator whose voice is distinctly different from the single character's speech. The opening, too, somewhat reminiscent of a fairy tale, introduces setting and time. Woolf's strategies of description, narration and evaluation (or commentary) are all compatible with fictional discourse. Another feature usually associated with literary text, considered by some theorists to be a defining feature, is unity. Reviewing some of the textual features already noted above, we can see the degree of intersentence cohesion that unifies the essay. We can also see how Woolf ties a surprising ending to the preceding text.

We may even construe the opening section to be a hint of the essay's closure by reading the early image of eternal rest that awaits 'over the hills', the 'Stainless and boundless rest', as euphemistically suggesting death – which Mrs Grey desires. The early 'pinning of clothes to lines' develops variously in the body clinging 'over a wire' and in the closing, 'we pinion it there'. Even 'mangling and ironing' may be associated with later images – the putting out of eyes and ears, and the 'nail through' the live rook. The birds' wild flight of the first paragraph, arrested 'Like a fling of grain' in the sixth paragraph, culminates in the rook nailed to the door. Like carefully planted seeds, such lexical echoes form chains of cohesive ties. There are others, such as the line image that develops into a cruel controlling force, or the door and doorway image, or the light and colour group. Much of the descriptive and also figurative language that carries us along is visual, as Woolf draws a picture in words. A progression of images engages the reader, leads us into the interior of Mrs Grey's world, then out again. The opening and closing paragraphs frame the story of Mrs Grey, giving it a larger significance.

This short piece that seems so loosely connected is highly unified. At places the lexical cohesion involves close, or 'immediate' ties (Halliday and Hasan 1976: 330), as related items occur in adjacent sentences, for example as 'week's washing' leads to 'Sheets and pyjamas'. Sometimes the ties are distant or 'remote' (331) with a good deal of material separating related items. Examples of such remote ties are 'a cruel invisible hand' (paragraph 3) and 'the tormenting hand' (paragraph 6); and 'sunshine' (paragraph 2) related to 'sunny' (paragraph 6) and perhaps also to 'colour' and 'lit up' (paragraph 8). Cohesive chains form as these recurrent words or variants weave through the text. Woolf uses words that collocate, tend to occur together, such as a group of words associated with laundering or with landscape. Still another, obvious feature of text unity occurs in the repeated pronoun reference to Mrs Grey, the many instances of 'her' and 'she'.

Woolf's use of conjunction also contributes to texture. She uses adversative conjunctions, especially those that signal reversal or contrast: 'though', 'however', 'but' and 'yet'. But there are also causal conjunctions, 'so' and the temporal, 'then' (see Halliday and Hasan 1976: 242–3 for types of conjunction). Such conjunctive elements point to a fabric of logical relations. Thus, we may not find a logical argument constructed according to formal rules, but we do find intersentential connections suggesting a logic of organization. Woolf creates connectedness and overall unity by means of recurrence, partial recurrence, reference, parallelism and conjunction.

While such unity may tighten the text, other features, such as metaphor, open it up. Ellipses and ambiguities invite readers to explore in their thoughts realms outside the text. In the opening passage, for example, ellipses in the expression 'the busiest, most contented' tease us to work through the possible classes of persons. Are they two separate, even contrastive classes, or are these a pair of features belonging to one group? Are they inclusive terms meant to specify humanity and therefore a hint of the universal move of the conclusion? Is Woolf already implying the audience she will later include in the class of people who put out 'the eyes and the ears'? And what does she mean by that figure? How are *we* responsible for Mrs Grey being unable to read or write, or 'hear the voices that have argued, sung, talked for hundreds of years'? Such is the conversation that Woolf initiates in her essay. The series of extraordinary images that conclude the essay are rich, indeed. They extend a reader's thoughts into other realms, perhaps politics, economics, ethics, and may even move us to add our voices to the exchange.

Woolf herself stresses the communicative aspect of literature. In 'The Modern Essay' (*The Common Reader* (1925)), she speaks of the importance of essays (such as Beerbohm's) that have the power to draw us back to them, to 'sit down with them and talk' (Woolf 1925: 218). And she argues, 'The public needs essays as much as ever, and perhaps even more.'

In that same meta-essay, Woolf explains, 'Never to be yourself and yet always – that is the problem' (1925: 217). Indeed, Woolf's voice permeates 'Old Mrs Grey'; we sense it in the conviction we hear but also in the emotion. The emotional charge of this piece signals its overlapping of expressive discourse, where primarily 'the reaction of the self is displayed' (Kinneavy 1971: 60). Expressive discourse is typically found in such genres as diaries, journals and autobiographies, as well as ordinary conversation (such as Mrs Grey's speech) and prayer – genres in which the individual's subjectivity dominates. In fact, in Woolf's diary there is a passage that suggests the essay 'Old Mrs Grey' comes directly from Woolf's experience. Recorded in her diary of Friday 16 September 1932 (Woolf 1982: 123–5) are Woolf's feelings about having 'botched the last-penultimate chapter of Flush', about a photo of her to be published by Wishart, the sale of a plot of land by neighbours, a dream of Angelica (her niece) dead, a walk through the downs, and the previous day's visit with 'L' to Mrs Grey. The entry illuminates much of the figurative language, narrative and dialogue sections, and the shifts of discourse style that characterize the essay, as well as the source of emotion that permeates it. Woolf expresses feelings about her writing and her personal reaction to aging. The photograph causes her anxiety as she writes, 'my legs show; I am revealed to the world (1,000 at most) as a plain dowdy old woman' (124). Even while recalling her experience of the beauty of England during her walk and writing, 'I almost felt my mind glow like hot iron – so complete & holy was the habitual beauty of England: the silver sheep clustering; & the downs soaring, like birds' wings sweeping up & up –', anxiety over the photograph intrudes and she adds, '(oh my legs in the snapshot)'. As is characteristic of diary writing, Woolf's language is private so that allusions like 'L' for her husband Leonard need to be referenced for the reading public. An associative logic structures the entry that is dominated by a speaking 'I' who makes intimate revelations.

As Woolf ends the long first paragraph of the entry she writes, 'This has a holiness. This will go on after I'm dead.' Her second paragraph is a summary evaluation of the summer, which despite her current anxiety has been a good one. She comments on the pleasure of being among friends: 'to feel the width & amusement of *human* life', and of the feeling that comes as she concludes the paragraph, when she can say 'Stop, & take out my pen'. Woolf ends with an affirmative afterthought: 'Yes, my thighs now begin to run smooth: no longer is every nerve upright' (124).

Woolf's diary displays her characteristic creativity, her unusual figures of speech, and a high degree of semantic coherence as she moves from a preoccupation with her own legs and anxiety about aging to the subject of Mrs Grey. The third and final paragraph records the visit that is the basis for the companion essay.

> Yesterday we took plums to old Mrs Grey. She is shrunk, & sits on a hard chair in the corner, the door open. She twitches & trembles. Has the wild expressionless stare of the old. L. liked her despair: I crawls up to bed hoping for the day; & I crawls down hoping for the night.' I'm an ignorant old woman – cant write or read. But I prays to God every night to take me – oh to go to my rest. Nobody can say what pains I suffer. Feel my shoulder' & she began shuffling with a safety pin. I felt it. 'Hard as iron – full of water – & my legs too' – She pulled down her stocking. The dropsy. 'I'm ninety two; & all my brothers & sisters are dead; my daughters dead; my husband is dead . . .' She repeated her misery, her list of ills, over & over; could see nothing else; could only begin all over again; & kissed my hand, thanking us for our pound. This is what we make of our lives – no reading or writing – keep her alive with parish doctors when she wishes to die – Human ingenuity in torture is very great.
>
> (1982: 124–5)

The diary reveals that there really was a Mrs Grey, not just a name chosen for its associations.[3] By comparing the two texts we can see how the visit becomes the central section of the essay, how the personal narrative of the diary becomes the more impersonal narrative of the essay. We can see how Woolf has re-arranged her material, re-ordering Mrs Grey's 'lines', and understand why the monologue of the essay has the feel of a conversation. We might even speculate on the origin of images from seed words like 'hot iron', 'safety pin' and 'torture'. We also find the precursor of the essay's closing. From the specific 'we' signifying Virginia and Leonard, Woolf moves to a first person plural that seems much more inclusive for the final sentence of the entry.

In his Editorial Note for *The Death of the Moth and Other Essays,*

Leonard Woolf explains that the first four, 'Old Mrs Grey' being the fourth, were written 'as usual, in handwriting and were then typed out in rather a rough state' (Woolf 1942: viii), unlike the longer critical essays which, he explains, Woolf revised several times before publication. Together, the pair – diary entry and essay – give us a glimpse of how expressive discourse may be, as Kinneavy argues, 'psychologically prior to all the other uses of language'. He proposes, 'It is the expressive component which gives all discourse a personal significance to the speaker or listener' (Kinneavy 1971: 396). In both diary and essay, style shifts hint at Woolf's shifting aims as she writes. As we have seen, the act of critiquing exposes that variability of discourse aims and styles.

Woolf experimented with notions of genre, her many-faceted works challenging us to find a 'pigeon hole'. Her fiction has been described variously as poetic, lyrical and visual. Her novels may be more lyrical than narrative, her essays more narrative than ideational. 'Old Mrs Grey' is at once literary, persuasive, personal and expressive, and unique. While the essay with its mix of styles presents a number of difficulties, it amply rewards a reader's efforts. Like the best of literature, Woolf's essay challenges us to understand our world differently.[4]

SUGGESTIONS FOR FURTHER WORK

1 It is best to approach genres as normative categories, rather than fixed entities. For example, most of us have learned to distinguish the following pairs of terms: fiction/non-fiction, prose/poetry, literary/non-literary. But in trying to set out features that distinguish these terms, we are likely to fall back on 'family resemblance'. Write an essay in which you explore by way of definition at least two of the sets of terms.

2 Study Woolf's complex discourse by making separate lists of the style features that are associated with specific aims: persuasive, literary, expressive, referential. For instance, one could argue that the description of Mrs Grey's condition is in part referential as it provides a reader with new information. You may place a feature on more than one list. When you have completed the lists, analyse them for patterns, such as shared features or overlap. Do the lists point to a primary aim?

3 Write an essay exploring the ethical dilemma Woolf raises. For instance, you may choose to spell out and explore logical steps

missing from 'Old Mrs Grey'. If necessary do some research, perhaps looking into medical or legal association journals or publications of ethical organizations. After exploring various aspects or sides of the issue, you may find you want to promote a particular position. If so, move to persuasion as you conclude. Keep a writer's journal in which you record your thoughts during the composing process.

4 Structure an argumentative essay in which you affirm or oppose euthanasia, assuming the same general audience as Woolf does, the general reading public. Using syllogistic form, offer the major premise in your opening paragraph, and your conclusion in the last paragraph. The body of your essay may demonstrate your supporting or minor premise(s).

5 Analyse how the essay moves from a focus on the physical aspects of Mrs Grey's old age to states of mind. Consider, for example, differences of vocabulary, figurative language and narrative perspective.

6 Is identification of gender important to the reading of Woolf's essay? Explore how the essay presents or reflects cultural constructions of gender. Consider, for example, how our reading might change if we substitute 'Mr' wherever 'Mrs' occurs.

7 Examine how the use of adjectives, adverbs and modals reveals Woolf's attitude towards her subject. As a first step, make a list of all value-laden terms that occur in the essay.

8 Explore some of the metaphors in Woolf's essay. Try paraphrasing them and then explaining their meanings.

9 For each of the categories that follow, develop a set of associated words that occur in Woolf's essay: landscape; laundry; house; health; religion/belief; death. Organize the lists of words into sub-sets wherever possible, such as sub-sets of sky and earth for landscape. Note: you may include a word in more than one category; also, include items that repeat each time they occur.

10 Select one or two paragraphs in the essay to study with regard to cohesion across sentences. Identify as many instances of cohesion as you can find. For each, indicate what item is referred to and whether it precedes or follows.

11 Compare Woolf's use of figurative language in the essay to the language of the companion diary entry. (You need not limit your study to the portion included here.) You might also compare instances of parallel constructions.

12 What changes in style, organization or logic do you find as Woolf moves from personal experience to public essay? What aspects of

the visit to Mrs Grey become prominent or get deleted? Consider the two references included in note 3, as well as the diary and essay.

NOTES

1 Kinneavy points out that such cultural contexts usually 'operate un-consciously' (1971: 95). He adds the distinction of situational context that includes the audience to whom the text is addressed, as well as contexts of time and place of publication. Halliday and Hasan (1976: 20) refer to the 'context of situation' that includes the 'speaker's and hearer's (or writer's and reader's) material, social and ideological environment'. They point to 'external factors' affecting a writer's linguistic choices, such as 'the nature of the audience, the medium, the purpose of the communication' (21). It is now current, especially in reader-response criticism, to distinguish also a reading context, which includes such factors as a reader's individual personality, age, sex, education and cultural background, as well as immediate conditions of the act of reading (see Fairley 1988: 293).

2 It may be useful at this point to introduce the distinction between aim and genre as clarified by Crusius (1989: 121): 'Aims are judgments or inferences about motive, often arguable, made during and after the fact of composition; genres are quasi-objective discourse types generally recognized by a language community or some group within that community.' Kinneavy uses aim as a way of sorting into four broad categories: reference discourse (which further divides into scientific, informative and exploratory), persuasive discourse, literary discourse and expressive discourse (1971: 63). For each language use he describes characteristic patterns of thought or logic, organization and stylistic choice (40).

3 Woolf writes of Mrs Grey in at least two other places. The woman is mentioned in the third paragraph of a letter Woolf wrote dated 15 September 1932 from Monks House, Rodmell, to Frances Marshall: 'It is an incredibly lovely evening and I wish you and Ralph were here to beat us soundly at bowls. Instead we have just visited an old woman [Mrs Grey, Rodmell] who made me feel a hump on her back and said it was full of water. But we should very much like to come to Ham Spray sometime whether you beat us or not' (Woolf 1979: 106). Years later Woolf records in her diary entry for Friday 27 July 1934 a conversation with 'Mrs B[artholomew]' and notes that woman's kindnesses, which include among others paying 'old Grey's insurance' and cooking 'a bit of meat for Mrs Grey – whose [maiden] name is Squelch' (Woolf 1982: 232).

4 I would like to thank the students who have kindly shared their responses to Woolf's essay, and in particular Hale Kipcak Binay who brought the essay to my attention.

REFERENCES

Crusius, T. W. (1989) *Discourse: A Critique and Synthesis of Major Theories*, New York: Modern Language Association.

Fairley, I. R. (1988) 'The Reader's Need for Conventions: When is a Mushroom not a Mushroom?', in W. van Peer (ed.) *The Taming of the Text: Explorations in Language, Literature and Culture*, London: Routledge.

Halliday, M. A. K. and Hasan, R. (1976) *Cohesion in English*, London: Longman.

Kinneavy, J. L. (1971) *A Theory of Discourse: The Aims of Discourse*, New York: Norton.

Woolf, V. (1925) *The Common Reader*, San Diego: Harcourt Brace Jovanovich.

—— (1942) *The Death of the Moth and Other Essays*, San Diego: Harcourt Brace Jovanovich.

—— (1979) *The Letters of Virginia Woolf*, volume five: 1932–5, New York: Harcourt Brace Jovanovich.

—— (1982) *The Diary of Virginia Woolf*, volume four: 1931–5, San Diego: Harcourt Brace Jovanovich.

APPENDIX

Old Mrs Grey

1 There are moments even in England, now, when even the busiest, most contented suddenly let fall what they hold – it may be the week's washing. Sheets and pyjamas crumble and dissolve in their hands, because, though they do not state this in so many words, it seems silly to take the washing round to Mrs Peel when out there over the fields over the hills, there is no washing; no pinning of clothes to lines; mangling and ironing; no work at all, but boundless rest. Stainless and boundless rest; space unlimited; untrodden grass; wild birds flying; hills whose smooth uprise continues that wild flight.

2   Of all this however only seven foot by four could be seen from Mrs Grey's corner. That was the size of her front door which stood wide open, though there was a fire burning in the grate. The fire looked like a small spot of dusty light feebly trying to escape from the embarrassing pressure of the pouring sunshine.

3   Mrs Grey sat on a hard chair in the corner looking – but at what? Apparently at nothing. She did not change the focus of her eyes when visitors came in. Her eyes had ceased to focus themselves; it may be that they had lost the power. They were aged eyes, blue, unspectacled. They could see, but without looking. She had never used her eyes on anything minute and difficult; merely upon faces, and dishes and fields. And now at the age of ninety-two they saw nothing but a zigzag of pain wriggling across the door, pain that twisted her legs as it wriggled; jerked her body to and fro like a marionette. Her body was wrapped round the pain as a damp sheet is folded over a wire. The wire was spasmodically jerked by a cruel

invisible hand. She flung out a foot, a hand. Then it stopped. She sat still for a moment.

4   In that pause she saw herself in the past at ten, at twenty, at twenty-five. She was running in and out of a cottage with eleven brothers and sisters. The line jerked. She was thrown forward in her chair.

5   'All dead. All dead,' she mumbled. 'My brothers and sisters. And my husband gone. My daughter too. But I go on. Every morning I pray God to let me pass.'

6   The morning spread seven foot by four green and sunny. Like a fling of grain the birds settled on the land. She was jerked again by another tweak of the tormenting hand.

7   'I'm an ignorant old woman. I can't read or write, and every morning when I crawls down stairs, I say I wish it were night; and every night, when I crawls up to bed, I say I wish it were day. I'm only an ignorant old woman. But I prays to God: O let me pass. I'm an ignorant old woman – I can't read or write.'

8   So when the colour went out of the doorway, she could not see the other page which is then lit up; or hear the voices that have argued, sung, talked for hundreds of years.

9   The jerked limbs were still again.

10   'The doctor comes every week. The parish doctor now. Since my daughter went, we can't afford Dr Nicholls. But he's a good man. He says he wonders I don't go. He says my heart's nothing but wind and water. Yet I don't seem able to die.'

11   So we – humanity – insist that the body shall still cling to the wire. We put out the eyes and the ears; but we pinion it there, with a bottle of medicine, a cup of tea, a dying fire, like a rook on a barn door, but a rook that still lives, even with a nail through it.

(from Woolf, *The Death of the Moth and Other Essays*, 1942)

11 'World enough, and time'
Deictic space and the interpretation of prose

Paul Werth

EDITOR'S PREFACE

Human beings always have their experiences at some place and at some time; they cannot have them nowhere. It therefore seems only natural that whenever we read about something happening, we try to conceptualize the background situation comprising the where and when of the event as well as the people and objects positioned in it. It is these apparently simple facts which form the starting-point of Paul Werth's well-argued proposal in this chapter to apply the theory of text worlds to the fictional universe projected in novels and short stories.

Though they are separated in time and space, the author and reader of a literary fiction are participants in an interpersonal communicative event, that is, a discourse. In this overarching discourse, author and reader undertake to work out or rather negotiate the meaning of what can be called an embedded discourse, which is the one presented in the novel or short story. Like any other discourse, it comprises a situation containing participants (at this level Werth prefers to call them characters) and objects, involved in all manner of relationships and positioned in a particular place and at a particular time. Through the medium of the actual text, all these discoursal constituents invite the reader to co-operate with the author in constructing a possible world, i.e. a conceptual space in which the fictional state of affairs occurs. It is this conceptual space which Werth calls the text world, that is, in so far as its deictic or scene-setting details are concerned. Since these world-building elements depict only the background of the narrative, we need to complete our mental representation of the text world by conceptualizing its foreground. Now, this is filled in by propositions or statements in the text denoting states, actions and processes which cause the story to move on. Werth calls such statements function-advancing components.

In processing this situational and function-advancing information, the reader makes use of frame knowledge. This is a cognitive structure of culturally determined assumptions and expectations developed from past experiences with similar situations, and stored and organized in so-called frames. The reader is also disposed to make inferences, that is, to draw conclusions from logical reasoning, so as to derive implicit information from textual cues in the discourse. All the information supplied by the text, together with the frames and inferences it has evoked, make up what is called the common ground. 'Common' because it forms the totality of information which the author and reader together think is necessary to comprehend the embedded literary discourse. Clearly, this common ground is not something stable because due to the constant flow of new information, frames and inferences, it will change all the time while the discourse proceeds.

Like the actual world, the text world of literary fiction has its own complex structure of modalities, in which some situations are factual and others are impossible or hypothetical. Another analogy with the real world is that the text world is inhabited by characters who can evoke memories, indulge in fantasies, express beliefs and wishes, state their intentions, and so create their own text worlds. Since these emanate from the text world which the characters are situated in, Werth categorizes them as sub-worlds. Actually, there are three basic types of sub-worlds: the type involving probabilities, possibilities, improbabilities, and impossibilities in terms of the modality structure of the text world; the type involving some mental activity on the part of one of the characters; and the type involving a disruption of the text world's dimensions of time (e.g. a flashback).

In terms of the point of view from which a story gets told, it is important that Werth makes a clear distinction between character-accessible and participant-accessible sub-worlds. In the former, the author delegates the power to create sub-worlds to a character, to whose mind the reader has privileged access through the medium of an all knowing narrative agent. In the latter, the author (or some unpersonified narrator) assumes this power him/herself and establishes a direct form of rapport with the reader. In fact, this turns out to be the predominant mode of narration in the first chapter of E. M. Forster's *A Passage to India* (1924/1984), to which Paul Werth has applied his text world model. The external position of the uninvolved narrator yields a panoramic and panchronic view of the novel's setting, Chandrapore town as a miniature of India in the 1920s. Through rich metaphorical sub-worlds, the narrator makes the reader aware that the geographical features of Chandrapore foreshadow the framework of British imperial rule in India and the ensuing social divisions and clash of cultures, which are the principal themes of the novel.

P. V.

The Mind, that Ocean where each kind
Does streight its own resemblance find;
Yet it creates, transcending these,
Far other Worlds, and other Seas;
Annihilating all that's made
To a green Thought in a green Shade.
Andrew Marvell, 1621–78
                    (Gardner 1957: 257)

WHAT IS A DEICTIC SPACE?

As the quotation from Marvell implies, the mind is indeed a wonderful instrument, occupying a central place in our mental universe. In fact, the mind is the mental universe, and in a very important sense, it is the universe which we perceive as outside ourselves as well. This is because everything we know, everything we perceive, everything we remember or imagine, everything we give significance or meaning to, is located in that abstract region we call the mind. Some of these processes, such as imagination, in some sense actually originate in the mind; others, such as memory and knowledge, are somehow stored there; yet others, notably our perceptions, seem to 'pass through' our minds. There is a universe outside ourselves, that is to say, but we can experience it only indirectly, by way of mental processing – in somewhat the same way that the air is full of radio and television waves, but we can only experience them when they are processed through a radio or television. This analogy is helpful, but only to a certain extent: a crucial difference between a radio and the mind is that the radio simply converts radio waves into sound waves; the mind, however, is an active instrument. It doesn't just convert one kind of signal mechanically into another; it sorts, classifies and, in short, interprets everything within its boundaries, whatever form this might be in: sight, sound, smell, touch, emotion, written language or spoken language.

In order to do this, the mind does indeed have to convert the incoming signals into a form that it can deal with. This form is called a mental representation. The precise nature of this representation is as yet unknown: it certainly does not consist of pictures, although something equivalent to images probably forms part of it, some of the time. What is interesting, though, is that once incoming sense-impressions have been converted into this format, they can be experienced again later – perhaps not with their full richness always, but certainly in the same mode that they entered the mind. Even more fascinating, perhaps, is the role that language often plays in this retrieval, or transfer, of sense-impressions. A single word can conjure up a whole experience, complete with sights, sounds and smells: 'seaside', perhaps, or 'Christmas'. And even more remarkable, language can introduce us to experiences we have never had. By reading or listening to someone else's language, we can be transported mentally to situations experienced by other people, or even to entirely imaginary situations. Literature, of course, provides the best examples of this. The main question I shall attempt to answer in this chapter is: how does this process actually take place?

Let us first answer, however, the question posed in the title of this section. Try to visualize the mental representation as happening in some part of the mind which is specially cleared for the job – a space, in fact. This space is a region of the brain, let us say, which has evolved to carry out this particular function. The first thing that must happen is that the characteristics of the situation to be represented must be defined. These are: where it takes place, when it takes place, who is in it and what is in it. (We must also keep in mind who is responsible for describing the situation – the reason for this will become clear later.)

These space-defining details are known as deictic elements: 'deixis' is the Greek for 'pointing' or 'indicating'. A deictic space is therefore one which has been defined in terms of place and time, and has characters and entities positioned in it. Many traditional novels and stories begin with such details, and their function is to orientate the reader – or, as I will now say, to help the reader build up a mental representation of the setting. Here is an example from the beginning of Thackeray's *Vanity Fair*:

(1) While the present century was in its teens, and on one sunshiny morning in June, there drove up to the great iron gate of Miss Pinkerton's academy for young ladies, on Chiswick Mall, a large family coach, with two fat horses in blazing harness, driven by a fat coachman in a three-cornered hat and wig, at the rate of four miles an hour.

(Thackeray 1848/1968: 39)

Here we can find all the deictic elements listed below:

• time: in the second decade of the present century, one June morning
• place: the gate of Miss Pinkerton's academy, on Chiswick Mall

- character: a coachman
- objects: coach, horses, hat, wig

Considering that this is just one sentence, there is a fair amount of information here, but most people will also be able to add to this from what they already know about some of the items mentioned. So, if you know that *Vanity Fair* is a nineteenth-century novel (in fact first published in instalments in 1847), then you can 'fill out' the time detail a bit more: between 1813 and 1819, if we take the reference to 'teens' seriously. If you have any knowledge about London, you may recognize the reference to Chiswick Mall. This kind of 'filling-in' knowledge is called general knowledge or frame knowledge. Moreover, you may be able to work out further information by applying logic or experience to what is explicitly mentioned. For example, if you know anything about the form of transport mentioned, then you may know whether four miles an hour is relatively fast, or rather slow. You may perhaps deduce from the fact that both the horses and the coachman are fat that they have no shortage of food, and that therefore their owner is rich, and so on. This process is known as inferencing.

Deictic information, frame knowledge and inferencing combine, then, to give the reader a very rich mental representation of the setting of a novel or story, as in example (1). Together, they constitute what I call the world-building elements of the text. But this, in most cases, provides only the background to the story. The foreground consists of the descriptions and events which propel the story forward. I call this the function-advancing component, and it is made up of language denoting states, actions and processes. Consider example (1) again: almost all of the deictic elements appearing in the list (which follows it) are further qualified by descriptions. The morning is sunshiny, the gate is great and made of iron, the academy is for young ladies, the coach is large and family-sized, the horses are fat and in blazing harness, and so on. Descriptions are state-propositions: they denote relatively permanent qualities. Actions and processes, on the other hand, always denote changes: movements, alterations, variations from one state to another. In example (1), we learn: 'there drove up . . . a large family coach . . . at the rate of four miles an hour'. This signifies a movement, from an (as yet) unknown starting-point and finishing, for now, at Miss Pinkerton's gate. The mental representation of this text in fact seems clear enough to diagram (see Figure 11.1).

In Figure 11.1, WB = world building, and FA = function advancing. Horizontal arrows signify descriptions (i.e. steady states), while the

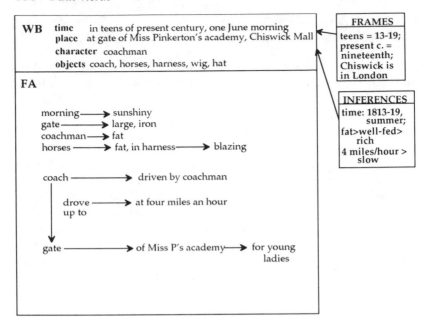

Figure 11.1 Vanity Fair text world

vertical arrow denotes movement. It represents, furthermore, a path-way, since that is what the coach is on, i.e. a line extending from its source to its destination, the gate. To the extent that (1) is an account of a scene, we could also have depicted it graphically, with little drawings or symbols denoting the (assumed) building with its gate, the coach, horses and coachman, and perhaps the road we may infer they were on. However, other elements would be, at the very least, difficult to picture directly ('iconically'): e.g. the time details, the geographical details, the movement (you would have to show it over several stages or 'snapshots', perhaps), the speed and even elements of the description (sunshiny morning, family coach, blazing harness). We might, of course, resort to agreed, or 'conventional', symbols (as on a map), e.g. ✻ for 'sunshiny'. But we already have a common system of conventional symbols, namely, language. All of these elements can, therefore, be portrayed linguistically, as in Figure 11.1, and that will be our preferred notation, since it is universally applicable.

Passage (1) is, of course, a very straightforward scene, viewed as if overlooked from some vantage-point. Thus, the descriptions of both the static elements and the movement are entirely external: there is no (or very little) evident subjectivity or mental activity going on here, but just observation. Furthermore, the only character mentioned (apart from Miss Pinkerton and her young ladies, who are presumably not actually present in this scene), namely, the coachman, is also not presented at this point as having a mental life: he just drives the coach and horses, dressed in such-and-such a fashion. Presently, we shall look at another passage, which depicts a more complex situation, but first, let us briefly discuss the question of the observer. The observer in the case of passage (1) is the author, we may say, and authors may be more or less obtrusive. Even the least obtrusive of writers, though, inevitably occupies some notional vantage-point with respect to the text world he/she is creating (think of the camera-position in a movie, for example). It is from this vantage-point that the basic deictic building-blocks of the text world are organized. However, authors often have not only locations in space and time, they also have opinions, and these opinions will colour what they select to talk about as well as the language they choose to talk about it. This is why I said earlier that, in many cases, we need to be aware that someone was responsible for creating the text we are reading, since the language chosen and the topics selected may well be slanted towards a particular viewpoint. We will see examples of this later, but now we may look at the more complex situation in passage (2):

(2) He looked further out to sea. A huge roller was forming out beyond the surf, one of those freak storm waves that gather the energy of a dozen smaller waves . . . the wave peak collapsed in a crash that shook the gravel beneath Brennan's feet and exploded in echoes against the face of the cliff above him.

The echo of a bomb.

They'd gone to Munich for the Fasching, the carnival, at Jane's insistence; she'd been worried for some months that he'd been driving himself too hard. In those days he was a case officer at the CIA station in Bonn . . .

They'd arrived Saturday morning; Saturday evening they started off for the Augustiner-Keller beer hall – Jane had a fondness for German beer – and, just as they were leaving the hotel, it started to snow. She'd insisted he go back up to the room and put on a scarf; he was recovering from a touch of bronchitis. Grumbling, he did so, while she waited on the hotel steps.

He was about to enter the elevator when the terrorists' car bomb went off on the other side of the street. The blast smashed his wife through the glass doors of the hotel entrance, and then drove her thirty feet across the lobby into a marble pillar.

(Jones 1990: 18–19)

In this passage, the text world contains the character Brennan standing alone by the sea-shore. The crash of a wave against the cliffs reminds him of the noise of a bomb, and propels him back to the memory of his wife's death in a bomb-blast in Munich. The flashback-world is built up with past perfect tense markers: 'They'd gone to Munich', 'she'd been worried', 'he'd been driving', 'They'd arrived'; and a time adverbial: 'In those days'. The plot-advancing part, though, settles down into normal narrative past tense. Since this is a memory of the character, it is presented as something which is inaccessible in the text world, so it does not carry the same reliability for the reader (a discourse participant), as a narration vouched for directly by the author (also a discourse participant). This inaccessibility is shown by depicting these parts as falling outside the text world space (see Figure 11.2). In this case, the sound of the wave crashing against the cliff triggers the memory of a bomb-explosion, by way of a metonymic link between loud noise and explosions. The memory is conveyed in the form of a flashback depicting a traumatic event in Brennan's life. Thus the sound of the wave causes a metonymic association with the sound of an explosion, and this

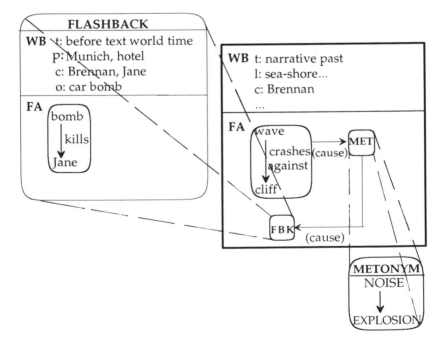

Figure 11.2 Warsaw Concerto text world

causes a flashback to an incident from memory in which a bomb explodes.

It was pointed out earlier that the flashback and the metonymy are depicted here as separate from the text world scene, though both taking their point of origin from it. This is because they represent sub-worlds: these are cognitive spaces, like text worlds, but which are conceptually distinct from the text world they arise from. Their distinctiveness can come about for a number of reasons: first, if they depart from the basic deictic parameters defined for the text world (e.g. a flashback, which departs from the time specification of the text world; direct speech is another kind of example); second, if they take place in a character's mind, rather than in the simple presentation of the author (e.g. the metonymy in Figure 11.2, which is in Brennan's mind, though triggered by something in the text world, and the resulting flashback is also in his mind; other kinds of example would be beliefs, hopes, intentions, etc., entertained by characters); third, when there is talk of probabilities, possibilities, improbabilities, impossibilities: none of these is 'real' with respect to the text world; rather they are speculations, and they too form sub-worlds. All the examples in (2) happen to be character-accessible sub-worlds; we readers have a privileged glimpse into the workings of a character's mind, thanks to the nature of fiction, but if we were really viewing this scene, we would only see Brennan standing on the cliff-top, and hear the noise of the waves. We know as readers that our ability to see inside Brennan's head is a fiction, brought to us by courtesy of an omniscient author. Apart from such character-accessible sub-worlds, though, there also exist participant-accessible sub-worlds, in which the author presents flashbacks, beliefs, memories, speculations, hypotheses, etc., directly and not through a character.

The author, of course, is a very important person in the process of creating a text world. But we should not forget that the author creates only a text; he/she will have a particular text world in mind, but there is no guarantee at all that the reader will manage to reproduce the same text world on reading that text. We cannot say that the author's text world is the definitive one, since, in fact, there is no such thing. We may say, therefore, that a text world does not come into being until each of the three elements – author, text and reader – are present. Since the interaction between an author, his text and reader X will be different from that between the author, his text and reader Y, a given text may correspond to many possible text worlds (though they may all be very close to one another). Furthermore, we may think of the text as providing the medium through which the author and the reader negotiate for a particular text world.

Let us now apply these ideas to a longer and more substantial text, the first chapter of E. M. Forster's *A Passage to India*:

(3)   Except for the Marabar Caves – and they are twenty miles off – the city of Chandrapore presents nothing extraordinary. Edged rather than washed by the River Ganges, it trails for a couple of miles along the bank, scarcely distinguishable from the rubbish it deposits so freely. There are no bathing steps on the river front, as the Ganges happens not to be holy here; indeed, there is no river front, and bazaars shut out the wide and shifting panorama of the stream. The streets are mean, the temples ineffective, and though a few fine houses exist they are hidden away in gardens or down alleys whose filth deters all but the invited guest. Chandrapore was never large or beautiful, but two hundred years ago it lay on the road between Upper India, then imperial, and the sea, and the fine houses date from that period. The zest for decoration stopped in the eighteenth century, nor was it ever democratic. There is no painting and scarcely any carving in the bazaars. The very wood seems made of mud, the inhabitants of mud moving. So abased, so monotonous is everything that meets the eye, that when the Ganges comes down it might be expected to wash the excrescence back into the soil. Houses do fall, people are drowned and left rotting, but the general outline of the town persists, swelling here, shrinking there, like some low but in-destructible form of life.

Inland, the prospect alters. There is an oval Maidan, and a long sallow hospital. Houses belonging to Eurasians stand on the high ground by the railway station. Beyond the railway – which runs parallel to the river – the land sinks, then rises again rather steeply. On the second rise is laid out the little civil station, and viewed hence Chandrapore appears to be a totally different place. It is a city of gardens. It is no city, but a forest sparsely scattered with huts. It is a tropical pleasaunce washed by a noble river. The toddy palms and neem trees and mangoes and pepul that were hidden behind the bazaars now become visible and in their turn hide the bazaars. They rise from the gardens where ancient tanks nourish them, they burst out of stifling purlieus and unconsidered temples. Seeking light and air, and endowed with more strength than man or his works, they soar above the lower deposit to greet one another with branches and beckoning leaves, and to build a city for the birds. Especially after the rains do they screen what passes below, but at all times, even when scorched or leafless, they glorify the city to the English people who inhabit the rise, so that new-comers cannot believe it to be as meagre as it is described, and have to be driven down to acquire disillusionment. As for the civil station itself, it provokes no emotion. It charms not, neither does it repel. It is sensibly planned, with a red-brick club on its brow, and farther back a grocer's and a cemetery, and the bungalows are disposed along roads that intersect at right angles. It has nothing hideous in it, and only the view is beautiful; it shares nothing with the city except the overarching sky.

The sky too has its changes, but they are less marked than those of the vegetation and the river. Clouds map it up at times, but it is normally a dome of blending tints, and the main tint blue. By day the blue will pale down into white where it touches the white of the land, after sunset it has a new circumference – orange, melting upwards into tenderest purple. But the core of blue persists, and so it is by night. Then the stars hang like lamps from the immense vault. The distance between the vault and them is as nothing to the distance behind them, and that further distance, though beyond colour, last freed itself from blue.

The sky settles everything – not only climates and seasons but when the earth shall be beautiful. By herself she can do little – only feeble outbursts of flowers. But when the sky chooses, glory can rain into the Chandrapore bazaars or a benediction pass from horizon to horizon. The sky can do this because it is so strong and so enormous. Strength comes from the sun, infused in it daily; size from the prostrate earth. No mountains infringe on the curve. League after league the earth lies flat, heaves a little, is flat again. Only in the south, where a group of fists and fingers are thrust up through the soil, is the endless expanse interrupted. These fists and fingers are the Marabar Hills, containing the extraordinary caves.

(Forster 1924/1984: 1–3)

We shall start by building up the basic details of the text world underlying passage (3). Remember that a text world is simply a representation of the cognitive space which the author and the reader are co-operating to form between them. For several reasons, this cognitive space is not a fixed, strictly-defined scene. First, no two readers bring exactly the same knowledge to bear in interpreting a text. Second, strictly speaking, even the same reader is in possession of a different body of knowledge on different occasions of reading the same text (since he/she will have done, experienced, learnt other things in the meantime) – and this applies to the author, too, of course, who we can think of as equivalent to a (somewhat privileged) reader. Third, the text itself is read through time, so it is accurate to think of the scene which it depicts as developing. When we also bring the function-advancing elements into the equation, which represent, for example, events, we can see that our representation must be thought of not as a picture or a photograph, but rather as a movie-film, made up of a large number of 'frames', succeeding each other in time.

Let us now go through passage (3), picking out the deictic elements which build up the successive frames of this text world. We can at least tentatively take it paragraph by paragraph. Paragraph 1 is mainly in the simple present tense: the text is rather like a travel guide, describing a place as it is currently. The place, of course, is the city of Chandrapore. There are no real individualized characters, only generics (the invited guest, the inhabitants, people). There are plenty of objects, but they are all either parts of the city, associated with the city or located close to the city. In a word, they are all metonyms of the city: the Marabar Caves, the River Ganges, the rubbish, bazaars, the streets, the temples, a few fine houses, alleys, etc. In the middle of the paragraph, there is a short interlude in the simple past, providing a short history of Chandrapore, and using it to explain the few fine features of the place. This is a kind of flashback, but a participant-accessible one, since it is presented as a straightforward fact by the author, and the reader can simply accept it as factual.

Paragraph 2 is rather similar, simply in terms of the kind of deictic elements used. It is entirely in the guide-book present (with just one exception: 'were hidden'). The place has changed slightly, in the sense that the vantage-point (the camera-position, as it were) has moved back, so that we are given a different, and more inclusive, perspective of the scene, with the city and the river now just components of a larger view. Again, there are no real characters, only generic types (Eurasians, man, the English people, new-comers), while the objects are again metonyms of the place in general (Maidan, hospital, houses, railway, river, land, rise, civil station, gardens, etc.). Paragraph 2 also has a kind of insert in the middle, but it is not any kind of flashback; rather, it is a re-evaluation of the description in paragraph 1, as seen from the different viewpoint. We can regard it as an application of the new focus, rather than reflecting a temporary deictic change (which is what a flashback does).

Paragraph 3 continues the same process: the deictic viewpoint changes again, bringing the sky into focus. The previous focus is reduced to a very small part of the new one (the vegetation and the river). The tense used is entirely present simple (with one apparent exception: 'will pale down'), and the place is the sky. There are still no characters, and now not even any generics. Objects are again metonymic with the sky: clouds, stars, vault.

Paragraph 4 is different. Again with one apparent exception ('shall be beautiful'), the tense is simple present. The place now broadens to include everything which has been focused on before, but from an all-encompassing perspective. There are now some characters of a sort, though they are not human (but, as we shall see, they are given human, or super-human, attributes): the sky, the earth, the sun. Objects are again metonymic upon these (flowers, the Chandrapore bazaars, horizon, strength, size, the Marabar Hills, the caves).

Let us now look at the function-advancing part of the text. Paragraphs 1–3 are almost exclusively descriptive: thus, the function being advanced is that of scene description. This explains why there is so much metonymy, a common feature of descriptions; it also tells us not to expect too many events, and such events as there are will be subsidiary in some way (e.g. 'new-comers . . . have to be driven down', encoding not a single event, but a routine happening). Practically all the function-advancing expressions, then, will be shown by horizontal arrows, depicting steady states (qualities). A notable exception to this statement, at least on the face of it, is the insert in paragraph 2, which is full of very dynamic vocabulary ('rise', 'burst', 'seeking', 'soar', 'greet', 'beckoning', 'build', 'screen', 'glorify'). Note, however, that all this activity is metaphorical, a point which we shall return to.

Paragraph 4, on the other hand, the culmination of this first chapter, presents a rather more active face than has generally been the case up until now (with the exception of the insert in paragraph 2). Thus, apart from physical activity verbs ('do', 'rain', 'pass', 'infused', 'lies', 'heaves', 'thrust'), which are again metaphorical, we have mental and abstract activity verbs also: 'settles', 'chooses', 'infringe', 'interrupted'. However, 'containing' (in the penultimate line of paragraph 4) is somewhat ambiguous in sense between a sort of activity (or process) – at any rate a dynamic use – and a stative verb denoting a steady state.

I shall now at this stage present a text worlds diagram for our observations so far, though at this point omitting the flashback in paragraph 1 and the metaphorical uses elsewhere. We will return to these subsequently, in our examination of the sub-world level. There are also other features which the reader will have spotted, such as the large number of negatives in paragraph 1. We shall have to see whether these too fall under the heading of sub-world accessibility. Figure 11.3 will be rather schematic – I shall in other words only include in it representative or general information.

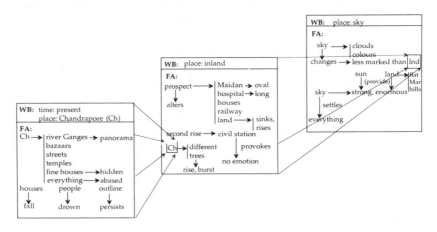

Figure 11.3 A Passsge to India text world (1)

Figure 11.3 should be interpreted like this: the scene is gradually described from a broadening perspective. The large squares represent separate, successive stages of this process. Since at each stage we are shown a wider vista, the later stages include the earlier ones, and are compared with them; the close detail of the earlier stages shrinks, as it were, to a more distant and simplified view (represented by a small square). The notation for this is meant to suggest the focusing of light rays by a lens – as in the viewfinder of a camera, for example.

As we shall shortly see, the notation for sub-worlds is rather similar: this is because there are important similarities between the concepts themselves. A focus, as we have seen, is a subsequent re-evaluation of a previous stage of text world, or part of it. A sub-world is a part of a text world which is outside the deictic definition which holds for that world. Both of them, then, are deictically distinct from their surrounding context: the focus because it is a return to an earlier viewpoint at a later stage, the sub-world because it is a departure to another viewpoint. An important difference, though, is that a focus is a concentrating of attention inwards, while a sub-world is an extension of view outwards. For this reason, the notation for the latter should be thought of as a cinematic projection (also, sub-worlds are shown with

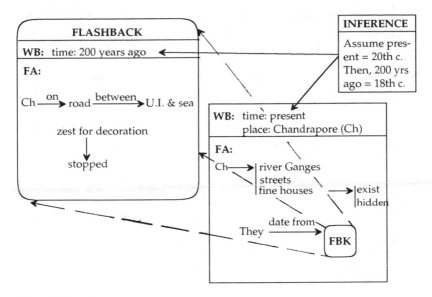

Figure 11.4 A Passage to India text world (2)

rounded corners). Let us look at a reasonably straightforward sub-world first, the little history lesson in paragraph 1 (see Figure 11.4).

The large square in Figure 11.4 is meant to be the same as the leftmost square in Figure 11.3, but it is displayed even more selectively here. The flashback is triggered by way of an explanation for the existence of fine houses amidst so much squalor. The deictic alternation in this case is the time-frame, which is two hundred years earlier. The inference-box deduces this as referring to the eighteenth century, which picks up the mention of the declining zest for decoration.

We may now turn to the question of the large number of negatives and related expressions in paragraph 1. Here is a list of them:

(a) straight negatives: 'nothing extraordinary', 'no bathing steps', 'not to be holy', 'no river front', 'never large or beautiful', 'nor was it ever democratic', 'no painting'
(b) negative modification: 'scarcely distinguishable', 'scarcely any carving', 'the very wood'
(c) words with negative meaning: 'trails', 'rubbish', 'shut out', 'mean', 'ineffective', 'hidden away', 'filth', 'deters', 'stopped', 'mud', 'abased', 'monotonous', 'excrescence', 'fall', 'drowned', 'left', 'rotting', 'persists', 'low'
(d) concessives: 'except for the Marabar Caves – and *they* are twenty

miles off', 'edged rather than washed', 'happens not to be holy', 'indeed', 'though a few fine houses exist', 'houses *do* fall, people *are* drowned, but . . .'

There are a number of questions which these expressions raise: first, what cumulative impression do they give? second, how does this actually work? third, how can we account for this? Opinions on the impression which this paragraph gives may very well vary, of course (see our previous discussion), but most readers are likely to agree that they carry away not only a picture of a dirty, squalid and totally unprepossessing place, but also that they share a sense of disappointment that such an exotic and promising location is so contrary to expectations.

Negatives and concessives work exactly in this way, in fact. Unlike positive sentences, negatives always operate in contrast to an expected state of affairs: expected in that it is normal or routine, or thought to be so. So, if you say 'John wasn't at Mary's party', this is in contrast to the previous idea or hope or expectation that John might have been at the party. If you say 'An aeroplane flew overhead', this is simply an observation; but if you say 'No aeroplane flew overhead', this must mean that you somehow expected one to. This happens throughout paragraph 1: 'There are no bathing steps on the river front'; the only reason for pointing this out is that in many other places along the Ganges, there are bathing steps. The same is true of words with negative meaning: you expect fine houses to be visible: these are hidden; you expect a river to flow, and wash its banks: this one merely trails along, and deposits rubbish freely. These expectations are cultural in nature: they come in fact from our knowledge-frames about India, rivers, cities, and so on. This is why the sentence 'There are no bathing steps on the river front' would be odd in a travel guide about Liverpool or New York (unless it were a guide written for Indians), while the sentence 'There are no ice-cream stalls on the river front', though perfectly true of Chandrapore, would nevertheless be extremely odd (yet for Liverpool or New York, perfectly normal).

Returning to the question of the effect all these negatives have, we can pick out one impression which will be important for our interpretation of the rest of the chapter, and indeed, for the whole novel, and that is the relative status and situation of the various groups of human beings in this place, as compared with the natural elements there. On the account of paragraph 1, human beings come out very poorly. The surroundings are squalid enough, and the inhabitants seem to be one with this degradation:

The very wood seems made of mud, the inhabitants of mud moving. So abased, so monotonous is everything that meets the eye, that when the Ganges comes down, it might be expected to wash the excrescence back into the soil. Houses do fall, people are drowned and left rotting, but the general outline of the town persists, swelling here, shrinking there, like some low but indestructible form of life.

(1984: 1)

They are equivalent, then, by the logic of this paragraph, to some lowly insect or microbe life-form.

Finally, how do we account for these phenomena in the model we have been using so far? Expectations, as we have seen, are part of the background of a text. The type we have looked at were cultural, and came from the frame-knowledge evoked by the entities and propositions in the text. Other kinds of expectations are built up out of personal experience of individuals and states of affairs: this also engenders frame-knowledge, but of a more personal type. Yet others come from what has actually been said and implied in the text itself: for example, if the text tells us that Bill, George and Susan are sitting on a couch talking about the World Series, we expect Bill, George and Susan to be present, even if they say nothing subsequently, until we are told otherwise. So, if the lights suddenly go out, and when they go on again, George says 'Susan's not here!' or 'Susan's gone!' or 'Where did Susan go?', this is because, like us, he expected her still to be there. To be brief, we can say that expectations form part of what is called the Common Ground of the discourse, the background knowledge necessary to understand not only the meaning of the words and sentences, but also the frames and inferences which they evoke. We can postulate, therefore, that negatives and concessives form sub-worlds also, since they constitute a departure from part of the deictic underlay of the discourse.

In order to account for this properly, we would have to show all the frame-knowledge which underlies the expectations in question. In fact, as has been my custom, I will be greatly selective in this explanation. However, there is an important point to be made first, and that is that there is more than one way of learning frame-knowledge. There are two, in fact. One is the usual way: by direct or indirect prior experience you acquire a set of facts, let us say, which are there in place when you happen to need them. So, for example, your knowledge about India might include images of people bathing in the Ganges, of richly carved decoration, of intricate buildings, and so on. The second way is by inference: because in some sense you know how negatives work, when you read 'There are no bathing steps on the river front', you immediately know that bathing steps would normally be expected, and you can add this deduced fact to your store. The result, of course, is identical.

In Figure 11.5, I shall assume prior knowledge, amassed in frames, and in contrast to which the negatives operate. Since frames encode all our general and personal knowledge, they may be expected to be very complicated affairs, overlapping and cross-referencing with each other in manifold ways. Some of these frames, furthermore, will not be based on straightforward classification (A is a B, A is part of B, A is a member of B), but rather on similarity, real or asserted (A is like B). This latter type is essentially how metaphor works. As usual, I shall not attempt to show anything like all this complexity in the diagram (see Figure 11.5), but will content myself with a rather schematic indication of the broad outlines.

Here is how Figure 11.5 should be read: the text world (still just the leftmost square in Figure 11.3) is shown with thicker lines. Around it are all the various types of knowledge with which we interpret the discourse in question: frames, containing general knowledge and connected information, including opposites (antonyms); inferences, or conclusions which can be deduced from other information which is present, and finally, the sub-worlds. The frames set up the complex network of expectations which we might hold about the set of topics under discussion; the text, by way of the negative sub-world, informs us where these expectations have been departed from. This leads us to draw a number of inferences about Chandrapore, and these inferences, via a conventional metonym ('a place is its inhabitants'), allow us to draw further inferences about the relationship between the city and its inhabitants. This then leads us to understand a metaphorical similarity between the inhabitants and the denizens of an organic heap of some kind.

I shall discuss one more point before drawing to a conclusion.[1] We have seen that the inhabitants of Chandrapore – the native Indians – come out of this description very badly. What about the other human beings in the vicinity (the British colonialists, and their assistants, the mixed-race Eurasians)? And what about the natural elements in the scene? The answer is that the other humans fare even worse. The political power-relationships mimic the height above sea-level (let us say): the colonialist English are at the top, with people of mixed race (the Eurasians) in the middle, and the native Indians at the bottom of the power ladder. We also carry a strong cultural assumption that humankind is at the top of the ecological scale – so below the Indians

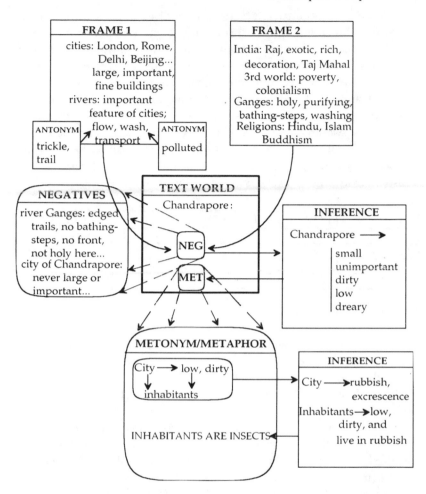

Figure 11.5 A Passage to India text world (3)

would be the local flora and fauna. This is the very common metaphor POWER IS UP.[2] However, this is not necessarily the pecking order from all points of view, as we are about to see.

In the first paragraph, the people of Chandrapore – that is, the native Indians – were characterized as mud moving, and the whole place was like some low but indestructible form of life. Compare this with the description of the Eurasians and the English in paragraph 2: the imagery describing their environment is predominantly geometrical and impersonal: oval, long, parallel, laid out, sensibly planned, disposed, intersect at right angles. The metaphor underlying these uses,

I suggest, is GEOMETRICAL IS LIFELESS. The natives by contrast may be a low form of life, but they are a form of life. In stark opposition to 'man and his works', however – both native and colonialist – is the vegetation. This is almost violent in its mobility and vitality: the trees rise, burst out, they seek light and air, and are endowed with strength, they soar and greet and beckon and build, and they glorify the city. The most powerful movement that mankind can summon up, by contrast, is swelling and shrinking. We can nevertheless say that MOVEMENT IS LIFE – the vegetation (and by extension the land, as opposed to the people) is what is truly living in this landscape. There is also an irony in the reversed topography (see Figure 11.6).

GROUP	POWER	TOPOGRAPHY	VITALITY
ENGLISH	TOP	SECOND (HIGHER) RISE	LEAST ANIMATE
EURASIANS	NEXT	FIRST (LOWER) RISE	NEXT LEAST ANIMATE
NATIVES	THIRD	GROUND LEVEL	MORE ANIMATE
VEGETATION	BOTTOM	IN THE GROUND	VERY ANIMATE

Figure 11.6 Power–vitality hierarchy

The vegetation is depicted as having movement – but oddly enough, it has no colour, except by implication (we assume it to be green normally, and brown when scorched – but this is nowhere made explicit). It is the sky which is the repository of colour, which is presented as associated with divinity (see below), hence presumably is a transcendental property. So the colour-scale adds an extra level, and subsequently follows the vitality scale: the sky at the top (colours fully specified), next the vegetation (colours strongly implied), then the natives (mud-colour, presumably), and finally the colonialists. The last paragraph re-defines the power hierarchy ('The sky settles everything') into what in business circles is called a 'flat structure': the sky has all true power; everything else is intrinsically powerless, and only enabled by association with the sky (see below). Thus we can say that, locally in this novel, COLOUR IS VITALITY, and we can draw further implications like EARTHLY POWER IS LIFELESS, EARTHLY POWER IS COLOURLESS.

The final two paragraphs of (3) reconcile the opposition in Figure 11.6 and at the same time render its earthly perspective obsolete: not only is the sky (which 'contains' Heaven, of course) described in terms of a temple ('dome of blending tints', 'stars hang like lamps from the immense vault'), and a kind of ultimate state of being, but it can also act divinely ('glory can rain', 'a benediction pass'). So, the land may be where the vegetation springs from, but it is the sky which is responsible for this ('By herself [the earth] can do little – only feeble outbursts of flowers'). Thus the vitality quotient – which, as we have seen, runs counter to both the topography and the political power – is actually in the gift of the sky. The sun infuses the earth with its power, and the vegetation reflects this directly. The native Indians, closer to the earth (even appearing to be made of it), benefit from some of this vitality, having at least life and movement, while the 'ruling classes', far away from the life-giving earth, lack vitality entirely. The sky, then, which is highest of all, restores the topographical metaphor: POWER IS UP, while at the same time 'explaining' the contrary direction of the vitality quotient. The colonialists are in a sense suspended between sky (strength) and land (size), thus partaking of neither. Figure 11.7 shows how these various metaphors combine to provide the underlying message – the sub-text – of this chapter.

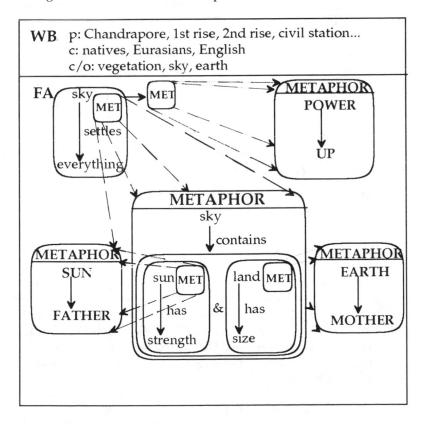

Figure 11.7 A Passage to India text world (4)

This is the logic by which these metaphors work, yielding a rich interpretation of this prose passage:

If power is up, then down is powerlessness; thus sky and sun are powerful, earth and things of the earth are powerless.
If the sun is the father, then the father has power; if the earth is the mother, then the mother is powerless.
But the mother breeds life, so the earth breeds life.
Thus entities near the earth have life, entities away from the earth lack life.
The sun gives light and colour, and the sun is powerful, so light and colour are the signs of power.
So, entities close to the earth have life, but lack power; entities closer to the sky have power, but lack life. Only the vegetation bridges the gulf between high and low: it combines life and power into vitality.

These are the inferences which may be drawn from the metaphorical sub-worlds which we have postulated for paragraph 4. I have not shown them in a separate box this time because of their length: but the procedure is similar to the rather simpler one we explored in Figure 11.5. In Figure 11.5, inferences drawn from the negative sub-world led to a specific underlying metaphor for the paragraph; in Figure 11.7, inferences drawn from a number of conventional metaphorical and metonymic sub-worlds lead to the specific metaphors underlying paragraph 4.

SUGGESTIONS FOR FURTHER WORK

1 Identify all the world-building elements and the function-advancing elements in the following opening passages from stories or chapters of novels.

(a) Dick Boulton came from the Indian camp to cut up logs for Nick's father. He brought his son Eddy, and another Indian named Billy Tabeshaw with him. They came in through the back gate out of the woods, Eddy carrying the long cross-cut saw. It flopped over his shoulder, and made a musical sound as he walked. Billy Tabeshaw carried two big cant-hooks. Dick had three axes under his arm. He turned and shut the gate. The others went on ahead of him down to the lake shore where the logs were buried.

(Hemingway 1925/1964: 283)

(b) A huge red transport truck stood in front of the little roadside restaurant. The vertical exhaust pipe muttered softly, and an almost invisible haze of steel-blue smoke hovered over its end. It was a new truck, shining red, and in twelve-inch letters on its sides – OKLAHOMA CITY TRANSPORT COMPANY. Its double tires were new, and a brass padlock stood straight out from the hasp on the big black doors. Inside the screened restaurant a radio played, quiet dance music turned low the way it is when no one is listening. A small outlet fan turned silently in its circular hole over the entrance, and flies buzzed excitedly about the doors and windows, butting the screens. Inside, one man, the truck driver, sat on a stool and rested his elbows on the counter and looked over his coffee at the lean and lonely waitress.

(Steinbeck 1939/1946: 4)

(c) Fog everywhere. Fog up the river, where it flows among green aits and meadows; fog down the river, where it rolls defiled among the tiers of shipping, and the waterside pollutions of a great (and dirty) city. Fog on the Essex Marshes, fog on the Kentish heights. Fog creeping into the cabooses of collier-brigs; fog lying out on the yards, and hovering in the rigging of great ships; fog drooping on the gunwales of barges and small boats. Fog in the eyes and throats of ancient Greenwich pensioners, wheezing by the firesides of their wards; fog in the stem and bowl of the afternoon pipe of the wrathful skipper, down in his close cabin; fog cruelly pinching the toes and fingers of his shivering little 'prentice boy on deck. Chance people on the bridges peeping over the parapets into a nether sky of fog, with fog all round them, as if they were up in a balloon, and hanging in the misty clouds.

(Dickens 1853/1971: 49)

2 Draw diagrams showing the text world and any sub-worlds for the following texts:

(a) The five men were spread out like the points of a five-pointed star. They had dug with their knees and hands and made mounds in front of their heads and shoulders with the dirt and piles of stones. Using this cover, they were linking the individual mounds up with stones and dirt. Joaquín, who was eighteen years old, had a steel helmet that he dug with and he passed dirt in it.

He had gotten this helmet at the blowing up of the train. It had a bullet hole through it and everyone had always joked at him for keeping it. But he had hammered the jagged edges of the bullet hole smooth and driven a wooden plug into it and then cut the plug off and smoothed it even with the metal inside the helmet.

When the shooting started he had clapped this helmet on his head so hard it banged his head as though he had been hit with a casserole and, in the last lung-aching, leg-dead, mouth-dry, bullet-spatting, bullet-cracking, bullet-singing run up the final slope of the hill after his horse was killed, the helmet had seemed to weigh a great amount and to ring his bursting forehead with an iron band. But he had kept it. Now he dug with it in a steady, almost machine-like desperation . . .

(Hemingway 1940/1964: 262)

(b) 'When I was a child I thought there was a dragon living here in an old dug-out down there among those trenches . . . .'

'Once I saw smoke coming out of a trench and I thought it was the dragon . . .'

'All the world hated my dragon and wanted to kill him. They were afraid of the smoke and the flames which came out of his mouth when he was angry. I used to steal out at night from my dormitory and take him tins of sardines from my tuck-box. He cooked them in the tin with his breath. He liked them hot.'

'But did that *really* happen?' [original emphasis]

'No, of course not, but it almost seems now as though it had. Once I lay in bed in the dormitory crying under the sheet because it was the first week of term and there were twelve endless weeks before the holidays, and I was afraid of – everything around. It was winter, and suddenly I saw the window of my cubicle was misted over with heat. I wiped away the steam with my fingers and looked down. The dragon was there, lying flat in the wet black street, he looked like a crocodile in a stream.'

(Greene 1978: 59–60)

(c) I decided not to go down to the cafeteria for breakfast. It would only mean getting dressed, and what was the point of getting dressed if you were staying in bed for the morning. I could have called down and asked for a breakfast tray in my room, I guess, but then I would have to tip the person who brought it up and I never knew how much to tip. I'd had some very upsetting experiences trying to tip people in New York.

(Plath 1963/1972: 43)

NOTES

1   This discussion is taken from Werth (1994).
2   See the discussions in Lakoff and Johnson (1980: chapter 4), Lakoff and Turner (1989: 149) on CONTROL IS UP; see also the latter, chapter 4, on 'The Great Chain of Being'.

REFERENCES

Dickens, C. (1853/1971) *Bleak House*, Harmondsworth: Penguin.

Forster, E. M. (1924/1984) *A Passage to India*, Harmondsworth: Penguin.

Gardner, H. (ed.) (1957) *The Metaphysical Poets*, Harmondsworth: Penguin.

Greene, G. (1978) *The Human Factor*, Harmondsworth: Penguin.

Hemingway, E. (1925/1964) 'The Doctor and the Doctor's Wife' from *In Our Time*, in *The Essential Hemingway*, Harmondsworth: Penguin.

—— (1940/1964) *For Whom the Bell Tolls*, in *The Essential Hemingway*, Harmondsworth: Penguin.

Jones, D. (1990) *Warsaw Concerto*, London: Futura.

Lakoff, G. and Johnson, M. (1980) *Metaphors We Live By*, Chicago: Chicago University Press.

Lakoff, G. and Turner, M. (1989) *More Than Cool Reason*, Chicago: Chicago University Press.

Plath, S. (1963/1972) *The Bell Jar*, New York: Bantam Books.

Steinbeck, J. (1939/1946) *The Grapes of Wrath*, New York: Bantam Books.

Thackeray, W. (1848/1968) *Vanity Fair*, Harmondsworth: Penguin.

Werth, P. N. (1994) 'Extended Metaphor: A Text World Account', *Language and Literature* 3, 2: 79–103.

12 Working with sexism

What can feminist text analysis do?

Sara Mills

EDITOR'S PREFACE

In an introductory note to his novel *London Fields* (1989), Martin Amis states that he considered *The Murderee* as a possible title for the novel before rejecting it for *London Fields*. The murderee is Nicola Six, who has the power of seeing into the future. She knows – and the reader knows – that she is going to be killed, though Amis misleads us about who the murderer is, and only reveals it to us in the surprise ending. In the meantime, Nicola, the 'love actress' (201), the 'performing artist' (202), is playing tricks on the two male protagonists, Keith Talent and Guy Clinch. There is a voyeuristic element about the way she drives Guy mad with desire by refusing to give herself to him, or rather giving herself to him literally inch by inch. This prolonged striptease or 'marathon seduction' (452) has the effect of delayed fulfilment for the male reader, with Nicola as a 'male fantasy figure' (260), an instrument for imaginary gratification. For the female reader, however, all this may well be – in the words of Amis's narrator himself – a 'thesaurus of miserable clichés' (325) and crude sexist stereotypes.

But can we be more precise about what is sexist and offensive in Amis's novel? One possibility would be to argue that its sexism can be located in the language, the linguistic choices that Amis makes. The proponent of this position would carry out a transitivity analysis (an analysis of the processes represented in the sentences and of the semantic roles played by the nominal groups), as developed by the well-known linguist M. A. K. Halliday; and one conclusion might well be that women in *London Fields* tend to be presented as sexual objects acted upon by male agents. Another possibility would be to contend that sexism resides within the more general ideological framework. Here it would be possible to study the extent to which the male protagonists including the narrator himself are 'written' by an ideology of macho behaviour – in the sense of John Fowles (1974/1986: 232–3), who makes the distinction between *writing* one's life as opposed to *being written* by a particular ideology.

In this chapter, however, Sara Mills argues convincingly that sexism is to be located not just in either particular linguistic expressions or within the general ideological framework but in cognitive structures which mediate between the two and which she refers to as *narrative schemata*. For instance, there is a basic schema of 'man rapes/murders woman'. Amis uses a variant on this schema, the sub-schema of the woman 'asking for it'. For Amis's heroine actually *wishes* to be acted upon, to bring about her own murder. Finally, Mills warns that such sexist schemata have to be resisted and deconstructed, because otherwise they can easily come to be accepted as part of a particular culture's commonsense model of reality.

J. J. W.

This chapter aims to focus on an analysis of a passage from Martin Amis's recent novel *London Fields* in order to answer the question of my title – what can feminist text analysis do when faced with sexist texts? Martin Amis is often viewed by feminists as a quintessentially sexist writer, but accusations of sexism, while necessary, do not help us to work with that sexism, to *do* something with it. It is because of my feeling that the term sexism is too general that I try in this chapter to narrow down on what constitutes a particular form of sexism within a literary text. In this way, I hope that the term sexism will be less a blanket accusation and more a description of a set of specific choices which can be located at both the level of language choice and propositional content and also at a higher discourse level. First, I set out how sexist texts may be defined and suggest various strategies which have been adopted so far by feminist linguists and literary theorists. Central to this discussion will be the notion that women are often portrayed as passive and as acted upon by a male agent. I then consider the way that a close analysis of the text's language can help the reader to expose the sexism embedded in a text, but I go on to argue that this alone is not sufficient, since sexism is not simply 'located' within individual language items in isolation. Thus, the final part of the chapter proposes that, in addition to analysis of language items, we look to larger-scale systems or schemata which determine the production of sexist language items. Thus, I am proposing an intermediate structure between the language items and the ideology of sexism. The chapter is therefore motivated by a dissatisfaction with analyses of sexism which either locate sexism in particular words or phrases, or locate sexism within a more general ideological frame-work. Instead I argue that there are structures which mediate between the ideology of sexism and particular words or grammatical choices.

The ideas developed in this chapter arose when I was reading a novel by Martin Amis: *London Fields*. Apart from feeling intensely irritated, depressed and bored by the book, because of the way female and male characters are represented, I also had a strange sensation of *déjà vu* while I was reading it – as if I had already read the book or that the plot had been borrowed from another novel. I felt irritated by what I perceived as the book's sexism, which seemed to me to pervade the book as a whole: the female characters seemed to be portrayed as stupid and as objects, usually sexual, and they seemed to be working towards their own destruction. The male characters also seemed to be lifeless vehicles of an ideology of macho behaviour. I was quite shocked that the options that the author had chosen for the female characters in particular were so retrograde, and yet at the same time I began to wonder why these characters seemed so familiar. I began to wonder what options were available to the reader when faced with sexism – was it simply a case of throwing down the book in anger, writing a critical review of it, advising people not to read it? Or could the reader perhaps work on this sexism in order to develop a theoretical awareness, not so much of the origins of sexism, but of the reasons that sexism is so repetitive, so familiar, so commonsense?

In order to examine the ways in which Amis's novel can be classified as sexist, let us first consider the opening passage:

(1) This is a true story but I can't believe it's really happening.

(2) It's a murder story, too. (3) I can't believe my luck.

(4) And a love story (I think), of all strange things, so late in the century, so late in the goddamned day.

(5) This is the story of a murder. (6) It hasn't happened yet. (7) But it will. (8) (It had better.) (9) I know the murderer, I know the murderee. (10) I know the time, I know the place. (11) I know the motive (*her* motive) and I know the means. (12) I know who will be the foil, the fool, the poor foal, also utterly destroyed. (13) And I couldn't stop them, I don't think, even if I wanted to. (14) The girl will die. (15) It's what she always wanted. (16) You can't stop people, once they *start*. (17) You can't stop people, once they *start creating*.

(Amis 1989: 1; emphasis in original)

The novel thus opens with a very knowing narrator who addresses the reader in a direct, intimate and informal way, letting the reader in on his plans. The short simple sentences imitate spoken discourse and the phrases in parentheses suggest an intimate tone of disclosure to the reader. At the same time that this passage signals itself as intimate, it also signals to the reader that it is a highly literary text, because of its playful use of language, for example: 'the foil, the fool, the poor foal' (sentence 12). The tone of this opening passage is very reminiscent of passages in John Fowles's work, where the narrator draws attention to the fictiveness of the story, but at the same time he suggests that he himself is not entirely in control of the story, in the process creating an element of shared knowledge and camaraderie with the reader.

But what struck me most of all was the word 'murderee' (sentence 9). I had never encountered this word before and yet as soon as I read it I knew that it referred to a female character and not to a male, and as I read further on in this opening paragraph my expectations were shown to be right, since the narrator refers to 'the girl' who will die (sentence 14) and her death is described as 'what she always wanted' (sentence 15). I was interested by the fact that when describing the murder of this female character certain linguistic choices were made around the question of agency. In order to try to locate more precisely the sexism within this passage, I would like to consider first some definitions of sexism by feminist theorists, and then I will go on to consider the way that agency can be represented.

SEXISM

Many feminist theorists have attempted to describe and combat sexism in texts. Sexism itself is a complex phenomenon which manifests itself in a number of different ways in language. Vetterling-Braggin (1981: 2) has stated that a statement is sexist 'if it creates, constitutes, promotes or exploits an unfair or irrelevant marking of the distinctions between the sexes'. In this way, language which presents the female as the 'marked' form and the male as the 'unmarked' or neutral form is sexist. Some feminist theorists have focused on the way that female characters are represented as a form of sexism, since they consider that female characters are treated in an altogether different way from male characters. For example, Kate Millett, in her book *Sexual Politics* (1969), demonstrated the way in which many male writers, such as Norman Mailer and D. H. Lawrence, depict female characters as if they only existed as sex objects for male consumption. Female characters are often described in sexual terms and are reduced to a catalogue of body parts, which the narrator (and the reader) survey in a voyeuristic way. Other feminist theorists, such as Judith Fetterly (1981), have focused on the way that texts address the reader as a male, and for her this constitutes a form of sexism. The implied reader of texts is, for Fetterly, male: women readers have therefore to decode texts as if they were masquerading as males.

Sexism is thus seen as something which can be detected through analysis of language and which somehow resides within the text. It is not necessarily seen as inherent in certain forms, as many critics assume, but it is seen as associated with certain language items, structures in texts or forms of address.

AGENCY

There has been a certain amount of feminist work on agency. Deirdre Burton's (1982) work on transitivity (that is, who does what to whom) has been very influential in feminist text analysis, in that her analysis demonstrates that certain systematic language choices in a text lead the reader to form certain kinds of overall impression. For example, Burton shows that if a writer chooses to describe a character using verbs which place the character systematically in the agent position only, then a certain type of text will result. For example, detective and murder stories frequently describe the detective using verbs of this type ('I followed'; 'I noted'; 'I traced', and so on). Burton concentrates in her analysis on the fact that many writers choose to use verbs to describe female characters which do not locate them in this agent position, but rather they are acted upon by other characters ('The doctor examined me'; 'The nurse leant over me', and so on). This leads to an overall view of the female characters as passive and as not having control over their lives. Burton's essay is useful in that she states so clearly that this language choice for female characters is pernicious and that there are other choices at the level of language items which could have been made. Other feminists have used her work and gone on to show that this choice at the level of transitivity may occur at particular narrative moments; for example, Shan Wareing (1990) has described the way that strong female characters, who are portrayed as acting in an independent way throughout a text, are often represented as 'acted upon' when sexual scenes are described. Thus Wareing shows that there are other narrative options for female characters but that they often conflict with narrative choices which are more clearly determined by sexist ideology.

As I have discussed in a recent essay (Mills 1994b), this type of examination of linguistic choices is extremely useful as an analytical tool, because it shows us that the choices that writers make about agency play a central role in the way that the general message of a text is constructed by the reader. However, it is nevertheless the case that the analyses generally tend to move from a study of language items to the positing of a more generalized sexism in too easy a way, and it is this move from language to ideology that I feel needs to be mapped out a little more. Tony Trew's analysis of the interface between language choice and ideology suggests ways in which this link might be made. Trew tries to urge us not to make too easy a link between linguistic items and overall meaning. He notes that:

> No simple one-to-one correspondence can be set up between the linguistic and theoretical processes, because the latter are structured sequences of the former, and can occur in various forms and because individual linguistic changes can occur in different kinds of sequence. A single linguistic transformation – like passivisation – does not have a fully determinate theoretical significance. But if it stands as the first in a sequence of changes that include deletion of agents, selective rewording, nominalisation and embedding . . . then that single linguistic change belongs to a structured sequence of changes, which as a whole has determinate theoretical or ideological significance
>
> (Trew 1979: 111–12)

Thus, it is not the individual language items themselves which have a particular meaning but those items in co-occurrence with other language items. Context and co-text here seem to be vital components in determining what particular language items can be said to mean. It seems to me therefore essential that in analysing individual language items, we consider them as part of a network of linguistic choices which can have particular ideological significance when those choices are taken as a whole. I would like now to analyse these choices in the passage from *London Fields* in order to consider whether there are linguistic choices which could be part of a larger network or ideological framework.

LINGUISTIC ANALYSIS

Let us look back to the passage from *London Fields* which I cited earlier in the chapter, and consider the way that actions and agency are represented. There are many ways of representing actions and who is responsible for them; take for example the following sentence:

(1) [The murder] hasn't happened yet (sentence 6).

In this example, the murder is described using the verb 'to happen'; this is a verb which does not reveal who has performed the action (the agent) and further, the verb makes the murder seem more like an event than an action, since generally things which 'happen' are those which are not motivated or decided upon, for example:

(2) The motorway accident happened because of fog (i.e. the drivers involved were not responsible for the accident).

If we re-write the sentence in example (1) to reveal who is plotting the murder, it is clearer that the agency in the text has been obscured:

(3) X hasn't murdered her yet.

In example (3), there is a human agent who appears at the front of the sentence (rather than the action itself appearing in this position) and he has responsibility for this motivated act. Sentences in close proximity in the text to example (1) back up this feeling that the murder is being described as if the person who is planning to commit the crime is not the person responsible; for example, the narrative continues, 'But it will. (It had better.)' (Sentences 7 and 8.) Here, it seems as if the narrator knows more about the murder than the murderer himself and it is he who wishes the murder to happen. If we consider another sentence from this paragraph:

(4) The girl will die (sentence 14),

we also see a similar kind of grammatical structure being used. Generally, when we are describing actions, the agent comes at the front of the sentence and the person who is affected by the action comes after the verb. Thus, in example (5), the person who performs the action is put in the position of the agent:

(5) X will kill the girl.

However, the choice which is in fact made in example (4) is to place the woman who is murdered in the position normally reserved for the agent, and this often has the effect of making the person who takes up this position seem in some sense to be the agent and to bear responsibility for the action.[1] Here again, a verb is chosen which does not foreground the agent – the girl will simply die, as if no-one brought about her death; it simply happened. Compare this to passive constructions which could have been used:

(6) The girl will be killed.
(7) The girl will be shot.

In examples (6) and (7), although the verbs do not reveal to us who has performed the action, they do suggest to us that the action was motivated – someone killed the woman, she did not simply die from natural causes as the verb which was used might suggest. Further to this, the sentence which follows example (4) in the text is:

(8) It's what she always wanted (sentence 15),

which again focuses on the girl and her wishes rather than the real agent of the murder.[2] Thus, the opening passage of this book seems to signal to the reader that she is responsible for her own murder, and that the murderer is actually only a poor 'foil' or 'fool'. In essence, the book is about the male protagonists, Keith Talent and Guy Clinch, and their involvement in the preparation for the murder of the 'girl', Nicola Six.[3] Nicola herself does not feature a great deal in the book and she is not described in anything more than very vague terms. However, the fact that she is described as wanting her own death began to remind me of a large number of other plots, specifically Muriel Spark's short story 'The Driver's Seat' (1970), where a female protagonist prepares herself for her own murder in a way which suggests that she had planned for it and wished for it. In a wide range of cultural images and texts there seems to be a message that women want things which are not in their interests; they are masochists – they are 'asking for it', and that the skilled interpreter will be able to read this message beneath the surface of women's outward behaviour.

There also seem to me to be a large number of plots in films where women are the victim of murders, and where the film opens with the murder of a woman as the problem which the film then goes on to 'solve'. Women characters are routinely stalked through empty office buildings and car parks and even their own homes in a way which does not seem to happen for male characters; when male characters are presented being stalked and killed they do at least have the means to fight back on equal terms with their killers. I found this complex of ideas around women being agents and being acted upon particularly in their own murders coalesced in the analysis of this passage from Amis and I have therefore tried in this chapter to find ways of describing what it is that is going on in this type of sexism. These types of narratives constituted sexism for me, but a peculiar and particular form of sexism which seemed much more specific than the general definitions that I had encountered in feminist work. I would like therefore to consider a way of describing the cognitive structures which I feel may be partly at work in the production of the linguistic choices which we located in the Amis passage.

NARRATIVE SCHEMATA

Robert Hodge and Gunther Kress, in their book *Social Semiotics* (1988), have attempted to look beyond a simple analysis of language items; they argue that 'a concentration on words alone is not enough' (Hodge and Kress 1988: vii). By this they mean that language items cannot be studied in isolation from the other language items with which they co-occur and also that language items, phrases or grammatical structures themselves cannot be seen as containing ideological meaning. They argue that 'to capture the contradiction characteristic of ideological forms, we will talk of ideological complexes, a functionally related set of contradictory versions of the world, coercively imposed by one social group on another on behalf of its own distinctive interests or subversively offered by another social group in attempts at resistance in its own interests' (Hodge and Kress 1988: 3). This notion of contradictory ideological complexes seemed to me to be of some value, since it is clear that the passage from Martin Amis does offer a message about the female character; but rather than thinking about it in terms of statements, as Vetterling-Braggin (1981) does as I mentioned above, it is possible to think of it in terms of a complex of statements which, taken together, combine to form an ideological viewpoint.

Hodge and Kress's book pointed out to me the necessity of some mediating structure between language items and ideology at a conceptual level. Although many theorists of ideology seem to feel that ideology works on individuals in a fairly straightforward way, it seemed useful to me to specify the way that there were many different elements within the ideology of sexism. As I mentioned earlier, Wareing (1990) has shown that it is possible for there to exist in a text two conflicting messages about female characters, one of which is an 'older' ideology which presents women as acted upon and passive within sexual relations, and the other which is a more 'modern' position which presents women characters as strong and active in the public sphere. It is clear therefore that sexism as an ideology is more complex than a simple representation of women in terms of a negative difference in relation to men.

What concerns me here is the way in which there may be certain narrative structures which lead to particular representations of women, and these narratives or schemata are the interface between language choice and ideology. In the study of artificial intelligence, the schema or scenario is a model of narrative format which individuals use to structure their thought and action sequences; these are stereotypical models for the processing of thought (see Brown and Yule 1983). Thus, the schema for going to a restaurant will involve opening moves such as entering the restaurant, being greeted by a waiter and asking for a table, and it will also map out the possibilities for ordering, eating and paying for food within the constraints of behaviour appropriate in restaurants. We do not generally need to think about the sequence of events within this train of actions because they form part of a larger structure which is familiar to us, because it is stereotypical. In some sense it is an idealized lowest common denominator of all the times we have been to restaurants, or have watched representations of other people going to restaurants.

In the same way, there are schemata for other events, and this makes it easier for us to deal with unexpected deviations from the schema, because we are able to deal with the general run of events automatically rather than having to consider each move in the narrative before proceeding. The notion of a narrative schema is obviously simplistic but it does help to explain the way in which there are certain plots which seem to us familiar and those which present themselves as marked or unfamiliar. Lynne Pearce (1993, personal communication) has examined the way that the narrative constraints of the romance determine the way that many people think about their relationships. She has found that it is difficult for people to think beyond the narrative frameworks which to them seem self-evident, for example, that one lives with someone that one falls in love with, that this entails monogamy and a downgrading of relationships with one's friends, and so on. Her work is an attempt to analyse the choices that people make in terms of their relationships in order for them to see that there are other choices that they could make. In a similar way, I was interested in the way that the narrative choices made by Martin Amis, which seemed to be part of an ideological complex, were difficult to 'see around' to find alternative roles for female characters.

Brown and Yule (1983: 247) note that in some strong versions of schema theory, 'schemata are considered to be deterministic, to predispose the experiencer to interpret his [sic] experience in a fixed way. We can think of racial prejudice, for example, as the manifestation of some fixed way of thinking about newly encountered individuals who are assigned undesirable attributes and motives on the basis of an existing schema for members of the race.' What I am arguing is that sexism is precisely operating at this level of schemata, but that in addition to there simply being ways of thinking about members of other groups, in this case women, there are narratives which involve certain ways of thinking about them. This does not mean that this is all that can be thought about women, but that these schemata are likely to be chosen in certain circumstances, even when there are other schemata which are more productive. In the instance under discussion, Martin Amis's narrator's choice of language items is certainly clearly brought about by the initial decision to present the female character as acting to bring about her own murder. Thus, it is not simply the case that the female character is acted upon, although that is important, but the fact that she wishes to be acted upon and paradoxically strives to bring that about. This seems to me to constitute a schema or narrative pattern which once embarked on entails in its wake all manner of linguistic choices and decisions. It is a schema which is familiar through a wide range of texts.

I would like now to consider what these narrative pathways or schemata might consist of. We can plot out the schema in the following way:

• An attractive female is described (often in a voyeuristic way).
• A male is described (the narrative takes his point of view).
• The male follows the female without her knowledge.
• The male plans to murder/rape the female (the reader has to share his point of view).
• The male manoeuvres/lures the female to an isolated place.
• The male murders/rapes the female.

This basic schema has a number of additional features which are optional, for example, it can continue:

• The narrator/detective/policeman hunts the murderer.

In some plots based on this schema, more time is spent on planning the murder than the actual murder itself: John Fowles's chilling novel *The Collector* (1963/1986), where a female character is stalked, held captive and then killed by someone who 'collects' her in the same way that one collects butterflies, is a good example of this; so is *London Fields*, except that here it is the murderee, Nicola Six, who plans her own murder. In yet other plots, the murder of the woman constitutes the initial problem which the rest of the text attempts to 'resolve', the murder itself only occupying a relatively minor part of the narrative.

Several features are interesting: first, that the plot necessarily has to be focalized on the male protagonist, that the female character has to be attractive, and that the murder/rape needs to be planned meticulously. If we follow Michael Hoey's (1980) narrative model and assume that narratives are constructed on the basis of a problem followed by its solution, we can see that the problem which the narrative proposes is the murder/rape of a female which is solved by the murderer being hunted and caught. However, a variant on this basic schema which can be seen in *London Fields* is that the problem is perhaps the female herself and the solution to this problem is that she assents to her own murder. There are various degrees of intensity of this narrative, so that women can be seen to be asking for intimacy, rape or murder when in fact their outward behaviour seems to signal that this is not what they want.

In much the same way as with racist knowledge, the reader has certain choices to make about these narrative schemata: whether to accept them as part of his/her knowledge and as commonsense or whether to react against them. This decision will depend on the reader's interests (in Hodge and Kress's sense) and their familiarity with other ways of thinking about the issues. There are some male readers who feel that it is in their interests to accept this schematic knowledge as part of their own knowledge; some male readers may not have come across knowledge which conflicts with this narrative in order to challenge it and think through alternatives; other males will reject the narrative, because they take pleasure in other narrative pathways for female and male characters, or because they have read feminist work and find some narratives retrograde and unchallenging. What feminist analysis needs to do is to focus on the way that this acceptance of sexist schemata works in the interests of some readers. Rather than simply dismissing the plot out of hand, it is necessary to map out in detail its constructed nature, so that these building blocks of thought are shown to be only one choice amongst many others. In this way, rather than readers feeling comfortable with this type of ideological complex, they will perhaps recognize it as a construction which they have the choice whether to accept or not.

CONCLUSION

It is clear that close textual analysis of texts which appear to be sexist is necessary to describe the characteristics of sexist ideology; however, what I have been arguing is that language analysis alone cannot help us make the link between language and ideology, because if we focus on individual language items we risk both excluding the context of the text and also the polyvalence of language items themselves. What is necessary is some intermediate stage or structure which determines the choice of language items. In this chapter I have tried to demonstrate that one of these structures might be narrative schemata. The familiarity I felt when reading this novel is due to the fact that narratives within ideological complexes like sexism are well-trodden pathways, which because of their familiarity take on an air of common-sense knowledge. It is only by describing these seemingly common-sense narratives that we will begin to expose their constructed nature and at the same time their perniciousness. This type of feminist analysis will, I hope, move us forward from blanket accusations of political incorrectness towards an analysis which is detailed enough to demonstrate to readers the way that certain texts offer us constructions which are retrograde; once those constructions have been described and 'made strange', it is to be hoped that readers will be able to find other narratives which are more productive.[4]

SUGGESTIONS FOR FURTHER WORK

1 Consider the plot of the novel by John Fowles, *The Collector*: how similar does the plot seem to the opening passage of *London Fields?* How closely does it adhere to the underlying schemata?

2 Make a list of all the plays, films, novels which are informed by this narrative schema.

3 Change the sex of the characters in the narrative schema, so that the male is female and vice versa. What changes are entailed? Can you think of any plots which are informed by such a narrative schema?

4 Describe other (narrative or non-narrative) schemata which make up our commonsense views of women and men. Find verbal and visual texts (literature, films, advertisements, etc.) which instantiate one or more of these schemata. Consider what linguistic choices might be determined by the choice of schema.

5 Consider, for example, the representation of child rearing in popular films. Analyse the way that males and females have specific roles in these schemata which are currently being re-defined and re-negotiated. What linguistic choices are entailed?

6 Consider a stereotypically machismo narrative – a war film or novel, an action film, etc. – and analyse the roles of both males and females within the narrative. What effect do these roles within these schemata have for the development of masculinity?

NOTES

1 For a fuller discussion of this point, see Trew (1979), Fairclough (1989) and Mills (forthcoming).

2 It should be noted that the term 'girl' here is used to refer to a woman.

3 Of course, because the writer is Martin Amis, there is a twist to the plot, and it is far less simple than this account might suggest; but the cleverness and mystery is located at the level of who killed the woman rather than at the level of her role in being killed.

4 This chapter is a substantially revised version of a section in my forthcoming book *Feminist Stylistics*, London: Routledge. I would like to thank Jean Jacques Weber for his extremely useful and constructive comments on a first draft of this chapter.

REFERENCES

Amis, M. (1989) *London Fields*, Harmondsworth: Penguin.

Brown, G. and Yule, G. (1983) *Discourse Analysis*, Cambridge: Cambridge University Press.

Burton, D. (1982) 'Through Glass Darkly: Through Dark Glasses', in R. Carter (ed.) *Language and Literature*, London: Allen and Unwin: 195–214.

Fairclough, N. (1989) *Language and Power*, London: Longman.

Fetterly, J. (1981) *The Resisting Reader*, Bloomington: Indiana University Press.

Fowles, J. (1963/1986) *The Collector*, London: Pan Books.

—— (1974/1986) *The Ebony Tower*, London: Pan Books.

Hodge, R. and Kress, G. (1988) *Social Semiotics*, Oxford: Polity Press/Blackwell.

Hoey, M. (1980) *On the Surface of Discourse*, London: Allen and Unwin.

Millett, K. (1969) *Sexual Politics*, New York: Doubleday.

Mills, S. (1991) *Discourses of Difference: Women's Travel Writing and Colonialism*, London: Routledge.

—— (ed.) (1994a) *Gendering the Reader*, Hemel Hempstead: Harvester Wheatsheaf.

—— (1994b) 'Close Encounters of a Feminist Kind: Transitivity and Pop Lyrics', in K. Wales (ed.) *Feminist Linguistics in Literary Criticism*, Woodbridge, Suffolk: Boydell and Brewer.

—— (forthcoming) *Feminist Stylistics*, London: Routledge.

Mills, S., Pearce, L., Spaull, S. and Millard, E. (1989) *Feminist Readings/Feminists Reading*, Hemel Hempstead: Harvester Wheatsheaf.

Trew, T. (1979) 'Theory and Ideology at Work', in R. Fowler, R. Hodge, G. Kress and T. Trew (eds) *Language and Control*, London: Routledge and Kegan Paul: 94–116.

Vetterling-Braggin, M. (ed.) (1981) *Sexist Language: A Modern Philosophical Analysis*, Littlefield: Adam and Co.

Wareing, S. (1990) 'Women in Fiction: Stylistic Modes of Reclamation', *Parlance* 2, 2: 72–85.

13 Strategy and contingency

David Birch

EDITOR'S PREFACE

Critical discourse analysis is a rapidly developing branch of linguistics which aims at revealing the implicit social, political and ideological mechanisms at work in spoken or written texts. Such mechanisms are implicit or hidden because people are not generally conscious of the causes and consequences of the ideologically loaded language they are using. They have lost this consciousness through a process of inculcation. By being persistently exposed to politically and socially dominant norms and values in numerous written and spoken texts, in the mass media, in books, etc., but also in their everyday conversations, people have been induced to naturalize their beliefs, to see them as normal, even to the extent of treating them as matters of mere common sense.

It will be obvious that hidden ideologies in texts cannot be directly inferred from their formal features. Therefore, to expose their ideologies, texts need to be treated as discourse, that is, they must be embedded in a context of social interaction, where speakers/writers and hearers/readers produce and interpret texts against a background of naturalized beliefs and commonsense assumptions. From this it follows that, though an analysis of the formal features of texts (phonology, lexis, syntax) may provide cues for their interpretation, their use in discourse, that is, as social practice, requires additional tools of analysis. These have recently been supplied by pragmatics, speech act theory, discourse analysis, the co-operative principle and politeness in conversational behaviour, cognitive science, artificial intelligence and the coherence principle, all of which, for that matter, lie at the root of the basic ideas of this book.

By way of an appropriate illustration of discourse as a strategic and political act, Birch asks us to consider a piece from *The Songlines*

(1987), Bruce Chatwin's fictionalized account of his travels in Australia. The title is one of the European renderings, the other being 'Dreaming-tracks', of the Aboriginal words 'Footprints of the Ancestors' or the 'Way of the Law' for the labyrinth of invisible pathways which meander all over Australia (Chatwin 1987: 2). One of the author's guides explains to him

> how each totemic ancestor, while travelling through the country, was thought to have scattered a trail of words and musical notes along the line of his footprints, and how these Dreaming-tracks lay over the land as 'ways' of communication between the most far-flung tribes.
> 'A song', he said, 'was both map and direction-finder. Providing you knew the song, you could always find your way across country.'
>
> (Chatwin 1987: 13)

The author is intrigued by the indigenous system of land tenure and land use, which appears to be based on the principle of collective experience, in contrast to the Western system, which is based on the principle of material acquisition. In consequence, his travel story actually becomes an account of a double journey: his physical wanderings through the Australian Outback and his intellectual exploration of the nature and implications of the Aboriginal songlines (Huggan 1991: 62).

The passage Birch has chosen for a critical analysis comes from the author's travelogue of his physical wanderings through the Australian back-country. One day at lunchtime he finds himself in a roadside pub, which turns out to be a microcosm of present-day Australia, in that it is a conglomeration of many races, nationalities and cultures. Therefore, it comes as no surprise that the author's description teems with character classifications such as 'truckies', 'Outback male', 'tourists', 'the blacks', 'a Spaniard', and a great many more. Since such character labelling has proved to be a powerful ideological weapon, Birch's critical analysis challenges our prejudiced views and naturalized interpretations, and brings home to us that we, as readers, are ourselves responsible for the meanings we construct from these labels, and not the author.

P. V.

Many analysts are now no longer interested in simply studying a text 'for its own sake'. Many now recognize that communication is a strategic and a political act requiring a critical approach to analysis, where we are no longer just interested in what communication is, but in why communication means; no longer just interested in what a text means but in how discourse means.

Traditionally, linguistic/stylistic analysis of texts argued that the structures of language could somehow be separated from language use, and, often, that particular language communities had a specific grammar of language which pre-exists social processes. This implied, of course, that language existed separately from the people who used it, and that language and its 'use' in society was, more often than not, a relatively *ad hoc*, and often arbitrary, process of making meanings.

There are problems with this traditional view because, generally speaking, the forms of language we 'use' are not freely chosen. Language choices are made according to a series of political, social, cultural and ideological constraints. These constraints mean that people can be manipulated, kept 'in good order' and assigned inferior/superior roles and status by a system of social strategies which involve power, order, subordination, solidarity, cohesion, antagonism, pleasure, and so on, all of which are an integral part of the control systems of societies.

Where there is control, there is conflict, and where there is conflict there is always politics. No act of communication, no matter how seemingly simple and innocent, can escape this politics. No act of communication – no act of language – pre-exists reality, and no reality, no matter how familiar, pre-exists the political/conflictual interactions and interpretations involved in communication. All communication is consequential, i.e. it has significance beyond its own form and structures, for the people and institutions involved in constructing and interpreting, not just the communicative act itself, but also the consequences of that act.

No act of communication is innocent. There are always consequences, and what that means, therefore, is that communication is always an interested activity. Understanding the interests that drive the construction and interpretation of communication, i.e. the way we make sense of the world, the way we determine the realities of the world, the way we make meanings for ourselves and others, and the way we control those senses, realities and meanings, involves us in understanding the politics of communication.

Those politics involve us in recognizing that as well as being consequential and interested, communication is also motivated. In other words, all acts of communication are designed not just to inform or to simply 'say' something, but are always, irrespective of the degree to which specific intent might be known by particular individuals, motivated to accomplish something.

Much of that accomplishment is naturalized by society, and institutions within society, through processes of inculcation, where, for the most part, people involved in accomplishing particular acts within communication would not consider that what they are 'saying' is actually 'doing' something at the same time. Many of the things we achieve and accomplish through communication seem so 'natural' to us that many of us would resist the idea that we are engaged in a political act when we are communicating. But we are. The politics that we are engaged in has simply become so familiar to us – so 'natural' to us, that we no longer see it as problematic or contentious. We no longer see it as politics at all.

The politics of communication has been naturalized to make it seem unproblematic, and the values of that unproblematic face of communication have been gradually inculcated into us over the years by the vested interests of those power groups and institutions within society that do not want the majority of people who communicate to be always fully aware of what they are doing. But all communication is situated in particular encounters, particular contexts and particular discursive frames. It is how communication is situated; why communication is situated; where communication is situated; when communication is situated and who it is situated with and for, which concentrates on the process of communication. This is a considerably more dynamic analytic procedure than simply concentrating on the what (or product) of communication.

And why do we need to be dynamic in what we do as analysts of text, language, communication and discourse? Because the whole process of making meanings is a dynamic one. Meanings do not exist outside of communication; they do not exist as finalized products available for use at any time – they exist only as part of a politics of interaction, involving people, society and institutions, struggling to privilege certain values over others, and battling to maintain, develop and extend power and status relations. In other words, communication is always contingent upon the ways in which certain groups, institutions, societies and individuals assign value to certain meanings. That value has nothing to do with fixed meanings in dictionaries, or 'natural' meanings that have developed over time. Value is always the product of conflict and struggle; of the powerful over the disempowered, and of processes of naturalization and inculcation.

What that means, therefore, is that communication – making meanings – is always a political activity long before it ever becomes linguistic. And what that, in turn, demands, is an analytic practice which is strategic long before it becomes linguistic. What that means, therefore, is developing ways of analysing the way we make sense – the way we make meanings – which go beyond the words and linguistic/stylistic structures of texts as such into the strategic twists and turns of discourse. It means developing an analytic vocabulary which, though it traditionally has not been part of linguistics/stylistics, can recognize that:

(a) Communication is always political before it is linguistic.
(b) Communication is always motivated, interested and situated.
(c) Communication is, therefore, always strategic.
(d) Communication always occurs in encounters and interactions.
(e) Communication is always about value.
(f) Communication is, therefore, always contingent.

To engage with these basic principles of communication as strategic and contingent within a framework of critical linguistics/stylistics, consider the following:

I had had to change buses in Katherine, on my way down to Alice from the Kimberleys.

It was lunchtime. The pub was full of truckies and construction workers, drinking beer and eating pasties. Most of them were wearing the standard uniform of the Outback male: desert boots, 'navvy' singlets to show off their tattoos, yellow hardhats and 'stubbies', which are green, tight-fitting, zipless shorts. And the first thing you saw, pushing past the frosted glass door, was a continuous row of hairy red legs and bottle-green buttocks.

Katherine is a stopover for tourists who come to see its famous Gorge. The Gorge was designated a National Park, but some Land Rights lawyers found a flaw in the legal documents and were claiming it back for the blacks. There was a lot of ill-feeling in the town.

I went to the men's room and, in the passage, a black whore pressed her nipples against my shirt and said, 'You want me, darling?'

'No.'

In the time I took to piss, she had already attached herself to a stringy little man on a bar-stool. He had bulging veins on his forearm, and a Park Warden's badge on his shirt.

'Nah!' he sneered. 'Yer dirty Gin! You couldn't excite me. I got me missus. But if you sat on the bar here, and spread your legs apart, I'd probably stick a bottle up yer.'

I took my drink and went to the far end of the room. I got talking to a Spaniard. He was short, bald and sweaty, and his voice was high-pitched and hysterical. He was the town baker. A few feet away from us, two Aboriginals were starting, very slowly, to fight.

The older Aboriginal had a crinkled forehead and a crimson shirt open to the navel. The other was a scrawny boy in skin-tight orange pants. The man was drunker than the boy, and could scarcely stand. He supported himself by propping his elbows on his stool. The boy was shrieking blue murder and frothing from the side of his mouth.

The baker dug me in the ribs. 'I come from Salamanca,' he screeched. 'Is like a bullfight, no?'

Someone else shouted, 'The Boongs are fighting,' although they weren't fighting – yet. But the drinkers, jeering and cheering, began shifting down the bar to get a look.

Gently, almost with a caress, the Aboriginal man tipped the boy's glass from his hand, and it fell and shattered on the floor. The boy stooped, picked up the broken base and held it like a dagger in his palm.

The truckie on the next stool poured out the contents of his own glass, smashed its rim against the lip of the counter, and shoved it in the older man's hand. 'Go on,' he said, encouragingly. 'Give it 'im.'

The boy lunged forward with his glass, but the man parried him with a flick of the wrist. Both had drawn blood.

'Olé!' shouted the Spanish baker, his face contorted into a grimace. 'Olé! Olé! Olé!'

The bouncer vaulted over the bar and dragged the two Aboriginals outside on to the sidewalk, across the tarmac, to an island in the highway where they lay, side by side, bleeding beneath the pink oleanders while the road-trains from Darwin rumbled by.

I walked away but the Spaniard followed me.

'They are best friends,' he said. 'No?'

(Chatwin 1987: chapter 8)

A theory of communication which considers language to be strategic and contingent before it is linguistic means that any analysis of the texts of that language will not be concerned at all with intrinsic meanings of a text, but with the ways in which a text might be read from different political positions. In that respect, analysis is no longer an attempt to 'recover' meanings by description, but is rather a social and political commentary on the way meanings are made to privilege particular ideologies and reading positions. Those ideologies and positions are often not fully known to us. Often we assume a shared knowledge of them. We imagine them – building up a picture of what we think – imagine – they might be like, reading the text through all the other texts we have ever encountered before and constructing, intertextually, what we imagine the appropriate meanings may be.

Just as we have to find ways in which to distinguish different communities in the way that they have been imagined as real, for example, as 'Australia', 'European Community', 'China', 'Japan', and so on, because it is only in the ways that these communities are imagined that they come to have any existence at all, so we have to imagine the existence of meanings as real, using intertextual knowledge to build up a picture of what we can usefully constitute as real in any given context. Just as no single nation or community is synonymous with all humanity, so no meaning is ever synonymous with a single reality – a single way of making sense – a single way of thinking about the world. Meaning, like the concept of nation and community, is contingent.

So, in reading the passage from Bruce Chatwin's *The Songlines*, ask yourself the question, 'Whose dictionary am I using in understanding the language of the text?' And then ask yourself, 'How many dictionaries am I using?'

Assuming, for example, we isolate a couple of lexical fields like place names: Katherine, Alice, the Kimberleys, Katherine Gorge, National Park, Salamanca, Darwin, and character classifications: truckies, construction workers, the Outback male, tourists, Land Rights lawyers, the blacks, a black whore, darling, a stringy little man, Park Warden, Yer dirty Gin, missus, a Spaniard, the town baker, two Aboriginals, the older Aboriginal, the other, a scrawny boy, the man, the boy, the baker, someone else, the Boongs, the drinkers, the Aboriginal man, the truckie, the older man, the man, the Spanish baker, the bouncer, the two Aboriginals, the Spaniard, best friends; no matter how familiar these classifications might appear to us, none of them are unproblematic and innocent. All are strategies of character labelling which are contingent upon different sets of values, different intertextualities and different regimes of reading. Familiarity with words, expressions, ideas and concepts can often lead us to suppose that we 'know' their meaning, and so therefore do not have to think any more about it. Often that 'knowing' is so comfortable to us, because of years of inculcation of particular values associated with a word or expression, that we no longer engage with how we make it mean. But a contingent theory of communication demands that we always engage critically with how we make meanings, how we imagine realities.

In that respect, then, we have to make a critical choice about how we interpret phrases like 'Yer dirty Gin', 'the older Aboriginal', 'the Boongs', 'a scrawny boy', 'the Spanish baker', and so on. That critical choice is contingent upon the values that we have already established for a particular world-view, or that we have never actually thought much about before. Because we are not talking here about Bruce Chatwin's ownership of the language of this text, and, therefore, his ownership of the meanings of this text, but the way in which we imagine the realities of this text when we construct a reading for it. In other words, we, as readers, are responsible for the meanings here, not Bruce Chatwin.

What that means, of course, is that we have to think rather more fully about what we are doing when we read than we might have done in the past. We have to deconstruct our reading as we go along so that we are always interrogating the text and the meanings we imagine for it so that we can construct an interpretation. And we can only do that by constantly asking what our interpretations are contingent upon – what set of values are we using? What are the politics of those values? What are the ways in which we have privileged certain values over others? The result will necessarily be a more critical awareness of the way we make sense, and a more critical awareness of the way we are often controlled by contingent values to make sense in particular ways.

So, for example, the strategic positioning of the character classifications in the passage above, might suggest, to some, an uncomfortable stereotyping of Aborigines, women, workers, Spaniards, white Australians, scrawny boys, but a relatively comfortable image of tourists and travel writers/narrators. Strategically there might seem to be a major divide between the character classifications, with a strategic imbalance between the regular occupants of the pub, and the more distanced/'sophisticated' tourist; between the white Australians in the pub, and the Aborigines; between the white people of the town and the blacks who are claiming back their land; between the 'uncivilized' value systems of the Outback pub culture of Australia and the 'civilized' value systems of elsewhere.

Issues of race, class, gender, stereotyping, justice/injustice, 'them/ us', comfort/discomfort, pleasure, masculinity, and so on, necessarily have to be a part of the way we think about communication as strategic before it is linguistic. The various character classifications outlined above, for example, demand that we think, not so much about the linguistic structure of the text, but the value systems we are drawing upon – the contingencies of communication – in order to imagine realities for them. We do this principally from an intertextual awareness long before we engage with linguistic structure. As a consequence, when we engage with this text – any text – we are constructing notions of who we are, and more specifically, who we consider others to be, out of our imagining of them as characters, communities, nations, races, ethnic groups, citizens, cultures, and so on. The consequences of this imagining, more often than not, involve us marginalizing, stereotyping and belittling the value of difference in order to privilege a particular dominant value of order.

We write cultures. We do not represent them in writing. They exist only in the many different ways we imagine them. So the questions to be asked of your reading of this text – any text – is 'Whose culture am I writing here?', 'What values am I privileging?', 'What values am I marginalizing/ignoring?', 'What are the strategies I am using to do this?', 'And why?' Consider some of the ways that you imagine Aboriginality; Spanish; Australia; Land Rights; dirty gins; Outback males; drinkers; truckies and construction workers; travel writers and narrators. Is 'your' culture the same as 'theirs' – if not, how not? Are these values contingent upon racism and bigotry? Are they contingent upon fairness and justice? Are they contingent upon multi-cultural celebrations, or ethnocentric narrowness? Is this passage comfortable reading for you? If so, why? If not, why? Should we as readers of fiction, travel writing – anything – get upset, annoyed, angry? Should we demand that the writing of cultures in this way – any way – bring about social and political change according to a dominant set of values that, for example, objects to the stereotypical presentation of women, blacks and Outback males? Should we demand that certain ways of writing culture – certain strategies of making meanings and privileging values – be changed? Or should we simply, as analysts, like the 'I' who opens this passage from *The Songlines*, stand back from the action, assume an innocent and dispassionate distance in order to allow us to describe already existing realities, rather than to imagine and construct, dynamically, those realities?

A lot of questions – but this is the nature of critical analysis – we need to interrogate the textual construction of reality in order to understand the ways we make sense. Because a contingent theory of communication is, at the same time, a theory of ideology. We make sense of the world by classifying the world discursively. This means challenging the assumption that the world has a 'natural' order and structure. The central activity of such a critical practice is a process of deconstruction and demystification which is concerned with discourse not as a linguistic reflection of social structure, but as an integral politicized part of that structure. All criticism is a political act. All criticism is an intervention.

So, for example, you may be interested in exploring a particular strategy, say of colonization because you are interested in intervening in the debate about constructing certain people as 'colonized others'. Your concerns may spring from a desire to right some wrongs; to bring justice to bear in unjust situations; to explore and interrogate the ways in which strategies of colonization persist and continue in societies long after the specific colonizers seem to have left the scene.

But, as *The Songlines* piece might demonstrate, strategies of colonization are a continuing cultural practice which involve a wide range of communities and individuals in the writing of histories, narratives, cultures and values, which are not necessarily their own. The chief effect of such strategies is to de-humanize people, and as a consequence of this, strategies of substitution are often brought into play, in order to substitute and replace 'undesirable' and 'inappropriate' values and cultural practices with 'desirable' and 'appropriate' ones; to substitute 'uncomfortable' values with 'comfortable' ones.

So, for example, what is your position when reading *The Songlines* piece? Do you consider the fight appropriate? Do you consider the 'stringy little man's' treatment of 'the black whore' appropriate? Would you seek strategies of substitution to make their behaviour more comfortable? More fitting to your own? Or does the textual frame of the Outback pub make this more appropriate than if these events took place in the textual frame of an evangelical meeting in urban Melbourne or Manchester? If your answer is yes, then answer the question 'Why?' What are the contingencies you are using to change your attitudes to particular communicative strategies within particular textual frames? Why should a strategy of colonization which marginalizes Outback males, black whores and Aborigines in general, with its criticism of certain types of behaviour and morals, and its own inherent violence against difference, be any more comfortable, or less comfortable, in different textual frames?

This notion of comfort/discomfort, and its associations with violent strategies of colonization, marginalization, appropriation, and so on, is contingent upon a belief that the colonizer operates regimes of truth which valorize their colonizing strategies as acceptable, appropriate and dominant. Of course, once we start thinking about such regimes of truth we then have to think very long and hard about the 'naturalness' of truth. Is white truth more 'natural' than black truth? Is European truth more 'natural' than Australian Outback truth? Is the baker's truth more 'natural' than the truckie's truth? Is the narrator's truth more 'natural' than the reader's truth? You may say that it is all (or should all) be the same, but of course, the politics of everyday life is that it very clearly is not the same. The strategies of conflict, struggle, power positioning, status relationships, control, and so on, that rule our everyday lives see to it that it is never the same. The 'naturalness' of truth is always contingent upon who has the most control of these, and other, strategies. Truth is a cultural practice. We write truth, as we write cultures, narratives and histories. Contingent communication is interested in how and why we write it as we do. We are talking, therefore, about truth as cultural practice. The question we must always ask is 'Whose truth?' because such truth – all truth – is always in the writing of any culture, a strategic positioning of one value over another, one person over another, one community over another, one society over another, one nation over another.

No one escapes these regimes of truth – no one escapes the strategies of control and power – no one escapes the contingencies. The institutionalized analysis of language, communication, style, literature, texts in general, has tried to escape in the past – continues to keep trying – because, for the most part, it fears the idea that all criticism is a political act, but as soon as we reposition communication as strategic and contingent, we have no choice – we have to engage.

SUGGESTIONS FOR FURTHER WORK

1 Consider the following extract from a talk-back radio show in Singapore. What do you consider to be the dominant and marginalized discourses here? What strategies are used to privilege particular values? What are these strategies contingent on? Whose values? Whose morals?

Host: Sasha, go right ahead.
Caller: Yeah, okay. Um good afternoon to everybody. I'd just like to um tell you about a friend of mine who –
Host: Sasha, just a minute uh, you, you're bit soft, could you – speak perhaps closer to the telephone, the mouth of the telephone?
Caller: Er – is this okay?
Host: Mmm, slightly better.
Caller: Er okay, um sorry about that. Yeah, it's just about a friend of mine whom, I would rather not mention his name – um – he is eighteen years old and – um – previously he's had a girl–boy relationship before – um he is a Dutch boy you see, so what happened was – um he recounted his story, he told me that – he's had countless girls before, and er – yeah, he's got steady relationships with some of them but all they seemed intent on is his money and not him as a

whole person. So instead of – trying to – look, I mean, focus his attention elsewhere, he – just got into this kind of homosexual affair, so – um – he's captain of a ship and er – um it's been going on for two years but um – I was just wondering because he's so young a, a guy, you know, and he's throwing away his life so when I asked whether he's gone for his lab test, he said 'no' because most probably he might be infected, you know, the chances are very, very high you see, so I was wondering if there is something I could do to help him.

Host: How does it, are, are, you very close to this particular guy, friend of yours?

Caller: Um well – we see one another occasionally, we're not that close –

Host: Mmm.

Caller: I mean, up to a certain extent, yeah we could be close, you see – he could talk easily to me.

Host: Right, and you want to help him in some way.

Caller: Yes.

Host: Well, I'm not an expert on these things, I'm afraid, Sasha, I, I really cannot um – tell you what to do but I mean, I, I do feel for you in that sense that – it's, it's very sad when you see someone whom you know, you know, living a dubious lifestyle and, and he might actually have that particular virus in him um but um he is obviously aware of the situation and of the danger, isn't he?

Caller: Oh yes. He did tell me once that he wanted to change his lifestyle – um and I was wondering if, you know, if he wants the help, I could give him my helping hand, you know?

Host: Mmm, maybe a support, some kind of support, huh?

Caller: Yeah.

Host: But er he's just disillusioned with life, right? By, by the sounds of it he's just disillusioned because you mentioned that the girls just want his money.

Caller: Yes, right.

Host: Mmm, er well, I really don't know what to say to that but er I'd like to thank you, Sasha, for calling in and sharing that particular incident with us, okay?

Caller: Okay.

Host: Okay then, thanks a lot.

Caller: Yeah, bye bye.

2 Choose any page from any newspaper you have access to, and

examine in detail the different textual frames involved in the various articles. What are the assumptions involved here? How much shared knowledge are we assumed to have as readers? How much of this shared knowledge is contingent upon value systems that you agree/disagree with?

T he mysteries unveiled. To step into Dreamtime is to step back into a world where folklore teaches that people searched for food by the dim light of the moon because there was no sun.

Here, old myths and traditions spring into life.

You'll see the origin of the sun explained like never before.

Learn how primitive tools and implements became effective food gathering and home building aids.

Experience a traditional campfire. Marvel at old carvings and paintings and ancient relics.

Discover a world we could only guess at, until now. Understand a civilisation that was extremely well advanced even before whites arrived.

A ncient and Modern side by side. The contemporary building which houses the Dreamtime museum, research and educational facilities, canteen and arts and crafts boutique was inspired by the sheer sandstone cliffs in the central highlands of Queensland. With a few visible windows, the interior of the building is enhanced by the magic of the natural environment which has been cleverly designed to create a feeling of deep mystery. Limestone Creek separates this formal section from the initiation rings, sandstone cave replica, burial sites, rock arts and gunyahs. And these are sheltered by a timber-lined billabong, adding to the overall atmosphere of authenticity.

Every individual facet of the centre has been designed to meet the needs of tourists while still retaining the integrity desired by traditional Aboriginals.

You will never forget the day you stepped into The Dreamtime.

A t last the dream comes true . . . And so the Waterlily Flower came into beautiful bloom . . . and the four leaves rejoiced in her happiness for the four leaves represented the four clans of the Darumbal Tribe. And at last the dream had come true.

For as it was done in the Dreamtime, on the very place where their ancestors and elders had made campsite, gathered for ancient tribal meetings and burials and established sacred initiation rings, the dream burst magically into life.

The Dreamtime symbol represents the Darumbal Tribe – the main tribe where the Cultural Centre is built. Their totem is the Waterlily Flower and the four leaves symbolise the four clans of the Darumbal Tribe.

T he vision becomes a reality. Dreamtime is Australia's largest Aboriginal Cultural Centre, a focus for both Aboriginal and Islander people to learn more about their heritage while sharing this knowledge with the world.

Set in some 30 acres of natural bushland, on ancient tribal sites. Dreamtime will help all Australians, all people, both students and adults, to understand Australia's first 40,000 years of civilisation.

ies of the discourse participants, including their attitudes towards each other, the permanent or temporary social relationship holding between them, their respective statuses and roles, as well as the degree of formality or intimacy of the situation in which the discourse takes place. In this connection, it will be clear that a shift in form of address following a change in the social relationship between people will normally affect their politeness strategies (see **politeness**). See also the entry under **vocatives**.

Adjacency pairs

Conversational interaction is characterized by turn-taking (q.v.), the switch in roles from hearer to speaker, and the other way around. This behavioural phenomenon is shown in such recurrent conversational patterns as adjacency pairs, which are connected pairs of utterances, produced by different speakers. Examples of adjacency pairs include question–answer, greeting–greeting, summons–answer, and so on. The sub-parts of these paired sequences are usually described as first pair-part and second pair-part. On the basis of social harmony and polite behaviour, we expect that the second pair-part is an appropriate response to the first. So an offer will normally be followed by an acceptance, rather than a rejection, and a summons by an answer (e.g. *Summons*: 'Janet!' *Answer*: 'Coming!').

Although adjacency pairs typically consist of sequences of two related utterances, they can also be expanded, for example, by other sequences inside them, which are therefore usually called insertion sequences. For instance, in the following dialogue, the answer to the question in the first pair-part is held up by an intervening conversational exchange:

> 'Can you tell me what is Angelica Pabst's room number?' Persse asked him. 'It's funny you should ask me that,' said Busby. 'Somebody just mentioned that they saw her going off in a taxi, with her suitcase.' 'What?' exclaimed Persse, jumping to his feet. 'When? How long ago?' 'Oh, at least half an hour,' said Bob Busby. 'But, you know, as far as I know she never had a room. I certainly never allocated her one, and she doesn't seem to have paid for one.'
>
> (Lodge 1984/1985: 56)

The importance of adjacency pair analysis is that it provides a structural framework which, if it is related to a proper context, enables the discourse analyst to draw inferences about what the paired utterances really stand for in case, as often happens, there is an

3 Consider the text opposite, taken from a glossy brochure advertising an Aboriginal Cultural Centre in Rockhampton, Queensland, Australia. What strategies of white colonization are operating here? What strategies of black colonization? Who is responsible for the writing of Aboriginal history here? Whose narratives are we talking about?

4 Consider the advertisement for HIV/AIDS awareness on the previous page. How comfortable is this text? What are the main strategies, do you think, for effecting comfort/discomfort? What are those strategies contingent upon?

REFERENCES

Atkinson, P. (1990) *The Ethnographic Imagination. Textual Constructions of Reality*, London: Routledge.

Birch, D. (1989) *Language, Literature and Critical Practice*, London: Routledge.

—— (1991) *The Language of Drama. Critical Theory and Practice*, London: Macmillan.

Chatwin, B. (1987) *The Songlines*, New York: Penguin Books USA.

Fairclough, N. (1989) *Language and Power*, London: Longman.

Hodge, R. and Kress, G. (1988) *Social Semiotics*, Oxford: Polity Press/Blackwell.

—— (1993) *Language as Ideology*, second edition, London: Routledge.

Huggan, G. (1991) 'Maps, Dreams, and the Presentation of Ethnographic Narrative: Hugh Brody's *Maps and Dreams* and Bruce Chatwin's *The Songlines*', *ARIEL: A Review of International English Literature* 22, 1: 57–69.

Kress, G. (ed.) (1988) *Communication and Culture*, Kensington: New South Wales University Press.

Kress, G. and van Leeuwen, T. (1990) *Reading Images*, Deakin: Deakin University Press.

Glossary

Accomplishments, Achievements, Activities

Accomplishments, achievements, activities and statives are four predicate-types which exemplify different inherent temporal structures of a situation. An accomplishment is a situation of some duration, with a natural endpoint (e.g. building a house, writing a letter). Achievements also have a natural endpoint but no duration (e.g. reaching the top, blinking). Both activities and statives have duration but no natural endpoint. The difference between activities (e.g. running, swimming) and statives (e.g. knowing someone, being tall) is that no input of energy is required to maintain the latter.

Actor, Agent. See **Transitivity**

Address, Forms/terms of

Our linguistic choices in social interaction are greatly influenced by all kinds of contextual factors (see **pragmatics**). Thus, the social setting of a discourse (q.v.) is one major factor in our selection of the forms (or terms) of address, which are the words or phrases we use when speaking or writing to or about each other. They include personal pronouns ('I', 'you', 'she'), first name ('Clare'), last name ('Smith'), title with last name ('Mrs Smith'), words denoting kinship ('mum', 'uncle'), titles as a sign of respect or honour ('doctor', 'your honour'), markers of intimacy ('darling'), offensive terms ('fathead'), and so on. The latter also include, for instance, any kind of address term discriminating against women, race, class or political and religious views.

Taking into account that forms of address vary from culture to culture, we can infer from them information about the social identit-

obvious mismatch between its two components (e.g. *Question*: 'Are you coming to my house-warming party tonight?' *Answer*: 'I've got an exam tomorrow'). See **co-operative principle**, **implicature**, **politeness** and **pragmatics**.

Appropriateness conditions. See **Speech acts**

Aspect

Comrie (1976: 3) defines aspects as 'different ways of viewing the internal temporal constituency of a situation'. For instance, the distinction in English between the simple past (they played football) and the past progressive (they were playing football) is an aspectual distinction and not a difference in tense, since both examples have past tense. The difference is that in the simple-past case, the event of playing football is seen as completed, with a beginning, a middle and an end, whereas in the past-progressive case, it is perceived as ongoing, with no explicit reference to the beginning or the end of their playing.

Camera

By means of the manipulations of camera angles, a particular shot can be identified with a character's point of view. The audience see what the character may be imagined to see. Therefore, point-of-view shots contribute to an understanding of the motivations of the characters and reinforce the audience's identification with their experiences (see Graddol and Boyd-Barrett 1994: 126–7). Compare the entry under **point of view**.

Coherence

People encounter texts with an assumption of coherence: an expectation that the sentences of the text – even if they are not linked by cohesive devices (see **cohesion**) – form a meaningful whole. For instance, on a poster reproduction of a painting above my desk I can see the following text:

> Dante Gabriel Rossetti
> The Tate Gallery – London

I use my knowledge of the world to make sense of this text and understand that this particular painting by Rossetti is exhibited in the Tate Gallery in London. In this way, I have restored coherence to what might initially have seemed a slightly incoherent (because syntactically incomplete and non-cohesive) text. See also **cohesion**, **pragmatics**, **text/discourse**.

Cohesion

Cohesion refers to the set of linguistic devices that bind a text together, that give it unity or texture. There are four basic types of cohesive relationships: reference, conjunction, lexical organization and ellipsis. Both co-referential expressions (e.g. pronouns referring to the same entity) and conjunctions such as 'and', 'but', 'therefore', tie together different parts of the text. Repetition of key words is one aspect of the lexical cohesion of a text. For ellipsis, see the separate glossary entry. See also **coherence** and **text/discourse**.

Coloured narrative

Coloured narrative is narrative coloured by a particular character's point of view; in other words, narrative invaded by subjective and expressive elements which have to be attributed to that character's orientation. See also **methods of speech and thought presentation** (especially **free indirect discourse**). Coloured narrative is a more comprehensive phenomenon which includes free indirect discourse, as the former can also occur outside contexts of speech and thought presentation.

Communication

In very simple terms, communication can be defined as the activity of transmitting and exchanging information between a sender and receiver by means of a signalling system. In human communication, this system can be, and in actual fact it generally is, a language. It is possible to take a mechanical view of communication: messages are encoded by a sender (i.e. a speaker or writer), transmitted through linguistic signs and then, on receipt, decoded by a receiver (i.e. a hearer or reader). Such a transmission model of communication assumes that the speaker/writer encodes meanings and that the hearer/reader will decode these in a predictable way. In other words, these messages, designated as 'texts' in linguistics, contain definite meanings which can be recovered by hearers/readers unproblematically.

This assumption must be based on an idealized conception of

human communication, because we know from our everyday experience that it is a lot messier and that meaning in texts is far from univocal. The motivation for this idealization must be that it provides linguists with a model of texts as neat, analysable structures, ignoring the unsettling factors of a real life social context in which meanings are far from being a matter of consensus.

The alternative view is, therefore, that meaning in texts, in spoken or written form, is never fixed but negotiated and re-negotiated in an ongoing process of socio-cultural interaction between speaker/writer and hearer/reader. In other words, when texts are treated as con-textualized 'discourses', different hearers/readers with different socio-cultural backgrounds or, for that matter, the same hearers/readers at different times in their lives, will interpret one and the same text in different ways.

Though, broadly speaking, it is this view of meaning in texts which underlies the principles of David Birch's contribution, he widens the reference of the term communication, which can be read here as discourse, by regarding it as a strategic and political act. This requires a critical discourse analysis (q.v.) which is not primarily interested in what texts mean, but in exposing how texts produce meanings which are determined and constrained by all kinds of political, socio-cultural and ideological forces.

Constraints

A linguistic term which is used to refer to the restrictions on the choices a speaker/writer can make from the structural (phonological, grammatical, semantic) and pragmatic (contextual) possibilities of a language. So structural constraints belong to language as a system of rules, while pragmatic ones specify the restrictions we put on our linguistic choices in social practice, that is, in a context of use. Compare **context**, **semantics**, **pragmatics**, and **sentence/utterance**.

One of the innumerable contextual constraints imposed on language users is knowledge of the socialized conventions of genres or discourse types (q.v.). Literature, for instance, can be seen as a specific range of genres or discourse types, each of which puts its own characteristic constraints on writers and readers alike. For example, a familiar genre constraint is the convention that the narrator in fiction or the lyric speaker in poems, though speaking as 'I', is not supposed to be the novelist or poet, but a literary construct.

Critical discourse analysts hold that the way we speak and write is shaped by the institutions of power in our society such as education, the family, the church, the law, the political parties, the media, etc., so that our language choices are not free but subject to all kinds of ideological constraints. Compare **critical discourse analysis**, and **ideology**.

Context

There are two types of context. The first of these is the linguistic context, or co-text, that is, the surrounding features of language inside a text, like sounds, words, phrases or clauses which are relevant to the interpretation of other such linguistic elements. The second is the non-linguistic context in which an utterance or discourse is embedded. In recent years linguists have become increasingly convinced that a sentence or text cannot be fully interpreted without appealing to situational considerations (see **discourse analysis**, **pragmatics** and the **sentence/utterance** distinction). As it is, the idea of non-linguistic context is quite complex and may include components like:

(a) the time and physical situation of the discourse;
(b) its socio-cultural situation;
(c) the general background knowledge required for the discourse to be understood;
(d) the identities, abilities, attitudes and beliefs of the speaker/writer and hearer/reader;
(e) the social relationships holding between the discourse participants;
(f) knowledge of the socialized stylistic conventions of the genre or text type (e.g. a neighbourly chat, a broadcast interview, a brochure, a television commercial);
(g) the association with other similar or related discourse types (compare **intertextuality**);
(h) the purpose and function of the discourse;
(i) the mode of communication (e.g. speech or writing), and the influence of other modes of communication (e.g. pictures, music and sound effects in advertising; see e.g. Cook 1992).

Conversational implicature. See **Implicature**

Conversational maxims. See **Co-operative principle**

Co-operative principle

According to the American philosopher H. P. Grice (1975), our conversations are characteristically co-operative efforts. Participants in a conversation recognize a common purpose, which is the efficient and effective use of language. They will therefore try to observe a general principle, which Grice calls the co-operative principle. This overall principle is broken down into four sub-principles or conversational maxims, which Grice groups under quantity, quality, relation and manner.

The maxim of quantity states that speakers are expected to provide the required quantity of information, neither too much nor too little.

According to the maxim of quality, listeners assume that speakers try to make their contribution one that is true.

The maxim of relation represents the listeners' assumption that speakers make an effort to talk to the point.

Finally, the maxim of manner holds that speakers are assumed to be clear and orderly, and avoid unnecessary obscurity and ambiguity.

In our worldly wisdom we may think these principles rather naïve because we know that in reality people may behave quite differently in their conversational exchanges. Of course, Grice recognizes this, but maintains that in their communicative behaviour people nevertheless assume that speakers observe the co-operative principle and its attendant maxims because, given the central goals of communication (e.g. giving and receiving information, influencing and being influenced by others), it is the reasonable and rational thing to do.

In fact, Grice's strongest claim is that precisely because rational speakers observe these unwritten maxims of conversational conduct, and expect their hearers to do the same, it becomes possible to mean more than we actually say. Grice provides the following example. A and B are talking about a mutual friend, C, who is now working in a bank, and A asks B how C is getting on in his job and is told 'Oh quite well, I think; he likes his colleagues, and he hasn't been to prison yet.' In the final clause 'he hasn't been to prison yet', B is conveying something that does not follow from the literal meaning of his words. What B is really suggesting or implying is that C is a potential criminal. Now, A can only infer this implied meaning by assuming that B obeys the co-operative principle and adheres to its maxims, in this case the maxim of relation. In other words, A assumes that B's uncalled-for remark about the prison, which at first seems irrelevant, must be relevant after all. The literal meaning of B's words is simply that C has not been sent to prison yet, but by using these very words he wanted A to infer that C is a dishonest person. Grice calls this inferred meaning a conversational implicature (see **implicature**).

Another type of implicature gives rise to what have traditionally been called figures of speech such as metaphor, irony, litotes and hyperbole. They are the result of what Grice calls the flouting or exploitation of the maxims. In such cases a speaker infringes some maxim so deliberately and ostentatiously that the hearer would simply be at a loss if there were no underlying assumption of the operation of the co-operative principle. Levinson (1983: 110) provides the following example. The sentence 'Queen Victoria was made of iron' blatantly flouts the maxim of quality (be truthful). Assuming that the speaker is co-operative and intends to convey something rather different, the hearer searches around for an interpretation (see **metaphor**) that can be related to the context of utterance: if said by an admirer it may be taken as praise (e.g. Victoria was tough and resilient); if said by a detractor it may be taken as a denigration (e.g. Victoria was inflexible and emotionally impassive).

Since implicature is something that cannot be entirely explained by a syntactic or semantic rule, this notion has had a profound influence on recent developments in pragmatics. See, for example, Leech (1983), Levinson (1983) and Mey (1993). Compare also the entries under **politeness**, **pragmatics**, **semantics**, **speech acts** and **syntax**.

Co-text. See **Context**

Critical discourse analysis

Critical discourse analysis (CDA) is a rapidly developing branch of linguistics which aims at revealing the implicit social, political and ideological mechanisms at work in spoken or written texts (see **ideology**). Such mechanisms are implicit or hidden because people are not generally conscious of the causes and consequences of the ideologically loaded language they are using. They have lost this consciousness through a process of inculcation. By being persistently exposed to politically and socially dominant norms and values in numerous written and spoken texts, in the mass media, in books, etc., but also in their everyday conversations, people have been induced to naturalize these beliefs, to see them as normal, even to the extent of treating them as matters of mere common sense. Consider, for example, this entry in the *Collins Cobuild English Language Dictionary* (1987: 957): 'It is natural for trade unions to adopt an aggressive posture'. As a matter of fact, critical discourse analysts tend to assume that the 'fixed' common-sense meanings in dictionaries are the result of a process of naturalization (Fairclough 1989: 95).

It will be obvious that hidden ideologies in texts cannot be directly inferred from their formal features. Therefore, to expose their ideologies, texts need to be treated as discourse, that is, they must be embedded in a context of social interaction, where speakers/writers and hearers/readers produce and interpret texts against a background of naturalized beliefs and common-sense assumptions (cf. **context** and **text/discourse**).

From this it follows that, though an analysis of the formal features of texts (phonology, lexis, syntax) may provide cues for their interpretation, their use in discourse, that is, as social practice, requires additional tools of analysis. These have recently been supplied by pragmatics (q.v.), speech act theory (see **speech acts**), discourse analysis (q.v.), the co-operative principle (q.v.) and politeness (q.v.) in conversational behaviour, cognitive science (see **idealized cognitive model**), artificial intelligence (see **image-schema, schema, knowledge base**), and the coherence principle (see **coherence**).

For a seminal work on critical discourse analysis, see Fairclough (1989); for a detailed application to literature, see Hodge (1990).

Deixis

Deictic expressions include such orientational words as 'I', 'you', 'here', 'there', 'this', 'that', 'now', 'then', 'today', 'tomorrow', 'yesterday', 'come', 'go'. What all these have in common is that they usually 'point to' particular aspects of the extra-textual situation (deixis is the Greek word for pointing, indicating). For example, the personal pronoun 'I' can refer to different entities on different occasions of use. In this way, deixis shows that the interpretation of utterances is crucially dependent on an analysis of the context. See also **context**, **pragmatics** and **sentence/utterance**.

Deviation. See **Foregrounding**

Direct discourse. See **Methods of speech and thought presentation**

Direct speech acts. See **Speech acts**

Discourse analysis. See **Text/Discourse**

Discursive frames

It is one of the basic tenets of critical discourse analysis (q.v.) that the production and interpretation of individual discourses are ideologically determined by, and are in fact only understandable in terms of, much larger discoursal frameworks, that is, conventional linguistic formations which reflect, recreate, and hence preserve, a particular social, cultural or political institution. These larger institutional discourses are often termed discursive frames or discursive formations. Consider, for example, the discursive frames of education, literary criticism, feminism, trade unionism, the quality and popular newspapers, etc. Compare **idealized cognitive model**, **ideology**, and **intertextuality**.

Ellipsis

Look at the following conversational exchange:

A: When are you coming?
B: In a moment.

B's reply is an instance of elliptical syntax, because some of the information needed to understand it ('B is coming in a moment') is not explicitly available, but has to be retrieved from the preceding linguistic context.

Experiencer. See **Transitivity**

Expressive constructions

Expressive constructions are linguistic constructions used to express, rather than report, a character's state of mind. For example, exclamations, hesitation words and emphatic repetitions are expressive constructions.

Face

Face is the self-image that is projected in public by a particular person. It consists of two facets: positive face, or the desire to be liked and respected, and negative face, or the desire not to be imposed upon by others.

Consequently, what any speaker says may threaten the face of the addressee, and it can do this in two ways: the speaker may threaten the addressee's positive face, by e.g. insulting him, or she may threaten his negative face by imposing upon him (e.g. by asking him for a loan of money). These two types of act are therefore called face-threatening acts (FTAs). See also the entries under **politeness** and **pragmatics**.

Felicity conditions. See **Speech acts**

First pair-part. See **Adjacency pairs**

Focalization. See **Point of view**

Foregrounding

In linguistic poetics textual devices such as deviation and parallelism are usually subsumed under the concept of foregrounding. Deviation refers to a writer's conscious or unconscious violation of some linguistic rule of phonology, morphology, syntax or semantics, or an infringement of a particular linguistic usage or of some literary genre or convention. Parallelism is in a sense the opposite of deviation, in that it is based on extra regularities rather than irregularities. This effect is usually achieved by repetitive patterns on any of the already indicated levels of linguistic organization. The theory of foregrounding claims that by using these unorthodox or highly patterned structures, the writer exploits the language aesthetically and as a result invites the reader to see a particular structure in a new light.

Frame. See **Schema**

Free direct discourse, Free indirect discourse. See **Methods of speech and thought presentation**

Genre

The concept of genre refers to different text-types, such as the essay, the novel, the lecture, etc. These are not universal, but culturally-specific categories, which are often divided into relevant sub-types (e.g. Virginia Woolf's 'Old Mrs Grey' belongs to the sub-type 'literary essay'). In chapter 10, Irene R. Fairley shows how Woolf's essay deconstructs culturally received notions of genre by diverging radically from the prototypical essay and incorporating many features of another related genre, the short story. See also **context** and **intertextuality.**

Given/new information

Given information is information that the speaker or writer assumes is known to the hearer or reader, whereas new information is information that the speaker/writer assumes is not known to the hearer/reader. Consider the following text:

The detective picked up a knife and a button from the floor. She put the button in her pocket.

In the first sentence, 'button' is introduced into the discourse as a new entity and is therefore referred to by means of an indefinite expression ('a button'). In the next sentence, however, it is referred to by means of a definite noun phrase ('the button') and is thus presented as a given entity, since by now the writer can take for granted that the button is information known to the reader.

Iconicity

The principle of iconicity (or imitation) stipulates that the order in which events are presented in a text corresponds to their order of occurrence in the real or a fictional world. Consider the following sentences:

(1) John wrote his autobiography and became famous.
(2) John became famous and wrote his autobiography.

The principle of iconicity leads us to interpret (1) as suggesting that it was John's autobiography that made him famous, whereas in (2) John only wrote it *after* he had become famous.

Idealized cognitive model (ICM)

Each conceptual metaphor (see **metaphor**) sets up an idealized cognitive model of a domain. For instance, in Doris Lessing's 'To Room Nineteen', the heroine understands neurosis in terms of a military invasion. This metaphor sets up an idealized cognitive domain of the self as a bounded space with an interior – occupied by the rational forces of the self – and an exterior, where all unconscious, irrational forces are located. Neurosis then involves an attack staged by the external forces in order to conquer the inner territory of the self.

Such an ICM is not a natural structure, but a highly ideological set of assumptions about how a particular aspect of reality works. It combines with other ICMs into intricate conceptual structures which constitute the commonsense or world-view of a particular culture or community. See also **pragmatics**, **schema** and **ideology**.

Ideology

An ideology is a complex of ideas which seems to form a conceptual unit and which informs the way we think about things in a stereotypical manner. There are many ideologies in competition on certain subjects: for example, in relation to women, it is ideological knowledge which suggests that women stay at home and look after their children, when the majority of women in Britain in fact go out to work. See also **critical discourse analysis**, **pragmatics** and **schema**.

Illocutionary act/force. See **Speech acts**

Image-schema

Image-schemata are the recurrent patternings of our everyday perceptual interactions and bodily experiences. For instance, whenever we breathe in or out, whenever we go into, or out of, a particular place, we experience the image-schematic distinction between 'in' and 'out'. Other image-schematic patterns are up–down, source–path–goal, balance, force, iteration and scalarity. We use these image-schematic patterns in order to make sense of new types of situations that we encounter in our daily lives. See also **pragmatics**.

Implicature

An implicature is an inference which the hearer has to draw in order to make sense of the speaker's utterance. For instance, in the following dialogue:

A: Do you know where Clara is?
B: There's a green BMW outside Jonathan's house.

B's answer does not seem to be directly relevant to A's question at first sight. However, if we can assume that Clara is the owner of a green BMW and that she knows a particular person called Jonathan, then we can infer what B probably means: he implies that it is highly likely that Clara is in Jonathan's house. This inference is what is technically referred to as an implicature of B's utterance. Compare also the entries under **adjacency pairs**, **co-operative principle**, **politeness**, **pragmatics** and **sentence/utterance**.

Inculcation. See **Critical discourse analysis**

Indirect discourse. See **Methods of speech and thought presentation**

Indirect speech acts. See **Speech acts**

Inferred meaning. See **Co-operative principle, Implicature, Politeness**

Insertion sequences. See **Adjacency pairs**

Intertextuality

Both in literary theory and discourse analysis, intertextuality has become a common term used to describe the way any spoken or written text, literary or non-literary, is produced and interpreted through our conscious or unconscious experience and awareness of other texts. These texts in turn will have their own intertextual dimension, and so forth. Obviously, the texts in such an intertextual network can relate to each other for all sorts of reasons. Topical coherence can be one of them: this very glossary, for instance, is related to a maze of texts (not only the ones cited in the references!), which are somehow concerned with the topic of this book. Another strong bond between texts can be the concept of genre or text type (q.v.). Thus, spoken or written texts and, for that matter, other modes of communication such as film, television and video, may be either genre specific (e.g. sermon, lyric, business letter, soap, western) or one genre may encroach upon another or others (e.g. mock-epic, parody, advertising).

Since critical linguists claim that all texts are ideologically informed, that is, have directly or indirectly been influenced by processes of political, social and cultural power, critical discourse analysis (q.v.) must be keenly aware of this phenomenon of intertextuality (Birch 1989: 155). See also **discursive frames**.

Invariance hypothesis

The invariance hypothesis formulates a constraint on metaphorical mappings. In metaphor, the source domain is mapped on to the target domain (see **metaphor**). However, the target domain may already have a pre-existent image-schematic structure (see **image-schema**). The invariance hypothesis now stipulates that when the source domain is mapped on to the target domain, the image-schematic structure of the target domain must not be violated.

Thus I can use the metaphor 'John is an elephant' to suggest that (e.g.) John has a good memory, but not to suggest that he has a trunk.

This is because the latter suggestion obviously violates the basic cognitive topology of the target (John) and hence is not imported.

Kinesic behaviour. See **Non-verbal conversational turns**

Knowledge base

This is a term used in artificial intelligence to refer to the systems of knowledge and beliefs which make up the common sense of an individual. The term is somewhat misleading, since obviously a knowledge base contains not only accurate knowledge of the world, but also mistaken or uncertain beliefs, attitudes, values, prejudices, etc. See also **pragmatics**.

Lexical repetition

There are three types:

(a) A re-use of the same lexical item, i.e. a word or a group of words: 'A fool, a fool! I met a fool i' the forest. A motley fool; a miserable world!' (Shakespeare, *As You Like It*, II.vi.12–13).
(b) A grouping of lexical items which are (more or less) synonymous. For instance, 'courage', 'fortitude', 'guts', 'nerve' and 'pluck' occur under the same entry in a dictionary of synonyms. However, complete synonyms are rare. There may be contexts which admit a choice of two or even more of these words without much difference, but most of them are only synonymous in certain contexts.
(c) A patterning of lexical items (usually termed a lexical set) which are not semantically synonymous but seem to be connected in our minds through association with a particular context of our socio-cultural or cognitive experience, which is usually designated as a semantic field. For example, 'demon', 'genie', 'centaur', 'satyr' and 'sea nymph' form a lexical set giving structure to the semantic field or concept 'mythical beings'. See also **lexical set**.

Lexical set

When there is a grouping of lexical items which are not semantically synonymous but associatively related because they tend to recur in similar contexts, the lexical items involved are said to form a lexical set. Actually, they give structure to so-called semantic fields, which are the areas of social and cognitive experience that exist in our culture. For example, 'appeal', 'prosecution', 'defence', 'plaintiff', 'defendant', 'accused' and 'witness' form a lexical set structuring the semantic field or concept of a court of law. See also **lexical repetition**.

Locutionary act. See **Speech acts**

Maxims of conversational behaviour. See **Co-operative principle** and **Politeness**

Metaphor

A metaphor is a mapping from one domain of experience, the 'source domain', on to another domain, the 'target domain'. In other words, it is a way of understanding the relatively unknown target domain in terms of a better known source domain. For example, in Doris Lessing's 'To Room Nineteen', the heroine understands neurosis in terms of a military invasion. So the structure of the 'military invasion' source domain is mapped on to the target domain of 'neurosis'. See also **pragmatics** and **co-operative principle**.

Methods of speech and thought presentation

The four main methods of speech and thought presentation are:

(a) Direct discourse: a linguistic style of speech or thought presentation in which a speaker's exact words are presented in quotation marks. Example: John said, 'I will be late tonight.'
(b) Free direct discourse: this style retains the pronouns and verb tenses of direct discourse but is not put in quotation marks or introduced by an attributive phrase.
(c) Free indirect discourse: this style is intermediate between direct and indirect discourse. It combines the pronouns and verb tenses of indirect discourse with expressive constructions characteristic of direct discourse. Example: John was worried. He would be late tonight.
(d) Indirect discourse: in this style, a speaker's thoughts or remarks are reported by another speaker. Example: John said that he would be late that evening.

See also the entry under **text/discourse**.

Naturalization. See **Critical discourse analysis**

Non-factive adverbs

Speakers may comment on the content of what they are saying by using an adverb that expresses some degree of doubt. Examples of such non-factive adverbs include 'apparently', 'conceivably', 'likely', 'possibly', 'seemingly', etc.

Non-verbal conversational turns

Sometimes the turns in a conversation (see **turn-taking**) are realized not by speech, but by facial expressions or body movements (for example, a smile, a frown, a nod of the head, feet-tapping). When in fiction such non-verbal turns are described in the narrative, they form in fact a conversational whole with the verbal turns. Communicative behaviour realized by body movements like this is usually called kinesic behaviour.

Parallelism. See **Foregrounding**

Patient. See **Transitivity**

Performative verbs. See **Speech acts**

Perlocutionary act. See **Speech acts**

Perspective. See **Point of view**

Point of view

Perspective or point of view is a key concept in literary criticism, but also one of the most confusing ones, as literary critics have tended to use it idiosyncratically. There is a need, therefore, to distinguish between the different senses in which the concept has been used.

There is, first of all, the question of 'who sees?' This is 'spatial' or 'perceptual' point of view, in other words the camera angle from which the story is viewed. See also **camera**

There is also the question of 'who speaks?' This second concept of point of view, 'linguistic' point of view, raises the problem of the narrating voice. See **methods of speech and thought presentation.**

A further aspect of point of view is what might be termed 'cognitive' point of view. Here we are concerned with the speaker's background beliefs and attitudes, and the way in which they influence the nature of her perceptions and interpretations.

Politeness

As anticipated by Grice (1975: 47), there is, besides the maxims of quantity (give the right amount of information), quality (be truthful), relation (talk to the point), and manner (be clear and brief), at least one other principle which participants in conversational exchanges usually adhere to: the politeness principle. This, too, may generate implicatures, that is, when in certain situations politeness rules are at work, additional meanings may be inferred which are not in the words of the utterance itself (see **co-operative principle** and **implicature**).

Politeness strategies frequently consist in using mitigation markers such as hedges (i.e. downtoners or qualifications to make an utterance less strong), hints, or other indirect speech acts (q.v.). Hence, the motivation of speakers for observing the politeness principle must be different from that for obeying Grice's maxims, which after all aim at the efficient and effective use of language. In fact, it appears that the principle of politeness sometimes overrides that of co-operation, particularly when contextual features such as power relations, differences in status or social distance induce speakers to depart from the direct and relevant speech acts required from them by the Gricean maxims. Consider, for instance, the indirectness of the utterance 'I don't suppose you would be prepared to stay in Edinburgh?'

On the other hand, polite forms are inappropriate, and are therefore meant to be ironic or sarcastic, in situations in which the speaker has direct authority over the hearer. For example, a parent saying to her child 'You wouldn't mind telling me how you have torn that hole in your trousers, would you?' Similarly, politeness appears inappropriate when there is an intimate relationship between two people. In such situations, the effect of polite forms can be, for instance, that the hearer feels 'cold-shouldered'.

Brown and Levinson (1987) have hypothesized that the main strategy speakers adopt in observing the norms of politeness in their conversational behaviour is based on the need to 'save face' and, at the same time, to prevent 'loss of face' (see **face**).

Clearly, norms of politeness vary considerably from culture to culture and from language to language.

In addition to Brown and Levinson (1987), another seminal work on politeness is Leech (1983). See also **pragmatics**, **sentence/ utterance**, **speech acts** and **vocatives**.

Pragmatics

Given its wide scope, the term pragmatics is hard to define adequately. Still, most linguists appear to agree that, broadly speaking, pragmatics is concerned with the meaning of language when it is used in a particular context. For instance, a moment's reflection will tell you that even a simple utterance like 'Meet me here tomorrow' cannot be interpreted solely on the basis of the linguistic or semantic meaning of its sounds, grammatical structure and vocabulary. Clearly, the meaning of the indicative elements (see **deixis**) 'me', 'here' and 'tomorrow' can only be determined when they are related to a real context of use from which we can infer the time and place of the utterance and the identities of the speaker and hearer (see **utterance** and **context**).

The contextual interpretation of such deictic expressions is the narrowest description of the domain of pragmatics. Since its broadest interpretation is that it studies, in principle, all the factors that influence our linguistic choices in social interaction and the effects these choices have on others, a pragmatic analysis of our example 'Meet me here tomorrow' will also investigate if the imperative construction of the utterance is appropriate, that is, if it is perhaps too abrupt or rude, taking into account the specific contextual factors such as the social relationship between the speaker and hearer, their attitudes, abilities and beliefs as well as the physical circumstances. Hence pragmatics intersects with a number of other areas of study including socio-linguistics (see **ideology**), psycho-linguistics, speech act theory (q.v.), discourse analysis (q.v.), conversational behaviour (see **co-operative principle, face, implicature, politeness, turn-taking**), cognitive science (see **idealized cognitive model**), artificial intelligence (see **image-schema, schema, knowledge base**), the coherence principle (see **coherence**), and rhetoric (see **metaphor**).

From this it follows that meaning in pragmatics is largely a matter of negotiation between speaker/writer and hearer/reader in a contextualized social interaction, whereas meaning in semantics, as Leech (1983: 6) puts it, is defined purely as a property of expressions in a given language, in abstraction from particular situations, speakers, or hearers. All the same, pragmatic meaning must not be conceived as an alternative to semantic meaning, but as complementary to it, because it is inferred from the interaction of linguistic or semantic meaning with context.

For fuller discussions of pragmatic theory, see Levinson (1983), Leech (1983), Green (1989), Blakemore (1992) and Mey (1993).

Presupposition

When I say,

The King of Belgium is rich

I presuppose (or take for granted) that there is a king of Belgium and I assert that he is rich. And when I say,

I regret that Jim left

I presuppose that Jim left and I assert that I regret this. An easy way of identifying presuppositions is to apply the so-called negation test: 'there is a king of Belgium' and 'Jim left' are presuppositions because they are also entailed by the negative statements 'The King of Belgium is not rich' and 'I don't regret that Jim left' (respectively).

Prolepsis

Prolepsis is the opposite of a flashback. Whereas in a flashback, a narrative event which took place earlier is recounted, a prolepsis is a flashforward, in which a narrative event which will only take place later is related as it were 'before its time'. Both flashbacks and prolepses are thus deviations from the 'normal', chronological presentation of events.

Purr words

These are words to which a particular linguistic community has attached very positive connotations or associations, whereas 'snarl words' have very negative connotations. Note that what is a snarl word for one community can easily be a purr word for another. For instance, 'Socialist' tends to be used as a snarl word by Conservative politicians and as a purr word by the political left.

Schema (cognitive)

The concept of 'schema' is derived from research in cognitive science and artificial intelligence. Cognitive schemata are sets of pre-structured actions which at a stereotypical level inform our thinking about certain spheres of behaviour. For example, the 'restaurant' schema suggests that, when people go to a restaurant, they assume that there will be waiters in the restaurant, that they will be shown some sort of menu, that they will be able to order some dishes from this menu, that after eating they will have to pay for their meal, etc. Many schemata, such as our background assumptions about male and female behaviour, are deeply imbued with ideology (see **ideology**). See also **pragmatics** and **speech acts**.

Second pair-part. See **Adjacency pairs**

Semantic field. See **Lexical set**

Semantic roles. See **Transitivity**

Semantics

Semantics is the study of the linguistic meaning of words, phrases, clauses and sentences, and of the systematic relations that hold between them. As such it is concerned with the meaning of language as a system of rules rather than language in a context of use. Compare **pragmatics**.

Sentence/Utterance

Though difficult, it can be useful to make a distinction between sentence and utterance. Traditionally, syntax is the study of how words, phrases and clauses are arranged to form meaningful relationships within sentences. A sentence is thus the largest unit of syntactic and semantic organization. When regarded as abstract units in this way, sentences belong to language as a system (see **semantics**). An utterance, however, is the concrete realization of a sentence in its spoken or written form in a particular context and therefore belongs to language in use (see **pragmatics**).

Snarl words. See **Purr words**

Source domain. See **Metaphor**

Speech act force. See **Speech acts**

Speech acts

Speech act theory, which was proposed by the British philosopher J. L. Austin (1962) and expanded by the American philosopher J. R. Searle (1969), claims that when we produce an utterance (q.v.) in an appropriate context, we perform a kind of act, i.e. a speech act. To be more precise, in the utterance of any linguistic expression we are characteristically performing three kinds of acts simultaneously:

(a) a locutionary act – the act of uttering a meaningful linguistic expression;
(b) an illocutionary act – the act of conveying some communicative purpose in uttering a linguistic expression, e.g. a promise, a threat, a reminder, a command, a greeting, etc.;

(c) a perlocutionary act – the act of achieving some effect on the hearer by uttering a linguistic expression.

For instance, the utterance 'You are acquitted of all charges' constitutes a locutionary act because it is a linguistic expression with a certain sense and reference. The same utterance may also perform an illocutionary act, that is, the speaker formally declares that the hearer is not guilty of some criminal offence. If this illocutionary act is produced by the right person in the right context and hence is successful in restoring the hearer's freedom, we have a perlocutionary act.

This example illustrates that certain conditions must be met if an illocutionary act is to be successful. So our communicative competence does not only enable us to determine the purpose or functional intention of an illocutionary act, but also to assess whether the conditions and context in which the act is performed are appropriate, e.g. does it have the right form in terms of a locutionary act? does it fit in with the surrounding circumstances? does it agree with the social relationship which holds between the speaker and the hearer? and so on. Conditions such as these on which the success of an illocutionary act depends are called appropriateness or felicity conditions. Any utterance which does not satisfy these conditions will be regarded either as infelicitous or, alternatively, may lead to a different interpretation, e.g. irony, sarcasm, a joke, etc., because both speaker and hearer are aware of its inappropriateness.

The utterance 'You are acquitted of all charges' also invites the suggestion that in our assessment of the type of illocutionary act which it represents and its felicity conditions, we are likely to make use of our social background knowledge, in this case of a courtroom situation (see **schema**).

Probably because of its communicative aspects, it is the illocutionary act (frequently also termed the illocutionary force of an utterance) which has received most attention in pragmatic studies of speech act theory. In fact, the term speech act is often used instead of illocutionary act, as for example in the term speech act force, which is frequently used as shorthand for the illocutionary force of an utterance.

Furthermore, a distinction must be made between direct and indirect speech acts. A direct speech act contains a performative verb, that is, a verb which marks the illocutionary force of an utterance explicitly. For example, in the utterance 'I must insist on paying for my share of the meal', the illocutionary force of 'strongly demanding something' is expressed by the performative verb 'insist'. Other examples of performative verbs are promise, command, request, object, warn, threaten, apologize, etc. Conversely, in indirect speech acts there are no such performative verbs present and the result is ambiguity because the number of potential illocutionary forces greatly increases. Thus, traditionally, sentences are classified into the following formal types (form = the grammatical structure, i.e. the locutionary act) and functional types (function = the communicative use a speaker makes of a sentence, that is, its illocutionary force when the sentence becomes an utterance):

FORMS		FUNCTIONS
Declarative	He paid for the drinks.	Statement
Interrogative	Did he pay for the drinks?	Question
Imperative	Pay for the drinks.	Command
Exclamatory	How nice of you to pay!	Exclamation

However, given appropriate contextual conditions, these grammatical structures may drop their characteristic illocutionary forces, and take on entirely different ones. For example, a declarative structure like 'It's cold in here' could, in certain contexts and dependent on the relationship holding between speaker and hearer, also be used to convey the illocutionary forces of a request ('Please close the window'); an order ('Close the door at once'); a complaint (e.g. if uttered by a hotel guest), and possibly others. Similarly, imperative structures can be used in offers, e.g. 'Have some more tea', wishes, e.g. 'Have a good time', and welcomings, e.g. 'Come in'.

It appears that identifying the illocutionary force of a particular speech act, in other words, inferring its implied meaning, can only be done if we assume that speakers/writers and hearers/readers work together to accomplish effective and purposeful communication or follow certain strategies of politeness. These assumptions are called the co-operative principle (q.v.) and the politeness principle (q.v.).

Speech act theory is one of the mainstays of pragmatics (q.v.) because it goes against the traditional tendency to study the meaning of isolated sentences set apart from the context (q.v.) in which they are uttered. For discussions of speech acts from the pragmatic angle, see Levinson (1983), Leech (1983), Green (1989) and Mey (1993); for a detailed application of the theory to literary discourse, see Pratt (1977).

Statives. See **Accomplishments**

Synonymy. See **Lexical repetition**

Syntax. See **Sentence/Utterance**

Target domain. See **Metaphor**

Text/Discourse

For many years, linguists have studied the structure and meaning of single sentences. In the last few decades, however, there has been a growing interest in the way sentences combine to form coherent and cohesive stretches of language (see **coherence** and **cohesion**). Though in this relatively new area of investigation the terms text and discourse have gained wide currency, there is no general agreement about their exact meaning and application. Some linguists would use text for a piece of written language, and reserve discourse for a continuous stretch of spoken language. Others appear to use the two terms interchangeably, talking about 'spoken and written text' or 'spoken and written discourse'.

Perhaps as a result of the recent multi-media revolution, which has to some extent blurred the dividing line between spoken and written forms, as well as through the evolvement of new theories, there is now a strong tendency among linguists to relate the terms text and discourse to the perspective of analysis they adopt. Thus, they talk about text, if their analysis is focused on intrinsic structural properties, that is, the linguistic features of the text, without taking into account its contextual factors. On the other hand, these linguists prefer the term discourse, if their analysis is not only concerned with linguistic aspects, but also with non-linguistic features such as the context of communication in which the discourse is embedded (see **context**, **critical discourse analysis** and **pragmatics**). Actually, in this sense of the term, discourse takes text and context together because they are seen as interacting generators of meaning.

It would have been convenient, if this clear distinction had been consistently adhered to in the recently established disciplines of text linguistics and discourse analysis. However, the fact of the matter is that there is a considerable overlap between the two fields of study. For instance, one standard textbook (de Beaugrande and Dressler 1981: 3 and 19) defines text as a communicative occurrence, restricting discourse analysis to the study of spoken texts, whereas another standard work (Brown and Yule 1983: 1 and 6) holds that the analysis of discourse is the analysis of language in use, and employs the term text to refer to the verbal record of a communicative act. Broadly speaking, it is in the latter senses that the two terms are used in the present book. More precisely, this book's predominant view is that any type of spoken or written communication should be regarded as a discourse, that is, as a communicative interaction between people producing and interpreting texts in a particular context.

In this broad sense, the term discourse removes the traditional boundaries between literary and non-literary texts, and therefore also covers narrative discourses like short stories and novels. These in turn comprise other embedded discourses, that is, the conventional presentations of a character's speech and thought. In accordance with the various degrees to which they are filtered through the narrator, the different modes of presenting speech and thought are termed free direct, direct, free indirect, and indirect discourse (see **methods of speech and thought presentation**).

In addition to the extensive introduction by Brown and Yule (1983) mentioned earlier, there is an accessible introduction to the concepts of discourse and discourse analysis in Numan (1993).

In critical discourse analysis (q.v.), the term discourse is used in a more loaded sense. Here this concept is typically regarded as a political and social tool, in that the meanings of language in communicative interaction are supposed to be determined by all kinds of social, cultural and political mechanisms.

Text linguistics. See **Text/Discourse**

Transitivity

Transitivity refers to the linguistic choices about who does what to whom, who is the agent and who is the affected of an action. For example, in 'Mary hit Paul', the nominal group 'Mary' plays the semantic role of actor or agent (the one who does something, who acts voluntarily), whereas 'Paul' is the affected, goal or patient (the one who undergoes the process, who is acted upon). On the other hand, in a sentence such as:

Mrs Grey saw something

there is no action but rather a mental process of perception. Therefore 'Mrs Grey' is not an actor, but may be referred to as the senser or the experiencer. For a complete inventory of these semantic or participant roles, see Halliday (1985: chapter 5).

Turn-taking (conversational)

A turn is the basic analytic unit in conversational analysis. In a conversation, usually one person speaks, then stops, then another person starts speaking, etc. These basic units of the conversation are called 'turns'. 'Turn-taking' refers to the point where one conversational participant stops speaking and another takes over. Conversation analysts are interested in studying the mechanisms which govern this system of turn-taking. See also **adjacency pairs, non-verbal conversational turns** and **pragmatics**.

Utterance. See **Sentence/Utterance**

Vocatives

When talking or writing 'to' people, we address them by using words or phrases like 'Jack', 'Mr Brown', 'Doctor', 'ladies and gentlemen', 'you fool', etc. Words used in this way are called vocatives. Some are restricted to formal contexts, some to informal ones. See further the entry under **address, forms/terms of**, which is an umbrella term covering these vocatives, that is, terms of address used in speaking or writing 'to' someone, as well as forms of naming people which are used in speaking or writing 'about' someone. See also **politeness**.

REFERENCES

Austin, J. L. (1962) *How to Do Things with Words*, Oxford: Oxford University Press.

Beaugrande, R. de and Dressler, W. (1981) *Introduction to Text Linguistics*, London: Longman.

Birch, D. (1989) *Language, Literature and Critical Practice: Ways of Analysing Text*, London: Routledge.

Blakemore, D. (1992) *Understanding Utterances*, Oxford: Blackwell.

Brown, G. and Yule, G. (1983) *Discourse Analysis*, Cambridge: Cambridge University Press.

Brown, P. and Levinson, S. C. (1987) *Politeness: Some Universals in Language Usage*, Cambridge: Cambridge University Press.

Comrie, B. (1976) *Aspect*, Cambridge: Cambridge University Press.

Cook, G. (1992) *The Discourse of Advertising*, London: Routledge.

Fairclough, N. (1989) *Language and Power*, London: Longman.

Graddol, D. and Boyd-Barrett, O. (eds) (1994) *Media Texts: Authors and Readers*, Clevedon, Avon: Multilingual Matters in association with The Open University.

Green, G. M. (1989) *Pragmatics and Natural Language Understanding*, Hillsdale, New Jersey: Lawrence Erlbaum Associates.

Grice, H. P. (1967/1975) 'Logic and Conversation', in P. Cole and J. L. Morgan (eds) *Syntax and Semantics 3: Speech Acts*, New York: Academic Press.

Halliday, M. A. K. (1985) *An Introduction to Functional Grammar*, London: Edward Arnold.

Hodge, R. (1990) *Literature as Discourse*, Cambridge: Polity Press.

Leech, G. N. (1983) *Principles of Pragmatics*, London: Longman.

Levinson, S. C. (1983) *Pragmatics*, Cambridge: Cambridge University Press.

Lodge, D. (1984/1985) *Small World*, Harmondsworth: Penguin.

Mey, J. L. (1993) *Pragmatics: An Introduction*, Oxford: Blackwell.

Numan, D. (1993) *Introducing Discourse Analysis*, Harmondsworth: Penguin.

Pratt, M. L. (1977) *Toward a Speech Act Theory of Literary Discourse*, Bloomington, Indiana: Indiana University Press.

Searle, J. R. (1969) *Speech Acts: An Essay in the Philosophy of Language*, Cambridge: Cambridge University Press.

Sinclair, J. (ed.) (1987) *Collins Cobuild English Language Dictionary*, London: Collins.

Index